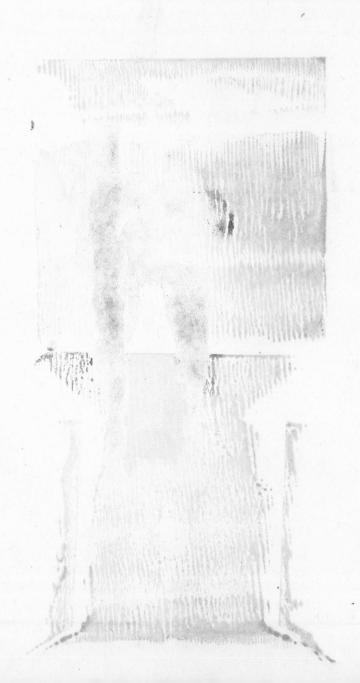

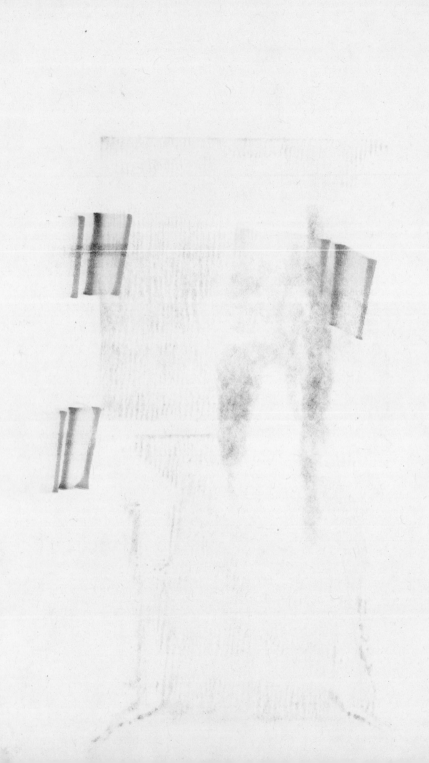

# CHANCE OR DESIGN?

# Chance or Design?

By

## JAMES E. HORIGAN

PHILOSOPHICAL LIBRARY

New York

Library of Congress Catalog Card No. 79-83605
SBN 8022-2238-2

MANUFACTURED IN THE UNITED STATES OF AMERICA

*To my Wife, Joan*

# Contents

# Author's Preface

In organizational design, this book consists of a number of chapters which, in material content, are quite distinctive from each other. Yet, in relation to several basic themes, there is a common bond between them. Like separate pieces of a jigsaw puzzle, a full understanding of what I have sought to accomplish may be best appreciated when all of the pieces have been joined together (by the reader) into a completed composition. It is by reason of this organizational necessity that a rather lengthy introductory chapter was required to provide, in addition to an overview of basic themes and objectives, an introduction to certain concepts which are carried forward later on in the book. Several of these, because of their early usage, may present the general reader with some initial difficulty. If so, I offer my apologies but note, however, that the subject matter of the book is cast against a background of thought expressed in philosophical literature which calls for some preliminary consideration in relation to such concepts.

In the final stages of the publication of this book, my attention was called to a new book written by W. H. Thorpe, a distinguished British biologist and Professor Emeritus of Animal Ethology at The University of Cambridge, entitled *Purpose In A World Of Chance\**. It was very encouraging to me (and I trust to the reader as well) to know that one of Professor Thorpe's main themes is similar in some ways to one of my own, i.e. that the universe is increasingly showing evidence

---

\* London: University of Oxford Press, 1978.

of design. What is assumed in greater degree as order and in some sense "design" by cosmologists and physicists, he notes, should also be apparent to biologists. Professor Thorpe's primary emphasis is on what he has found to be recent inferential evidence of design in the biological aspects of living organisms, in particular reference to the appearance of a wonderful "programmed" complexity of things at the molecular level, as well as to increasing signs of purpose reflected in animal mental performance in evolutionary development. He sees this as requiring more than what simply may be called "mechanism." As to the latter, he finds new significance in the philosophical views of A. N. Whitehead, Sir K. Poppers, and others. While my book undertakes (Chapters 10-12) to set forth some of these views and to offer proof in support thereof, it is yet not with the descriptive detail that a person of Professor Thorpe's special expertise may provide in this area. In comparison, my book gives greater emphasis (for reasons to be mentioned) to evident design found on the cosmic and inanimate side of nature—with perhaps less than one-third of the book devoted to biological evolution and related subjects. In this sense, our respective works are complementary to one another with respect to the theme as mentioned. On the cosmological side of things, Professor Thorpe's view of an origin of the universe is one which carries the imprint of order, coherence, and a preexisting "mental" primary aspect and, in this regard, is similar to thoughts of this writer as expressed in a number of chapters.

# Acknowledgments

There are numerous and diverse references to be found in this book which relate to the sciences, philosophy, and to what is sometimes called "natural theology." Many scientists, whose expertise has been a source of reference, may be surprised to find that acceptable knowledge derived from their respective areas of observation has been organized into a broad and unified general picture of the phenomena of nature in relation to the matter of origin. I am indebted for their individual and collective contributions which, either knowing or unknowing to them, have helped to make this book possible.

A measurable amount of time that would have been required in research to prepare a work of this nature was made unnecessary by reason of staff assistance at the excellent library research facilities made available to me (in order of usage), in England: The London Library, The Reading Rooms at the British Museum, and The Science and Technology Division (High Holborn) of the British Library. In the United States: The Public Library of Denver, The Library of Congress in Washington, D. C., The Public Library of Houston, The Main Public Library of Kansas City, Missouri, and The Main Public Library of the City of New York. To all of these, I am indebted.

During the early days of my search for background material, I was aided in no small degree by a number of modern publications that carried forward the theme of "intelligent design" that had flourished in an abundance of writings of the eighteenth and nineteenth century. A number of these are referred

xi

to in this work, including one in particular of several decades ago entitled "The Evidence of God in an Expanding Universe" edited by John Clover Monsma (E. P. Putnam Sons) and being a collection of brief essays by some thirty scientists as related to their respective fields. It is an interesting comparison to an eight volume work of the early nineteenth century published in England and known as the "Bridgewater Treatises" to which prominent men of science of that day contributed their views on design. A number of individual works of the current century were also helpful to this writer with respect to particular aspects of the general subject, as one will become aware in the chapters to come.

I am indebted, as well, to many friends in the U.S.A. and in England who lent their encouragement which helped to provide the will as needed to overcome the personal sacrifice involved in the production of a work of this nature and magnitude. I am especially grateful for the constructive suggestions and comments made by George C. Keely and Donald E. Crossland in their review of drafts of chapters in the final stages of completion. I further wish to especially acknowledge the typing and proof-reading services of Mrs. Edmond V. Osuch, in particular her attention to detail, and similar assistance provided by the Dageforde sisters, Betty and Judy. My son, Daniel, and daughters, Susan and Nancy J., also rendered helpful assistance in editing and proof-reading portions of various early drafts, and always present were help and an expression of encouragement from my wife.

All quotations are acknowledged as to author where they occur and, as to both author and publisher, in the bibliography at the end of the concluding chapter. I am grateful for the many permissions received for the use of excerpts and materials where appropriate.

JEH

Denver, Colorado, 1979

# CHANCE OR DESIGN?

# 1

# Introduction

The age-old question of the cause of the origin and development of the universe remains unsettled. This is evident from the existence in the world today of two opposing views. There is the materialistic view that the universe was created solely by the mindless working of chance and accident ("chance"). Then there is the religious view of an intelligently designed and purposeful creation ("design").

In this era of unparalleled scientific discovery, the search for meaning is a preoccupation of many people throughout the world. The controversy as mentioned serves to confound such a quest. There is a groping about for an objective standard from which man may either renew or set aside some of those human values which have helped to guide and mold his very nature. These values have been increasingly drawn into question by those who claim that man is simply a randomly evolved creature of chance and of no special significance. To those of no particular persuasion in the matter, the on-going conflict seems to hang in suspense as though dependent on further discoveries into the yet unknown.

There are many who feel that science, as a medium through which the secrets of the universe are unfolding, may eventually provide the key to the origin of the universe and to a final resolution of the basic question. To them, it is felt that both ancient and modern arguments of a philosophical or theological nature, based on pure reason or on religious belief and experience, have somehow failed to eliminate the existence of the controversy. The claimed absence of hard evidence, it

1

would seem, underlies the present day dispute between religious and materialistic thought.

Be that as it may, there is far more plausible evidence today of an empirical (fact-related) nature that bears on the question than was available to us at any earlier time. Science has shed significant new light on the subject to a degree that is inadequately recognized. By combining both new and earlier knowledge, we have, in the meaning of Plato, "come out of the cave," so to speak. The past three or four decades alone have made a measurable difference. We have acquired a more advanced picture of the contents and workings of the universe. Empirical knowledge of the planet on which we live, and of the universe beyond, has literally taken flight and exploded. It is believed that the discoveries of science in this century alone have far exceeded the total of the discoveries of man from the dawn of human history. Our present understanding of nature, its processes and mechanisms—especially inanimate (non-living) nature—has replaced centuries of relative ignorance.

We now have a rich and abundant source of new factual information which, if duly recognized for what it is worth, should serve to satisfy those who look for evidence of a nature that would support a definitive conclusion on the subject.

This may first be appreciated (as a matter of background) in the recognition that the progressive growth in human knowledge as mentioned is of itself phenomenal. In the first place, the planet Earth itself has been rather fully explored. Through the results of a wide-range of scientific fields of endeavor, man has realistically taken things apart. He sees the means and manner of the Earth's construction, how it holds together, what its constituents are and how they affect us, how it operates and what makes it function as an entity in support of life, how it is differentiated, what is fit and suitable to life, the uses to which it may be put by man, where and how it relates to the cosmos at least in a general way, and so on. The remaining mysteries relating directly to the Earth and its environment as yet to be explained in various fields of science, in fact or in theory, do not overshadow the basic fact that we have come a long way indeed in "knowing" our planet and in recognizing the basic design concepts involved in its formulation. Then, too, as the new parade of recently discovered particles of the "invisible" world of the atoms reveal an ever-enlarging picture of things, man has become more acutely aware of the complexity, rather than simplicity, of nature than ever before thought possible. Even into the far reaches of a vast universe, where man has looked more intently in recent decades to the appearance of things for analogies to intelligence and where cosmic "disorders" have appeared to be intermixed with a well-defined order of great magnitude, an amazing new level of observation (that is, in relation to a half-century ago) has significantly broadened our scope of understanding and knowledge.

It is a broad objective of the work to show that, in consequence of our greater enhanced knowledge and understanding of Nature's phenomena, a coherent picture of an intelligently designed creation is to be seen far more clearly and convincingly than ever before, and that the modern materialistic view of a creation by pure chance and accident is an unsupportable, if not an irrational, alternative. This is to be premised alone on the kind of knowledge that comes from present-day observation, rather than from reference to biblical or other religious sources which lie beyond the research and intended scope of this work. It is thought, however, that skeptical readers will seriously consider such sources, if, on reading this book, they should become convinced that the proposition as stated has been upheld.

Man is in a position—never before achieved—to approach the question with a new enlightened sense of confidence from an empirical standpoint; that is, from the observed "effects" of the universe toward a realization of the ultimate cause of things. Such an approach, due to its premise in factual observation, is not new by any means. It has commanded respect over the centuries from philosophers, theologians, and scientists. It is known as one of three classical methods of "proof" by which man has sought to show, independently yet in support of biblical belief and religious experience, the existence

3

of a designing God of the universe. It is, as well, the one kind of argument that is more open to change in keeping with progressive improvements in our observation and knowledge.

There is compelling reason for a fresh evaluation of this form of argument. It is not, as some critics have suggested, a weak or meaningless one, nor should it be deemed to be founded on limited observation and knowledge of an earlier day with respect to which logical and philosophical criticisms have been raised as a one-time final appraisal of the matter. Not only are the facts in observation today clearly incomparable to those of the past but, more importantly as we shall see, our present-day knowledge-level of phenomena has added a broader, significant, and additional dimension in which we may now view the matter overall.

But do we lack the clarity to know, asks a contemporary British philosopher, Thomas McPherson, "what are the criteria for order and disorder, or for design and the absence of design in the universe?"[1]* It is frequently said that there are things or phenomena which, while suggestive of design or order, may not be that at all, but rather be something quite different which may be mistaken for design. Then, too, one could have expected to find, even in a "chance" created universe, a degree of phenomena which could give the appearance of design. This, because the opportunities in the vast reaches of time and space are thought to be unlimited. A. E. Taylor, for instance, considered it objectionable to say that something in nature has "the marks of design." "This presupposes," he said, "antecedent knowledge, before the question is answered, what sort of thing a universe due to intelligent design would be, and what sort of thing one due to no design would be."[2]

Such a criticism suggests that we are unable to discern that this world is designed since we do not know what other worlds are like. It points to the absence of an actual observation of a causal condition for the origin of things. It was, in the past century, mostly directed in meaning to empirical arguments

---

* Quotes herein from "The Argument from Design" used with permission of Macmillan (London and Basingstoke).

4

based on the appearance of things by analogy to intelligence, but was (and is) further based on arguments made by the philosophers David Hume and Immanuel Kant that appeal to a lack of human experience and knowledge outside of our own particular world on which comparisons of similarity may be made. In these particulars, a contemporary writer, Robert H. Hurlbutt III, has expressed the criticism of Hume in this way: "The world is a particular; it does not belong to a species; it is unique; it is on the surface not a member of a class of machines."[3] The implication is that we are unable to say that this world shows intelligent design for lack of similar comparisons. Yet, if the modern hypothesis in science is correct that life, including intelligent life, exists throughout the universe, our world may be other than singularly unique. It may well be "a member of a class" or a "species." Indeed, that hypothesis is based on strong evidence of similarities throughout the universe on which comparisons have been made as a projection of our own experience. The criteria of design are no longer to be seen as "earthbound." Certainly, the basic building blocks of the universe, the atoms (together with associated cosmic phenomena and laws), circumscribe what other worlds *could be like* and our world is only one physical projection of what they are inherently capable of constructing elsewhere. As to be considered in Chapter 5, the atoms stand on their own as remarkable evidence of a designed universe. Even many of those of the materialistic view admit to the "miracle" of their very existence. Then too, even though we do not know specifically what other worlds are like in our universe, we may now see at least the essential similarity of circumstances for design in the observed cosmology of the universe (Chapter 8). As to what any other universes, past or present, may be like, we have no present knowledge to use as a basis of comparison, of course, but this in no way detracts from the appearance of design that is increasingly evident in this one.

The criticism, in any event, raises the question of certainty in the matter of proof with respect to design (and chance) in a speculative way. While the matter of absolute certainty is indeed a problem, as we shall consider, the above criticism itself presupposes a much more limited view of the inferences of design in both our world and universe than is to be presented here. It was more viable (as a criticism) in a different age when we had far less criteria and observational experience on which to view the subject. We are far closer today to understanding design from non-design in a most reliable way that calls to mind a suggested answer to this criticism put forth in a well-known and respected treatise of nearly fifty years ago by F. R. Tennant. He made the point that "if trust-worthy evidence of design in the limited portion of the universe that we know were forthcoming, a world-Designer would be 'proved,' and our ignorance as to other parts would be irrelevant."[4] Today, it is more relevant to ask whether we have not attained the "trustworthy" evidence of the nature suggested, even if not in terms of final certainty.

But how is it possible to assert that the universe was designed, rather than not designed, simply from observations to be derived from the phenomena of the natural world? Have not philosophers, such as Hume, Kant, Voltaire, and others, made it clear that one may not logically "prove" the existence of a Designer of the universe from the mere observation of the "effects" of things in nature that may give the appearance of design? In consequence, have not many present-day writers, as well as those of the past, mainly looked upon empirically-based "design" arguments as unfounded, meaningless, weak, or even "dead?" Does not modern science, as it elaborates more fully on the processes and mechanisms of the natural world, deem it inappropriate to look for explanations in terms of a supernatural cause?

The absence of direct and positive proof of an empirical nature of the existence of a Designer of the universe does present a problem in absolute proof. No one today, to our knowledge, has actually observed, tested and verified the existence of a Designer in the ways of scientific methodology, nor in accordance with any other means of empirical observation. In formal logic and in the strict methodology of science, direct and positive observation and verification is a pre-con-

6

dition to acceptability in terms of absolute certain proof. To many materialists, it has even been made a pre-condition to the acceptance of any kind of proof of design. This latter objection, which does nothing to explain anything, silently overlooks the astounding growth in human experience and its improved reliability which, when taken together with the amazing growth of inferences to design, tear at the foundations on which the objections stand.

A great many of the prevailing or "well-accepted" theories of modern science are inferred, inductively, from observations of nature where final, direct, and positive observation is lacking; that is, on the basis of observation of effect to cause, rather than from cause to effect. It is a well-recognized approach that may well lead to the ultimate and certain proof of things, not only in science, but in other fields as well. The alternative is to ignore, contrary to human reason, what we learn from observations of fact that point in a certain direction in relation to experience. The scientist, for instance, turns to regularities and invariances in nature in seeking to verify a theory. This is the sort of criteria that today appears to give strong support to the design argument to be advanced herein, as we shall see. In this, however, it needs to be emphasized that the weight to be given indirect proof, in the absence of direct and certain proof, is a matter of circumstance and degree depending on a great number of relevant factors. This quite often includes the quantity as well as the quality factor, and the reliability of presumptions which arise from the inferences that are, in turn, based on actual observed facts. But the more the presumptions involved are based on reliable and high-quality observation of an undeviating nature, as those to be endorsed herein, the less likely and more highly improbable the chance of error.

The basic approach to be made here will be to draw from science itself, its discoveries, and the accumulated knowledge that is today available—from atoms to cosmological phenomena—from genes to man—to organize into meaningful interpretation an empirical argument of the nature and scope as mentioned. We will examine various fields of science without

7

the constraint or inhibition that ordinarily divides them into separate compartments of expertise. The argument will spread across a broad spectrum of knowledge. The subject properly requires consideration on such a basis and the emphasis will be more on the end-results of present scientific knowledge of natural phenomena that bear significantly on the question rather than, as in science, to describe how and in what manner the constituent parts of it are technically put together and operate.

In making this approach, we will have to trust to science with respect to much of the modern "knowledge" it has given to us and to fully recognize that some of this is based on prevalent theories and hypotheses which often-times turn out to be something quite different in terms of certain knowledge, or even in terms of reality itself. One theory or hypothesis is not, of course, as trustworthy as another in this regard. It is unnecessary for our purpose here, however, to presage that revolutionary changes will occur in the current established or prevailing theories of science. Our point of reference here is necessarily the present and, even so limited, it is highly improbable that the disproof of some generally acceptable scientific theories and hypotheses to be relied upon would be significant in terms of the broad sweep of the phenomena to be considered. If, as one example, the unresolved controversial problems with respect to the modern theory of biological evolution were to be resolved in some ways against the theory in consequence of future discovery, it would not seem to matter. The picture of design to be presented herein is not to be seen as dependent on the outcome of the controversy. If, for instance, life was born in a far less distant period of time than the evolutionists say is possible on the basis of the fossil record and present time-dating mechanisms, it would be even more remarkable as evidence of design. Yet, it would not in any manner diminish the picture of design that is nevertheless in evidence in the processes that are said to have been at work for billions of years to bring about the same result. Furthermore, in relation to an eternity of time (that is, if time be eternal) a billion years would seem more like a few minutes on the human time-scale.

Any approach that is founded on the view of an assumed compatibility between modern science and the intelligent design of things leads necessarily to a synthesis, and one may reasonably ask whether the material to be presented herein furnishes a sound basis for a timely and needed reconciliation between modern science and religious thought, in a general sense at least. The scope of the material that is to be joined together in meaning is broadly comprehensive in scope. The instant effort may, perhaps, come as close to achieving such a desired objective as lies within our present ability so to do. Yet, the final answer may depend on the degree of credibility or merit that may be accorded to modern scientific knowledge and thought to be considered in relation to the arguments to be presented. For if both be sufficient in their premises, the reconciliatory linkage would seem to be far more than simply supportable as a reasonable conclusion.

The emphasis herein, except in later chapters, will be focused largely on inanimate (non-living) nature and associated cosmic phenomena. That is, the "stuff" of which the universe (including life) is made and the forces which govern its activity. This has been the more neglected area as concerns the meaning of "design" with respect to which so many of our modern discoveries have related. Comprehensive "design" arguments of earlier centuries were primarily related to animate (living) nature and the inanimate side of things received about as much attention as the animate will receive herein. How strange it is that, in this late 20th century, the picture of design has rounded out in such a fashion. The inanimate side of nature is, as well, the broad arena of existence that is unaffected in its substance and activities by Darwinian processes of natural selection. This should, on its face, tell us something meaningful about the many criticisms of design arguments over the past century that have sought to support the view of a chance creation largely on the basis of such processes. In later chapters, we will proceed to relate inanimate to animate nature in a way that will engage, among other

9

things, a serious consideration of the evolution of living things in the context of design in an updated and, in some ways, different manner than in the earlier arguments to design.

In several ways the picture of design may now be shown: Firstly, in a modern, unified and comprehensive way that adds great new credibility and scope to so-called probability arguments favoring the view of a designed universe. Secondly, in a way that, by reason of our advanced empirical knowledge, recognizes an important advancement has been achieved in what may now be meaningfully considered to show "design"— a broader and more significant new dimension to the subject.

Turning in the first instance to the comprehensive aspect, it is to be noted that this work is organized in a manner which will later on, chapter by chapter, set forth many of the important inferences that were advanced by writers in earlier empirical arguments to show design and, incrementally, to call attention to important new inferences to design that have come to light in consequence of modern discovery. The result is an overview of the relevant phenomena of nature that permits a modern grasp of the subject overall—one that is not limited, as in the case of the earlier design arguments, to the knowledge of the day and, in the case of more recent arguments to design, to certain specialized fields of knowledge. These built-in limitations essentially preclude the insights that are available from a broad, unified, and unrestricted presentation of the subject. It is difficult to see how an approach to the proof of design could be adequate and fully effective unless it undertakes to encompass, insofar as is practicable, the whole of nature as it is seen to bear on the question. Only in this way does one allay possible criticisms based on questions arising from incompleteness.

As we shall see, strong new empirical inferences favoring the view of an intentionally designed creation have increased significantly, indeed precipitously, in this century. In the course of time, scientific discoveries have progressively and unerringly unfolded a more definitive picture of the intelligent design of things. When considered together with old inferences, the view of a designed creation becomes far more than simply a "reasonable" view. It becomes, on the overall record to be made herein, the view that is exceedingly well-justified and empirically well-substantiated.

If the universe had been created by "chance," one might have expected, in keeping with the steady growth in discovery and knowledge, that some worthwhile new inferences of "non-design" would have come to the front. That is, imperfections or "flaws" in nature of some significance to counterbalance the appeal to design. Instead, the present-day critics of design are still claiming the same old inferences of "imperfection" that concerned the ancient Greeks. Surprisingly, by reason of our greater understanding of the nature of things, many of the so-called imperfections are being viewed quite differently in science, as we shall consider in Chapters 6 and 9. Indeed, some (if not all) of these may now be viewed as not constituting imperfections at all. Still others are now showing up as strengthening, rather than weakening, the view of a well-designed world. Those who would point to imperfections in human nature (such as evil and its consequences) may well be surprised to see how this phenomenon is shown to be increasingly isolated on its own, as though indicative of design and purpose, from the rest of the phenomena of nature which today reflects a remarkable degree of design.

These startling developments in one direction (a continual unfolding over time of almost countless new inferences to intelligent design of an empirical nature, a continual erosion of inferences formerly claimed to show the contrary, and a seemingly barren situation on new negative evidence that may be rationally inferred against design) are confirmatory of what one should expect to find in an intelligently designed universe and precisely the opposite from what one would expect in an accidental one. There is no satisfactory explanation for this distinctively unilateral and progressive trend toward the inductive proof of the intelligent design of things. If, in the post-Darwin era of the last century, such a trend had been foreseeable, it would have presented a formidable reply to the outspoken critics of the then limited view of a designed world.

It does suggest that man should become less influenced or concerned by the present-day application of the formalisms of eighteenth century philosophical and logical criticisms directed against an empirical approach to the ultimate proof of the origin of things. Such criticisms never sought to withhold spiraling proof of a factual nature on the subject, rather they served to negate the logical finality or certainty that such proof could offer in the manner of this approach.

The criteria for showing "design" herein will not be limited to calling attention to the things of the world of nature that, by analogy to the things or objects of human contrivance, appear on their face to have required the ingenuity of a higher creative intelligence to bring them about under the so-called old "argument from design" (Chapter 3) that prevailed in the days of the critical philosophers Immanuel Kant and David Hume. This old argument, in some ways, resembles the currently popular and speculative argument that extraterrestrial beings have visited our planet in the past on the strength of analogies between the appearance of things and the workings of intelligence. Nor will the criteria herein be limited in less degree under the so-called wider or re-structured "fitness" design arguments of this century which have pointed not so much to analogies (as in the case of the old argument from design) but to the existence of "innumerable" reciprocal and harmonious relationships in nature that make life possible and supportable on Earth (Chapter 4). These several representations to design, although engaging somewhat different-sided approaches to arrive at the same conclusion, were far more confined in scope and meaning than required today.

Indeed, the fact that we may now triangulate "design" from different empirical modes of broad-based reference is the sort of confirmatory evidence that should impress scientists who, in keeping with the scientific method, look for regularities and invariances from different bases of observation to the correctness and acceptability of theories. Thus, the general fitness or harmony argument as mentioned serves to verify the older analogy argument and, while each of them overlap and rely on the so-called law of probabilities, the former extends (in substance) rather beyond the latter as a general empirical approach to the matter of proof (Chapter 4). The new broader perception to be next considered, while most similar in some ways to the fitness argument, nevertheless stands distinctively on its own to verify each of the others, and vice versa. While all of them are based on inductive reasoning and probabilities, what widely accepted theory in modern science (inductively concluded on the basis of probabilities) will be seen as more objectively supported on the record to be presented herein? The protective "logical" shield (Chapter 3) that has sought to preclude the importance of design arguments for centuries is to be seen as impaired by the varying kinds of underlying factual observations which point to the same conclusion. The critics of the past were never faced with a triad of proofs with which to pin-point or triangulate the identity of an unknown "source" or cause, nor with the degree of reliable accuracy that science has come to find from its investigative experience which relies on multiple facets of observation for verification.

A most important and broader next-progression of an argument to design has been established and is now clearly in evidence. This results from the cumulative new discoveries and knowledge of the past four or five decades taken in combination with earlier indicia of design. It is an empirical approach that stretches beyond both the analogy and general fitness arguments in a way that closes old gaps in proof, shows a positive directional aspect in Nature, and completes the composition of design full circle in relation to the physical aspects of our planetary environment and, prospectively (as we shall see), beyond. The "innumerable" appearances of design in terms of the fitness of the environment for the existence and development of life become a portion only of an aggregate whole of what may now be rationally perceived in the design of things.

Of all discoveries of science that have accumulated over time, none should be considered more remarkable (whether so recognized or not) than that of the existence of a very special, purposive, and functional reciprocity *alone* between the creative ingenuity of man, his mind and consciousness,

13

and non-living matter and its associated phenomena. The potential for this most meaningful and unique mind-matter relationship was latent in material substance and related phenomena before the coming of man and, as we shall consider in some detail in Chapter 7 and to an extent in other chapters, the phenomenon itself has been found to be remarkably directional and complete by the discoveries of science and by our greatly enhanced understanding of the substances, processes, and mechanisms of nature.

The mind and consciousness of man, and his particular physical characteristics, permit a full functional utilization of highly suitable environmental phenomena in whatever course or direction his creative thought and ingenuity chooses to carry him. This is not a simple matter of the adaptation of man to what many have described as a "hostile" environment. It goes far beyond mere adaptation and the environment is not only compatible, rather than hostile, but is apparently designed (as we shall see) to perfection in relation to the potential in man, his mind and consciousness; and this, with a remarkable degree of variety and diversity. Considering the basic plan of its construction, constituency, and operational function in relation to man, the Earth's physical environment is of such a nature (Chapters 6 and 7) that it is inconceivable science could suggest anything better without introducing imperfections in its activity and system overall. It is remarkable that, not so long ago, such a statement would have been unfounded. But the world is, as we shall see, a perfectly complementary and well-prepared "stage" for man's purposes in a truly progressive sense, having yet to be found wanting in the provision of a physical environment that contains all the necessary elements, forces, and conditions, severally and in combination, to the attainment of his ever-enlarging objectives. It precedes adaptiveness in the usual selective evolutionary sense as generally understood. This, in a special and affirmatively contributing way that reflects the clearest sign of the advance foresight and intelligent design of things. It would be wrong to equate the uniqueness of this phenomenon with the Earth's environment alone. One of the more respected of the hypotheses of modern science is that the potential for such a reciprocity is latent throughout the wide expanse of the universe; that is, wherever this universally existent phenomenon may coincide with consciousness and intelligence.

The foregoing is not to say that design arguments of an earlier day, especially "fitness" or "harmony" arguments as mentioned, did not point to many relationships of a special nature between man and his earthly environment. This, in addition to the main emphasis placed on the matter of environmental compatability to the origin and survival of life. The knowledge formerly available, however, simply presented a quite incomplete picture which lacked the broader significance and new meaning that may now be derived from more modern knowledge on the mind-matter relationship and its positive fitness and directional aspect.

Does it not signify the importance of man, his mind and consciousness, in a universal scheme of things, that Nature's bounty within his grasp and in all its fullness (including inanimate, animate, and associated phenomena) may be seen to point directionally and specifically to him alone as though he were the central apex of intersecting vectors? Our present-day observation, based on the comprehensive overview of nature to be set forth herein, shows not only the regularity and invariant directionality of this phenomenon but, in addition, reflects the significance of man and his intelligence (together with its associated values) as a special object of creation. This is saying something quite different, empirically, than simply drawing analogies or calling attention to "innumerable" harmonious inter-relationships in nature that make for the existence and development of life. Not even light, gravity, or other known cosmic phenomena in the universe share the obvious significance of an equally far-reaching and penetrating mind and consciousness which appears to have the potential capacity to not only perceive and find meaning in it all, but to harbor the potential for becoming increasingly involved. Perhaps any failure on our part to recognize the empirical significance of this remarkable mutuality between man and the phenomena of nature may be attributed to our

15

tendency to take things for granted, being, as we are, an integral part of the creative process itself.

The suggestion that man, like the elephant, the grasshopper, or the fruitfly within their respective domains, has alone imaginatively fashioned a parochial view of an ordered or designed state of affairs for himself that bears no relation to either reality or to other possible views as may be derived from differing aspects of mental reference, has been carried much too far to merit credibility. Certainly on the fringes of uncertainties in knowledge to be found in the various fields of science, the question of reality versus illusion is most marked and perhaps a great deal of what is thought to be of a certain order, or point of view, will prove to be illusory in terms of ultimate truth. The same may also be said (in a broad universal sense) of present interpretations of man with respect to certain phenomena that may now be thought to represent reality exclusively on a given matter. While one may expect a certain amount of imaginative unrealism in human subjectivity, yet (as noted by Pollard) Nature itself is not a product of the human mind. In no small degree, man's ordered mentality is a mirror reflection of the design and order that already exists outside in the world of nature and, in a relational sense between man and his environment, man had no mental or physical control over the latent characteristics of Nature as presented to him. It had to be uniquely reciprocal in the first place for order, or even an illusory viewpoint of order, to be made possible in the manner in which it almost endlessly and singularly complements man's range of creative activities. Examples of the scope of many of these activities to date are briefly summarized in Chapter 7, and it would be difficult indeed for one to successfully challenge these as being unreal or illusory. Then, too, the facts we will be taking into account in support of "design" are, for the most part, facts which have essentially become established as "facts" from scientific methods used in observation. It is not simply a matter of 20th century imagination, for instance, that real space astronauts in their real spaceships have ventured some distance into "the void of space." While the astronauts, circling in their spaceships, unlike the ordinary inhabitants of Earth, have received a different perspective of an Earth that resembles a tiny and beautiful marble-looking object there is indeed greater significance to be attached to the very fact that, by reason of the real reciprocity between man and his natural world, they have been able to acquire such a different view.

The relational significance of man to his environment in a sense of design may best be appreciated when it is first realized that, historically, the main emphasis in early design arguments related mostly to living organisms—the animate side of nature. There, the appearance of design by way of analogy in relation to intelligence is rather overwhelming and no one, even today, would seriously dispute this. Hilde S. Hein, for instance, in her recent book "On the Nature and Origin of Life" pointed out that living organisms, "both structurally and functionally, appear to be designed for a purpose; that the parts are so organized as to suggest that there is a goal or end to which they are subordinate."[5]* But design, in this sense, is not attributed by the materialists in this post-Darwin era to intelligent design, but rather to selective processes of organic evolution that are said to have randomly brought about meaningful end-results in living systems. The materialists simply do not see design in the origin and workings of such processes.

On the inanimate (non-living) side of nature, in contrast, the old "argument from design" fell short of explaining a great deal that appeared to be irrational, disordered and reflective of non-design. Even the above-mentioned post-Darwin "wider" or re-structured design arguments of this century continued to leave open to empirical criticism this entire aspect of apparent non-design. The world of inanimate nature has continued to be viewed today by materialistic thinkers as generally random, indeterministic and disordered. The order and design to be found, rather than being seen as attributable to a supernatural cause, is simply considered the random by-product of ordinary

---

* From "On the Nature and Origin of Life," © 1971, by Hilde S. Hein. McGraw-Hill Book Company. This and quotations at pages 30, 159, 174, 181, and 193 used with permission of the publisher.

17

laws of physics and chemistry that have a capacity to make for order, coupled with the application of man's ordered mental existence—itself said to be the by-product alone of random evolutionary processes.

Reginald O. Kapp called attention to phenomena in inanimate nature that reflect randomness and disorder. He said that "so long as we look only to the untouched world of lifeless things we find examples of every conceivable contour, every degree of simplicity and complexity, every mixture of ingredients, every possible size and shape of things, etc."[6] By way of example, he pointed to the size and arrangement of stars in the heavens, the height of mountains, the constituents of the atmosphere, the proportions in which the elements are mixed in rocks, the width of valleys, the speed of rivers, the outline of continents, and so on.

Today, however, the view of an inter-mixture of phenomena in inanimate nature in our world that shows both disorder and order (chance and design) is fast disappearing. We are now able to see order and design equally as well on the non-living side of nature as on the living side of it in a manner that closes the gap and ties up the loose-ends. Our point of observation of the "effects" of nature has advanced significantly, as mentioned.

The *intrinsic nature* of inanimate substance and related phenomena has come to the front to give a highly complete and more substantive picture of design. A picture which shows that the varying form, shape, size, composition, simplicity, or complexity of things which, on their face, may reflect (by analogy) disorder, irregularity, imperfection, or the like, are not that at all intrinsically. Rather, the function, utility, fitness, accommodation and suitability of inanimate phenomena with respect to life in general and to man, his mind and consciousness, in particular, is the most important consideration in this regard. There is little indeed within the realm of man that is today "untouched" by evident design in one or the other of these aspects. In consequence, the world of lifeless things in all its myriad and countless forms, is to be seen on its own as much too well presented, differentiated, coordinated, and

18

correct to be reasonably attributed to either outmoded notions of disorder and non-design or to purely mechanistic explanations of the nature mentioned.

While the emphasis on design throughout this book will be placed more on the "end-results" to be found in nature, rather than on the "means" or mechanics for the achievement of such ends, several general observations on mechanics are here pertinent to a general understanding of certain of the design concepts to be introduced.

The apparent uncertainty in atomic particle activity (i.e., an inability to specify simultaneously both the position and the velocity of an orbiting electron) which gave rise to the theory of indeterminism (or uncertainty) in modern science, and hence to an argument in support of the view of a random chance creation, would now appear to be something quite different in an ultimate sense of reality. This, by the ever-enlarging evidence of purposeful end-results of such activity at higher levels of material aggregation. This may be seen in relation to the small part of the universe with which we are most familiar and, while yet obscure or quite speculative in many ways, in less known regions of the universe. The rigid determinism of earlier classical Newtonian concepts, as thought to have been discarded in the main by the principle of uncertainty, appears to have merely furnished the general outline of what may now be seen in far greater detail—and the detail, as well as the general outline, lends credence to those (such as the late Albert Einstein, for instance) who have questioned that the principle may be the result of our ignorance or, at least, that the ultimate reality of cosmic and inanimate activity, in a space-time continuum, must somehow be quite certain or deterministic.

Whatever the ultimate reality of the means of the achievement of purposeful end-results, the observed facts at hand, as we shall see, defy the idea of chance and accident as final cause. If indeed the concept of indeterminacy is not fraught with an aspect of our ignorance, there is no reason in science why the Designer of the universe should not have chosen such a means to an end. So noted the physicist William G. Pollard

19

in calling attention to the law of probabilities and the enormous number of atoms in the universe which, being limited in kind and in their statistical aggregating alternatives, achieve dependable and invariable certainties in their results.[7] A. S. Eddington, the late renowned British astronomer, similarly noted that the prospective predicability of events is much the same in practical application (as applied in science) whether final results are achieved under either a deterministic or indeterministic concept.[8] And while this is so only within a range of tolerances which Sir James Jeans referred to as "loose-jointedness,"[9] there are few, if any, loose-joints to be found in the end-results of cosmic and inanimate phenomena to be comprehensively reviewed herein (nor in the overall sense of animate phenomena to be described). Whether or not by the operation of statistical law in accord with a measure of indeterminacy within the range of the few kinds of atoms and basic universal laws, the end-results speak for themselves and are no less remarkable, creative, and quite deterministic.

Yet, to many, the question of "how" the material substances, energy, and cosmic forces were designedly linked together to bring about the present physical state of affairs in the universe is not fully or satisfactorily answered by statistical means, as mentioned above. It does not seem quite right to them, whether on religious or other grounds, to equate the remarkable harmony and precision to be found in our world with a generally loose and uncoordinated run of matter and energy. This, notwithstanding the enormous opportunities in a vast time frame for the occurrence of deterministic and meaningful statistical results. The view of the intelligent design of things seems (although not necessarily so) to call for a more specific directional principle for the selective guidance or coordination of certain of the cosmic and inanimate phenomena of nature into channelized activities and meaningful function. Much of the phenomena to be described in chapters 5-10, for instance, seems to call for such a principle. It is when we turn in emphasis to animate nature in Chapter 10-12, that we begin to see why and how, in a designed scheme of things, so-called natural selective processes were engaged with

20

a somewhat less degree of determinism in terms of end-results.

By no means has science precluded the possible discovery of a more specific guidance or coordinating aspect with respect to the phenomena of nature.

Although quite speculative, it would seem to this writer that some interesting "clues" of an empirical nature have recently come to light which suggest the possibility of a correspondence between matter and a designing Mind; that is, a yet unknown manner of linkage which may account for the sort of precise results in nature that would seem to come alone from direction and coordination rather than simply from statistical selection over time. Could there be an *atomos mentis* (Gr.; Lat.), or atom-mind relationship, to complement other known forces in conjunction with the activities of the atoms, the basic building-blocks of matter, in the attainment of selective modes of material organization? Implicit in the question is the thought that the atoms could be internally programmed to respond to external conscious activation, together with the incidental thought that an array of seemingly superfluous material in the universe as a whole is yet "unselected" in such a manner if, indeed, such material does not serve some other function or purpose of which we are yet unfamiliar.

The atoms already display an aspect of "programming" when, by reason of their make-up (as to be considered in Chapter 5), they combine selectively with the same or certain other kinds of atoms to form the 92 different chemical elements in nature with their distinctive qualities. When we take into account, as in later chapters, how a great many of the elements (alone and in their aggregations) bear a significant relationship to the existence and support of life, and (as we shall see) have a remarkable and very special relationship to man, his mind and consciousness, it is perhaps not too unreasonable to speculate that the atoms, individually or in their combinations, could also be "programmed" to interact in some manner with creative intelligence to allow for a measure of guidance. If this were to be the case, could there be a more simple and reasonable explanation of a means engaged in the intelligent design and construction of a life-productive uni-

21

verse? After all, if we are to believe that the universe was intelligently designed in the beginning, it best appeals to our common sense to believe, as well, in a continuing linkage between the initiating creative intelligence, the elements and forces, and the ultimate creations. It has far less appeal, on the other hand, to think there would be a later total disassociation between these factors. Any kind of "programming" aspect attributed to the atoms and their particles, however, would certainly be viewed in materialistic thought as unprovable and explicable alone in terms of "ordinary" physics and chemistry, devoid of mentality, and essentially random in occurrence. Yet, so long as the atoms were considered to be quite simple internally and comprising few elementary particles that were readily understandable in their nature and function, the materialistic view had more to offer in its support. But the nuclear physics of the past decade or so has revealed what has been described as a "zoo" of many newly discovered elementary particles deep in the interior of the atom, many of which we can hardly identify, much less understand what precise role or function they play, if any, in the nature of things. There are theories indeed but no generally acceptable theory has come forth to satisfy our quest for meaning. Some of them have such brief lifespans that one could be reminded of electrical thought impulses. At any rate, the point to be made here is that science has not closed the door by any means to a possible *atomos mentis* correspondence.

The empirical basis for such a speculation, in addition to what may be implicit in the foregoing, would seem to come from several somewhat divergent lines of modern scientific knowledge or thought. In the first place, it is to be noted that a growing number of prominent evolutionists take the view that some form and degree of behavioral awareness or consciousness in living organisms (more identifiable or associated at higher levels) plays an indirect (if not direct) role in evolutionary change in form, structure, or function. This latter will be more fully considered in Chapter 10 and it is perhaps sufficient here to say that a leading zoologist, Sir Alister Hardy of England, and some others are convinced that conscious behaviorism is an important factor (acting within the Darwinian System) that should be recognized as an additional selective process in evolutionary theory. While the intended meaning of conscious behaviorism in this respect is not conceived in terms of the speculative idea of *atomos mentis* as suggested, it does show (to this writer) a step or an inference in that direction as a possibility that should not be ruled out. As we shall see, there are some supporters of this view who feel that an element of "mind" may be universally present even in elementary particles, atoms, living cells, etc. Hardy does not incorporate this suspicion into his way of thinking other than to suggest it is something to be borne in mind as a possibility, presumably in conjunction with his further view, discussed in Chapter 10, that a creative element is somehow linked with a mental aspect arising from the physico-chemical nervous action in the mind-body relation, and playing a role in evolution in the Darwinian sense. The puzzling question to be answered, he asks, is "how?" It would seem to this writer that to account for consciousness in the evolution of a living organism over time, if such a concept is valid, a higher intelligence-linkage would be required than to fully account for this as consciousness in the organism itself; that is, in the matter of seeking and attaining meaningful and functional end results. It should be noted here, however, that the modern theory of biological evolution does not appear to recognize the existence of this so-called additional proposed selective process as mentioned.

The randomness that is considered to be operable in various ways in association with evolutionary processes could arguably be deemed inconsistent with this writer's idea of a conscious directionality in evolution. Yet, as we shall consider in some detail in Chapters 10 and 11, there are a number of favorable inferences to support the position that such processes are themselves intentional and purposeful in an overall context.

To some extent, as well, a recent discovery (to be discussed in a later chapter) that points to a sort of conscious self-determination even at the lowly level of genes in the DNA molecule of the living cell, seems to carry somewhat of an implication that an aspect of the mental may be operable in near proximity to the atomic level of things involved with life processes.* The discovery suggests that the genes seek to protect themselves against change and, while this does not rule out the possibility of an explanation of a purely mechanistic nature, it does give rise to a strong suspicion to the contrary.

Even parapsychological phenomena, if and to the extent believable, seem relevant to this question, such as extrasensory communication associated with thought (telepathy) or discernment (clairvoyance). This would, of course, presuppose some manner of linkage between human awareness and a higher or at least different level of awareness. This could be carried even further into the extensive experimentation and research under way throughout the world today (albeit not without skepticism) having to do with such mind-matter phenomena as the movement of physical objects including, for example, the claimed transferable mental powers (telekinesis) of Uri Geller in the bending of metal objects. The very idea of a transferability between thought or awareness and something we attribute to the material world fits quite well with the speculation of a mental guidance factor of the sort as mentioned. While the precise linkage aspect, if any, is unknown, it is not difficult to carry this back at least into the precedent sub-atomic world, not only because all material substance, as far as we know, emanates therefrom, but there

---

* This is not to suggest that this writer embraces the new controversial theory of *sociobiology* to the effect (at least in one version of it) that the genes of DNA are self-determined "ends" of themselves, rather than "means" to more physically organized and advanced living things (such as man). Quite to the contrary, this writer sees both the atoms and the genes as merely being "means to ends" if for no other reason than that the genes, at their level of existence, do not remarkably harmonize and interrelate, in scope at least, with the end-products of the atom-composed world of inanimate nature. The potential for meaningful linkage between the inanimate and animate worlds of nature occurs, as we shall see, at the higher level of the end-products of both the genes and atoms. The genes, of course, are absent from the activity of the atoms and their productions on the inanimate side of things. This carries the strong implication that an external intellect essentially guided both atoms and genes to meaningful inter-related end-results, and the extent to which this may have been programmed in advance is the more significant question.

24

is (as we shall explore in other chapters of this book) keen evidence today of remarkable design and coordination in cosmic and inanimate nature that is as strong as that which is to be found on the animate side of things; that is, evidence of a kind which infers that mental awareness preexisted from the time of origination of the particles and early events in the universe, and the precision involved in the achievement of end-results that are appropriate to life might best be explained in terms of selective intelligent coordination.

When phenomena of the foregoing nature (even though still subject to question) are considered in conjunction with yet other phenomena, such as that of an apparent correspondence or likeness between the human mind and a "higher intelligence" in pure mathematical abstractions (discussed in Chapter 7) and the many precise and meaningful end-results to be found throughout nature that imply external guidance, the idea of a powerful mental coordinating factor (i.e. God) in selective atomic aggregation seems less speculative.

As our knowledge has advanced immeasurably with respect to the story of cosmic evolution, including the lifeless world of things, as a perfectly compatible aspect to the story of the evolution of living things, there is far greater reason today for the combination of the two intertwined aspects of nature as a single process of creation and being; that is, in the rendering of any fair and valid portrayal of the origin, development and progression of life. Eric C. Rust and others have already raised the question as to whether both aspects should not be treated as one.[10] When this is done, an overall coherency and intelligibility in nature most strikingly shows intelligent design. It is believed this will become increasingly apparent to the reader in the chapters to come.

It is important to ask whether the literature on biological evolution in relation to life does not mislead one who is not versed in the sciences as concerns the subject matter of this book, i.e., chance or design. It frequently omits an entire dimensional aspect of universal evolution (i.e. cosmic and inanimate evolution) that ties it all together and gives it meaning. True, the separatism of this field of study aids in its independent research and investigation, but both aspects of evolution show "design" and appear to have converged invariantly in our world on a common goal—a central and dominant focal point as mentioned—man, his mind and consciousness. Even though the two aspects of nature are quite varied in their results, the borderline between them has become quite thin in this modern day, and this is so recognized in science as evidenced, for example, by the overlapping research in biochemistry and biophysics. Indeed, it will be strongly argued in later chapters that the view of intelligent design simply provides the best explanation for the very existence of such phenomena as the origin of self-replication in living organisms; the cognitive nature of the protein molecule and the basic genetic code representing inheritable information, the structural pattern for species differentiation, the life cycles, the tolerance aspect in the makeup of living things that allows for freedom to adapt, the goal-seeking and goal- achieving tendencies of living organisms toward functioning and purposive end-results, mind and consciousness, etc. Some of these are sought to be explained in science in terms alone of presently asserted or recognized natural selective processes, but others are inexplicable in such terms.

What may be said to be conceptually "new," in a positive way, in favor of a chance creation? Perhaps this question assumes that there has been something significantly positive in the past in favor of the view of "chance." We will, in Chapter 2, review arguments that have been advanced in materialistic thinking that are said to support such a view. As we proceed from there, we will continually test and weigh these arguments against the evidence of an empirical nature in support of the view of an intelligently designed universe. In the end, we will find that the materialists of this day are entirely wrong in suggesting that the view of a "supernatural" origin is a matter of unfounded "belief." It is "chance" that deserves such a labeling. The empirical evidence for an intelligently designed universe is not only well-founded, but far stronger than ever before.

Any consideration of the idea of a designed universe raises, of course, the question of purpose. To hold that the universe was intelligently designed is to expect that an intelligent Designer would have had reason and purpose to bring the universe, and all that lies within it, into existence. The remarkable purposefulness we will consider in the natural world herein is of itself not demonstrable of ultimate purpose. When one seeks to argue to the existence of an ultimate Designer of the universe on the strength alone of inferences arising from present-day empirical knowledge, and without resort to biblical or other religious references, it restricts one's possible avenues of explanation of purpose that could otherwise be available. No doubt some will find this approach to be in error. It does not mean, however, that theologians, philosophers, and scientists will not be free to draw views as they see fit from the material presented herein in a "not so" restricted manner. Interestingly, though, the phenomena we will consider does give a strong hint of ultimate creative purpose with respect to man's destiny in a rather surprising way—vis á vis an elimination process—in the manner described in Chapter 9 and, in a somewhat different context, in Chapter 8.

If one accepts the view that the world bears the marks of creative design, are we to turn to some "life force" within nature, as in the case of the so-called God of Spinoza,* or to religious belief and experience as exemplified in the biblical God? On the basis of the empirical record as to be shown, it would be most difficult indeed to say that the conditions that were requisite to the makeup of our known world could have been fulfilled other than by a unified creative essence that exists externally to it, in whole or in part. There are far too many antecedents, component parts, active forces, subdivisions of general laws, and precise relationships in the nature of things that would otherwise be far too disjunctive of one an-

---

* The 17th century philosopher, Baruch Spinoza, according to David Bidney,[11] viewed man as part of the order of nature and not as a special creation exempt from its universal laws—a notion of an impersonal, non-transcendent creator of the order of nature and dwelling within nature itself rather than outside of it—essentially "the impersonal God of the scientist, a God who may be conceived as the object of 'intellectual love,' but who, unlike the God of the Old Testament, did not reciprocate man's love and had no special concern with the welfare of the individuals."

other unless harmonized into a functioning whole. This is to say nothing of the advance forethought, knowledge, and incomprehensible power required to bring it all about in the beginning. The prescription, therefore, for our very existence is seen, in this writer's view, to empirically require the elements that we have come to attribute to the biblical God.

The empirical undertaking here is somewhat narrowed when one recognizes that the origin and development of the universe calls for an explanation on the basis of either (1) unintended chance and accident, or (2) intended design. No other alternative is possible. We should not lose sight of the fact that one or the other alternative expresses the truth and reality of the matter. Even if there should be found a curious blend of chance and accident with intended design in some ways, this would necessarily involve intended design. Yet, arguments are to be found on both sides of the question to the effect that one or the other is not an alternative possibility. These, however, are indeed extreme views that, when seen empirically, have no basis in logical necessity. But, of course, logical necessity, credibility, and reality may be quite different things. The next chapter will undertake to place into better focus the fundamental issues between the views of a chance or designed creation. In this way, we will be in a better position to distinguish more clearly between them.

# 2

## Chance or Design?

Like "a great lottery . . . our number came up in the Monte Carlo game."[1] This statement as to the origin of man "by chance" was made by the late Jacques Monod, the Nobel Prize winning French scientist, in his recent book entitled "Chance and Necessity." The concluding paragraph of the book summarized this view as follows:

"The ancient covenant is in pieces; man knows at last that he is alone in the universe's own feeling of immensity, out of which he emerged only by chance."[2]

The late J. Bronowski, the mathematician and author of the widely acclaimed best-seller *The Ascent of Man,* in his earlier book *The Identity of Man,* described a modern and perpetual heresy as follows: "An unbroken line runs from the stone to the cactus and on to the camel, and there is no supernatural leap in it. No special act of creation, no spark of life was needed to turn dead matter into living things."[3] In the Epilogue to *The Meaning of Evolution,* G. G. Simpson said: "Man is the result of a purposeless and materialistic process that does not have him in mind. He was not planned. . . ."[4] These views are representative of a rather widely held materialistic concept that there is no other explanation for the whole of the universe, including the existence of life, other than that of accidental causes arising from pure chance. It is a view that is, of course, in direct opposition to the view of an intelligently designed and purposeful creation. As Leslie

Reid observed in his book *Earth's Company,* the materialists look upon the origin and development of life "as the product of blind forces, denied of a recognizable plan, undirected by any approximation to what we call mind, organized on the basis of chance, which itself is governed only by the law that governs the tossing of a coin."[5]

The possibility that the remarkable universe might be compared to results achieved from "a single throw of the dice" is permitted in logic, according to F. R. Tennant. "Yet," he said, "common sense is not foolish in suspecting the dice to have been loaded."[6]

The "chance" theory of creation grew out of the original speculation of the existence of the atoms by the Greek, Democritus, in about 400 B. C. Greek atomism, according to John W. Dowling, envisaged that the atoms were invisible solid units of varying sizes and shapes, and possessed of original motion that could be transferred to other atoms by impact. They were also seen as clouds of particles swarming through an infinity of space and with a capacity to link together in a random manner.[7] The concept, he noted, came to be known as the Epicurean Hypothesis (after the Greek philosopher, Epicurus) which did not require, for its thesis, any explanation based on a supernatural cause. The basis for the Hypothesis, according to John Hick of the University of Birmingham in England, is that the universe consists of a finite number of atoms moving about at random that, in infinite time, will sooner or later fall into a self-regulatory combination and development of order.[8] In a somewhat broader sense, Hilde S. Hein considers it to be fundamental to the view of materialism that whatever takes place in the universe "is due to some affectation of matter" and that the explanation of life "requires no supplemental laws and principles beyond those which are sufficient to explain the non-living universe."[9]

Isaac Asimov, the well-known science writer, in his book *Only a Trillion,*[10] called attention to the manner in which the atoms can only form a limited number of combinations with one another and, of that limited number, some are more probable than others. He carried forward this combining propensity of the atoms into the build-up of a nucleoprotein molecule (the basic unit of life) to criticize, as some others have done, Lecomte du Noüy's 1942 best-selling book *Human Destiny*.[11] Du Noüy, in applying the calculus of probabilities to argue that the odds favoring the "random" formation of a single nucleoprotein molecule were so unbelievably remote that "chance" was an impossible alternative to a designed universe, did not take into account the selective combining propensity of the atoms as mentioned. Asimov simply ascribed the origin of this molecule to the "unblind workings of chance," rather than to the "blind" workings of chance, because of the limitations and probabilities involved in atomic aggregation.[12]

The proponents of the view of a chance creation turn to odds-limiting mechanisms in nature that appear to enhance such a view. Indeed, in an intermediate sense, the remarkable capacity of the few kinds of atoms involved in life processes to come together in only limited ways and combinations does serve to minimize the range of odds against "chance" in the incredulous "lottery" referred to by Monod, and to significantly alter the usual fifty-fifty odds ratio one would expect to result from "the tossing of a coin." But while this propensity does appear to give an "unblind" aspect to atomic aggregation, is it really to be seen as an argument for chance instead of design? In an ultimate sense, these explanations only serve to deepen the search for answers.

The elements of the atoms that are claimed to be the result of chance in the construction of the universe as we know it show strong inferences of an empirical nature in support of pre-conceived knowledge and design. We will, later on in Chapter 5, give consideration to this in a broad context. Here it is sufficient to say that the amazing atoms are anything but "trivial" or "ordinary" and the same may be said with respect to the laws which relate to their activity. Quite precisely from the beginning, they possessed the latent potential capacity to fulfill, as is today quite evident in our part of the universe (and, if we trust the modern scientific hypothesis of the probability of life as a common event elsewhere, then through-

31

out the universe) specific assignments, functional means-to-ends relationships and, in their material creations, to be meaningful, fit, suitable, and useful in one way or another for life in general, and for intelligent life in particular. How did they acquire such an amazing and fit potential capacity as mentioned if not by design? In terms of chance, there is no reason for their existence.

What, then, is to be said for the multitude of laws and forces in nature that complement and fashion the activity of the atoms and their elements? Were these, too, "unblind"? The materialistic explanation is that they exist by happenstance and, in addition, the point is made that, except for a few cosmic constants or laws of mostly a statistical nature, science has reduced these to a few basic universal laws in an ultimate sense, i.e., the laws governing celestial mechanics, the quantum theory of matter, and Einstein's general principles of relativity. There is a continuing search to reduce even these few to a basic single principle. Somehow, it is thought, the more simple and reducible the laws of nature, the more trivial these laws seem to become and, hence, the more acceptable the idea of a chance creation. But such a view overlooks that the efficiency and economy in the application of a "few" ultimate universal laws is what one could reasonably expect in a well-designed universe. This is to say nothing of the design suggested in that such few ultimate laws could be divided, extended or modified into a great multiplicity of diverse secondary aspects, e.g., into different specialized channels of function and activity to purposive ends. Although written in a somewhat different context of meaning, there is relevance here to the thought-provoking comment of Eugene P. Wigner, the Nobel Prize winning physicist, that: ". . . it is not at all natural that 'natural laws' exist, much less that man is able to discover them."[13]

On the inanimate side of elemental matter, everything is to be explained, according to materialistic thinking of today, on the basis of simple "physics and chemistry." Life, as a by-product thereof, is said to be the "outcome of an elaborate organization based on trivial ingredients and ordinary forces."[14] The design and evident purposefulness of living things is

32

thought to be the result of an interplay of chance with the selective processes of organic evolution. This interplay, it is said, simply carries forward from the point where physico-chemical activity was productive of first life, and this, without any need of calling on a supernatural cause for explanation. All of this is another way of saying that uncontrolled material systems are themselves creative of order. According to Reginald Kapp, the materialists see in such uncontrolled systems "a capacity for creating order . . . when we think, when we feel, when we plan for the future, it is solely . . . the result of the interaction of material systems."[15]

Such a view was not a dogmatic materialistic article of faith when expressed in a quite different manner and context by Immanuel Kant in the eighteenth century. Kant felt that the old argument from design could not "prove" the substance of ultimate cause and the contingency on which it is predicated unless it may be demonstrated that the things in the world "would not of themselves be capable of such order and harmony, in accordance with universal laws, if they were not in their substance the product of supreme wisdom."[16] Howsoever implausible it may seem, this view is the very crux of the issue between chance and design in this late 20th century. It is an issue which affects, once again, the question of certainty with respect to design (or chance) on the basis of empirical observation.

The element of *time* is the necessary catalyst, so to speak, by reason of which it is said the particles and atomic elements, interacting with physical forces and laws, were able to randomly produce any and all of the living and non-living phenomena of the universe. This is a kind of extension of the century-old analogy that if a million or so monkeys pounded typewriters continually for billions or even millions of years, they would eventually duplicate at random the complete poetic works of Goethe or the sonnets of Shakespeare, or both of these. Given the present view that the known universe is estimated to be some 16 to 20 billion years in age, and the Earth some 4.6 billion years old, the occurrence over time

33

whereby matter evolved into the present state of affairs from accidental circumstances is said to have become a reality.

But the universe as we know it is composed of limited kinds of ingredients, as well as relevant forces and laws, that are of themselves uncannily suitable to the remarkable end-results (including intelligent life in at least one portion of it) with respect to which time is to be reckoned and related. The elementary particles, the atoms themselves and their elements, and the associated forces, had to have the right organizational and other characteristics for specific kinds of properties and potential results that, in coincidence with time, could produce the remarkable universe as we know it. Then, too, certain key atoms of the lighter elements are said to be first traceable to events that occurred in near-proximity to events that are related to the origin of the universe. Even though the nucleation of different kinds of atoms from more elementary particles has been an on-going cosmic process, the 16-20-billion-year multiple of time does not readily allow for chance to have gained a foothold in countless critical antecedent aspects; that is, the lighter elements of the atoms and the principle of their internal structure that allows for chemical transformation, together with their latent remarkable potential capacities as mentioned, had already been firmly established in the very early stages of our expanding universe before enormous random-time opportunities for chance may be said to have entered the picture to influence their nature and destiny. It is not alone a question of whether all of the events that have occurred since the origin of the universe are, in the manner of expression of Nigel Calder in his book "The Key to the Universe," "a fulfillment of the potentialities of the various particles and forces."[17] It is as well, as in Kant's view, a question of whether an organizing God of the universe was the responsible agency to bring it all about in the first instance and to activate the various particles and forces that have made possible the contents and workings of the universe. Not to be overlooked, of course, is that the raw materials and forces included the potential for life, and special meaning in relation to life, particularly as we shall see in relation to intelligent life as we know it. But do the results of the observable events and activities speak adequately for themselves?

While the early events associated with the particles and cosmic forces are obscured from present observation, the end-results of the whole have opened up to far greater observation. If we look beyond the initiating phenomena, it is apparent that a great deal of what we will be considering herein did not flow as a matter of course from ordinary physics and chemistry; that is, without the development of countless non-causal relationships that had to correctly fall into place in order to realize the potential of life as a meaningful event. This is saying something different than simply that everything may be "explained" in physical and chemical terms, as a common denominator.

The materialists feel that the workings of chance, in the course of universal events over time, were not overwhelmed from a probabilities standpoint; that is, beyond the realm of credibility. Yet, there are few indeed who would take issue with Monod when he asserted: "The *a priori* (beforehand) probability that the inorganic and organic structure of the universe arose by chance is next to zero."[18] Does this not express a basic inconsistency; that is, to say that life arose by chance, and yet to also say that the advance predictive probability of this happening by chance was next to nothing? Apparently not, in a sense of observation.

This is because we are today looking backward in time (*a posteriori*) on this event of the origin of life so that it may be reasoned that the law of probabilities as to its happening does not now apply with the same degree of persuasion as it would have done if we were contemplating things contingently and looking forward. This is the "subtle illusion about events" to which the great Danish philosopher, Soren Kierkegaard, referred.[19]

Yet, the question of the persuasive effect of the law of probabilities on the prediction of an event that has already happened—as related to the origin of the universe and of life—does not give an empirically better or more logical reason in support of the idea of a chance creation over that of

35

a designed creation, and we are still left with the need for an explanation as to "how" and "why" it all happened in both an ultimate and intermediate sense. As we shall see, the idea of a chance creation is still an overwhelming improbability in contrast to the alternative of a designed creation from the very nature of things.

How, then, do the materialists account for the ultimate *first cause* of the known universe? Quite simply—they do not. They believe, however, that energy and matter existed from the time of the origin of the known universe, if not before, and, although itself inexplicable on the basis of natural causes, are more reasonable and plausible if considered to have been fortuitous than to appeal to an unobserved intelligent Designer as ultimate or first cause. "It is just as easy for them," observed the zoologist Edward L. Kessel, in a critical essay on such a view, "to suppose that the universe has always existed as to believe in a God who has always existed."[20] In this view, the "why" of things does not enter the picture and there is simply no need to answer the ultimate question put by Eric Mascall, the British theologian and scientist, i.e.: "Why is there a world at all?"[21]

Those adhering to the materialistic view of the universe are not moved by non-empirical (non-factual) pure reason arguments of the nature of St. Thomas Aquinas ("First Mover") or of St. Anselm (that the very conception of a God involves its existence), or by profound concepts as expressed by the physicist George Earl Davis, that "no material thing can create itself."[22] Nor do they seem amenable to the logic of the recent argument of Richard Taylor that there must be a reason for the existence of any material thing; but that logical necessity does not require a first cause for an existing creative essence in the universe from which all else has emanated.[23] Not even the force of the argument of Jules A. Baisneé makes a dent in the materialistic view. He said: "The more perfect cannot originate from the less perfect except through the intervention of a cause possessing at least the same degree of perfection as is found in the effect."[24]

Let us now turn to another form of criticism of the view

36

of a designed universe. Perhaps the one that is most frequently advanced is of an empirical nature. It is said that there are too many imperfections and disorders evident in nature which impugn the kind of perfection one would expect from an all-intelligent Designer who, to use a phrase of John Hick, is "skilled in the art of world-making."[25]

Thus, at one time or another, it has been said that earthquakes, the eruptions of volcanoes, cyclones, tornadoes, floods, droughts, famines, and other forms of natural catastrophical events cannot be attributed to a benign or skilled Designer; that the topographical irregularities on the surface of the Earth, such as mountain ranges, or the very existence of deserts, arctic areas, tropical jungles, and other seemingly "inhospitable" places reveals imperfections in nature so as to be inconsistent with a purposive intention; that geologic history is strewn with the record of "mistakes" of extinct species, such as the dinosaurs, which implies some fundamental error in design; that evil exists throughout the world in the form of human wickedness, cruelty, unhappiness, disease, death, suffering, controversy, war, and the like that also reflect unfavorably on the idea of a skilled Designer.

In a modern-knowledge context, many of these claimed "imperfections" may be seen in an entirely different light as indicated in the introductory chapter. This, as we shall consider in Chapter 9, is a fact of new significance to the view of an intelligently designed universe.

In this century, a new empirical form of argument has been put forward by the materialists. This, in result of the unraveling in science of the basic secrets of the DNA (deoxyribonucleic acid) molecule represented by the self-copying double helix structure that is familiar to most of us. It provides the code on which hereditary information is passed on from generation to generation in living organisms. It has been found that the genetic code mechanism is free in the sense of allowing for change (gene mutation, recombination, etc.) in DNA upon which natural selective evolutionary processes are said to act. An aspect of "chance," so to speak. This, however, within rigid genetic structural constraints. In Chapters 9-11,

37

we shall see how this aspect of chance in DNA fits quite well into a designed scheme of things, and that intelligent design may be seen as providing a better explanation than chance for the origin of DNA and its activity. As a materialistic argument it is somewhat similar to that based on the principle of indeterminacy in science, as mentioned in the introductory chapter.

There are still other types of arguments that have been engaged to provide a negative view to the idea of a designed and purposeful creation of the universe. In matter of fact, the materialists have brought forth a Pandora's box of arguments. Conceptually, they reflect a high degree of human ingenuity. In brief summary form and in addition to what has already been noted in this chapter, it is said that: there is no direct and positive evidence of an intelligent Designer and inferences of an empirical nature to the contrary are scientifically unverifiable or logically unnecessary and, therefore, should be disregarded; there is no other acceptable form of rationalization other than that derived from the discipline of scientific method, i.e., that real knowledge comes only from facts proven by observation, experimentation, and testing for verification; value judgments which relate to the existence of an intelligent Designer of the universe are inadmissible as the consequence alone of subjective (personal), if not illusory, observation; biblical "beliefs" are nothing more than just that; and that common sense and intuition are alogical.

Having thus summarized above the major tenets of the materialistic view of a "chance" creation, together with a brief outline of arguments which are frequently raised to negate the view of a designed and purposeful creation, we are now in a better position to compare in a discriminating manner, in this and in remaining chapters, the differing views.

The view of a designed creation, in a modern empirical context, has found general expression in various ways. Leslie Reid, for instance, has referred to "the unity that binds the manifestations of nature into an integrated whole, each one of these manifestations depending on the others with an intimacy that besides being vitally necessary is also frequently mutual."[26] A somewhat similar manner of expressing the view of design was made by F. R. Tennant when he said: "The forcibleness of the world's appeal consists . . . in the conspiration of innumerable causes to produce, by their united and reciprocal action, and to maintain, a general order of nature."[27]

The so-called old argument from design and more recent "wider" empirical arguments to design will be briefly considered in the next two chapters, respectively, as important background to the above and to the arguments to be developed later on. I should like to emphasize again the basic importance of these arguments, not only from the cumulative standpoint, but to show as well the rather substantial "leap" in the empirical evidence favoring design during the course of nearly three centuries and, more particularly, in the past half-century. At the same time, this permits an opportunity for one to realize how much more of natural phenomena the view of chance has had to absorb and to seek to account for than in earlier times. Preliminary to all of this, however, some basic observations are pertinent.

Essentially, arguments raised in support of a view of a "chance" creation of the universe are negative and unilateral in character. That is, arguments found in its support are mostly negative against the view of design, rather than being positive in support of chance. As an idea, chance has neither a firm foothold to a beginning, nor does it have an ending, in what is claimed for it in an empirical way. This includes the contention that chance alone is responsible for evolutionary processes as relate to living organisms which, as we shall consider in Chapters 10-12, may reasonably be best explained when viewed in the context of foreknowledge and intelligent design. As an idea, chance comes from nowhere and gets into difficulty as soon as it confronts the alternative of design. If there were not a vast multitude of high quality inferences and presumptions favoring design, it might be different. But this is not the case. Those who would say that the idea of chance is exclusive of itself and that the idea of a designed universe is not a valid possibility or probability have to explain away both the strong cumulative and the ever-increasing new proofs of an empirical nature favoring the latter and, at the same time, furnish either certain or at least convincing proof in support of chance. This they are unable to do.

In view of the fact that so many are turning to science today for explanations concerning the unknown, we should here briefly consider some widespread attitudes with respect to the views we have been considering. There is a great deal of modern literature which suggests that science has, indirectly at least, been a willing agency through which the view of a chance creation has been preferentially nurtured and left open to acceptability. It would seem that suggestions of this nature spring largely from the fact that quite a few in the scientific community adhere to an admonition, in keeping with the scientific method, to totally disregard any inquiry of a nature that would involve the concept of a supernaturally designed and purposeful origin of things. No such admonition, unfortunately, is outstanding as concerns the idea of a chance creation, even though, empirically, it is a view that fails the disciplinary test of scientific methodology.

As only one example of the foregoing, Alfred S. Romer, the eminent zoologist, asserted, in his book "The Procession of Life," as though restating an unwritten code of ethics, that "a scientist should attempt to explain the pertinent phenomena of nature in terms of natural laws" rather than "to resort to unprovable hypotheses of supernatural agencies being involved in the story of evolution."[28] This is a way of saying that the existence of a Designer of the universe is unprovable in accordance with the strict methodology of science as an objective discipline requiring observation, experimentation, testing, and verification to prove the certainty of facts. Perhaps, in another sense, it is a way of saying, subjectively, that empirical inferences of a supernatural should be left entirely to metaphysics and to religious belief and experience.

Certainly, scientific methodology does serve a most valuable purpose as perhaps the only method in which science may develop the absolute certainty to which it aspires. But the fact that science has chosen such an approach for its own purposes should not deter anyone from recognizing the probative evidentiary value of inductive proof and thought with respect to the fundamental question herein. Ironically, the useful discipline of scientific method to conclude the results of scientific investigation is by no means the sole method used in science, or outside of science, in determining whether or not facts which are founded on empirical observation are reasonable or generally acceptable even though, because of lack of direct proof, they fall short of certainty. In fact, as previously mentioned, scientists themselves accept as "established" and "plausible" a great many fully unverified theories and hypotheses in various fields of science. As noted by Eric C. Rust, many scientific laws "are of the nature of statistical averages in that they describe the probabilities but not the certainties. Determination is replaced by probability."[29] A most recent example of this is in the field of elementary particle physics where theoretical projections have been employed to develop theories of the existence of unseen particles in the proton nuclei of the atom called "quarks." Difficulties were encountered. In the throes of uncertainty, Yoichiro Nambu, a theoretical physicist on quarks, said: "If a particle cannot be isolated or observed, even in theory, how will we ever be able to know that it exists?"[30] And yet, the search continues in science for unobserved and unseen particles with no certainty of their existence.

The position in science that, in the use of its methods, the only theories or hypotheses that may be acceptably formulated are those which carry the possibility of ultimate proof of certainty is not only presumptuous as concerns the question of design but is a rather faulty argument, to say the least. This, in that "possibilities" that are acceptable in science for further investigation for probative value may never, in the end, be more than just that. There is no need for science to turn a "blind eye" to any and all empirically based inferences and presumptions to design that are in evidence throughout the whole fabric of natural phenomena. This is to say nothing of the fact that the system of the scientific method of proof does not stand alone as the only system of logic and understanding available to mankind.

41

It would seem that such a position is highly undesirable to scientific inquiry itself for, if indeed the universe was designed (and even the most pragmatic scientists cannot deny at least the possibility), it was done creatively in a manner that should furnish clues to aid in new discovery. This work will at least suggest, as well as give support to, the view that some of the mysteries in science today may be best explained empirically by resort to design. Nature appears to have taken the course of the best solutions from a design standpoint in both the inanimate and animate sides of things. Science, while continually chasing down countless hypotheses and theories that may, or may not, be blind alleys should not be ignoring the possibilities evident on the subject of design and perhaps should turn to "think" design. This is not at all an unreasonable suggestion when one considers the broader context in which design may now be viewed.

A few examples may serve to impress the point. A few decades ago, natural gas was being flared from oil wells, and helium, later on, from gas wells, both as "waste" substances of no real known utility. Where was the advance thought that, in the design of things, these substances might someday serve mankind in countless useful ways (as is now evident) just as many other natural phenomena and substances of the environment formerly considered superfluous, are now seen to relate to man in terms of fitness, suitability, and utility? As another example, let's take the Moon, as a neighboring object that, according to space scientists, holds the key to future interplanetary space travel. Before landing the first space vehicle there, could we have thought of design? As it turned out, the soft surface on the marias of the Moon—like damp sand—was of such a nature that it provoked the comment from the English science writer Adrian Berry that it "might have been made for descending spacecraft . . . something which would arouse one's suspicion in the direction of intelligent design."[31] Then again, we can all recall the great anticipation that accompanied the return to Earth of rocks and soil from the Moon. What turned out to be "unexpected" about the Moon's surface rocks and soils should have been "expected"—and precisely so at that, had any thought been given to "design"—as we shall discuss in Chapter 6.

These few examples could be multiplied many times over in relation to man's discoveries of the unknown. It is implicit in a great deal of the phenomena to be considered in later chapters and, specifically, in reference to certain of the great paradoxes in biology to be considered. It all adds up to the point that many in science today are making a serious mistake in limiting their field of empirical observation to exclude the possibility at least of the intelligent design of things. It is not unreasonable to predict that science in general will come to realize this in time. In matter of fact, my research reflects that perhaps a majority of scientists of today do not appear to be making this exclusion. In the physical sciences, in particular, there seems to be an ever-growing appreciation that accidental causes are inadequate to explain the magnificent design and organization in material substance that comes from continuing discoveries into the secrets of nature. Perhaps this growing awareness is typified in Nigel Calder's description of a group of theoretical nuclear scientists at the CERN laboratory who "seemingly take up pen and paper to commune with the universe trying to think how they would have organized the particles of matter had they been God."[32]

The foregoing is not to be regarded as a modern-day resort to the "God of the Gaps" criticism made by many scientists against the religious community in the post-Darwin era of the last century whenever "unknown" phenomena was attributed to a Designer of the universe. There is today, as we shall see, a strong empirical basis in fact to explain natural phenomena and even to fill certain gaps in scientific knowledge with answers that imply creative design. The criticism that is rightly justified today has to do with what might be called a resort to "Chance of the Gaps." For more than a century now, as a turn-around from the post-Darwin era, the materialists have been relying on this theme to explain away all of the "knowns" and "unknowns" in science.

There is no good reason why we should not draw a judgment founded on circumstantial proofs and strong presumptions arising from clear inferences to design. The degree of subjectivity or objectivity involved in such a judgment, in this work, may be seen, in part at least, as dependent on how science itself views many of its own theories and hypotheses that are to be relied upon in support of design. It is important to emphasize that, in inductive reasoning, direct evidence is not always required to permit the making of a sound and logically-premised judgment. It depends on many other factors which, among other things, may include varying degrees of quality, quantity, reliability, etc. As suggested above, it would seem unscientific of itself to ignore facts which have an empirical basis in observation. We do not always have, of course, the complete satisfaction that our judgments are correct when the evidence is not direct and positive. But here again, this is a matter of degree insofar as the uncertainties are concerned. The best we can do, according to George E. Davis, "is to make intelligent inferences from what we know."[33]

The next chapter will be devoted to a brief descriptive analysis of the so-called old argument from design and this includes, together with the next following chapter, some consideration of revised and wider versions of the old argument. As I have indicated, the empirical evidence with respect to both the ideas of chance and of design is to be viewed cumulatively as related to one or the other of the two opposing concepts.

# 3

## The Argument from Design

In result of a revival of the Epicurean Hypothesis in the 17th century, following a period of decline, a number of books of an empirical nature on design were written to counter the non-supernatural appeal of the Hypothesis which, as we have seen, pictured the universe as having been produced simply by a random concourse of atoms. The writers turned to the sciences of the day in order to make the point that the whole of Nature required the handiwork of a designing God, i.e. the biblical God, notwithstanding the views on the reality of the atoms.

John Ray, in 1691, in specific reference to the Epicurean Hypothesis, wrote a comprehensive design argument, the so-called argument from design (meaning, as noted previously, an argument from analogy).[1] This was followed by other works of similar nature as, for example, those of William Derham in 1730[2] and the more famous work of William Paley in 1804.[3] Later, in 1836, the eight volumes of the so-called Bridgewater Treatises entitled "The Power and Goodness of God as Manifested in the Creation"[4] were published. These included the separate works of eminent British scientists of the day (as related to their respective fields of specialty) setting forth a great deal of the then known natural phenomena that was suggestive of a "designed" creation. As John Hick has noted, one cannot help but be very much impressed by the phenomena of the natural world that attracted the attention of these writers.

The argument from design was related primarily to the

drawing of analogies with respect to natural objects or other phenomena, including living organisms and functioning parts or features of such organisms (as, for example, the eye, the brain, animal metabolism, the ear, camouflage and mimicry in animals, glands, and so on) that, on account of their intricacy or complexity, form or shape, or purposeful means-to-ends relationships, gave the appearance by analogy to artificially contrived objects, artifacts, or machines of human construction and intelligence (as, for example, a building, a watch, a machine, and so on). Thus, just as a machine is known to be the product of human intelligence, so also natural objects, such as the eye, heart, etc. closely resemble the sort of work that one would attribute to an intelligent cause. The famous "design" analogy of William Paley with respect to a watch is quite demonstrative of the concept of the old argument from design. He said:

> Suppose . . . I had found a watch upon the ground and that I had never seen a watch made . . . [and] . . . had never known an artist capable of making one . . . that when we come to inspect the watch, we perceive . . . that its several parts are framed and put together for a purpose, e.g. that they are so framed and adjusted as to produce motion, and that motion so regulated as to point out the hour of the day; that, if the several parts had been differently shaped from what they are, of a different size from what they are, or placed after any other manner, or in any other order, than that in which they are placed, either no motion at all would have been carried on in the machine, or none would have answered the use, that is now served by it . . . the inference . . . is inevitable that the watch must have had a Maker . . . [who] . . . at some time or at some place or other . . . formed it for the purpose which we find it actually to answer; [and] who contemplated its construction, and designed its use.

The inductive reasoning aspect of the argument from design was described in the form of a syllogism by Robert E. D. Clark as follows: "Everything that exhibits curious adaptation of

46

means-to-ends and is such that we know whether or not it was the product of intelligent design, in fact was the product of intelligent design. . . . The universe exhibits curious adaptation of means-to-ends. . . . Therefore, the universe is probably the product of intelligent design."[6]

For some reason it has been widely thought that these early writers were limited to analogies relating to natural objects of the general nature as mentioned. This is not the case. Their works described a surprising number of inter-connecting relationships, suggestive of design, found both in the living and in the then less known inanimate worlds of nature. A few examples from the books of Paley and Ray may give the reader a kind of brief insight into the variety of their arguments.

Ray pointed out such things as the variety of colors of infinite use in distinguishing objects and for adding beauty to the world; the variety of trees of differing textures, hardness, and other qualities to serve man in differing ways; the variety of rocks and stones with a wide range of characteristics suitable to the construction by man of shelters and other edifices; the variety of metals to serve different purposes and functions (interestingly, the rarity of the element of gold was regarded as necessary to "man's conduct of trade"); the variety of herbs for their medicinal quality; the abundance of edible fruits and vegetables and their distribution and variety; the natural occurrences of papyrus to early civilizations which enabled the spread of written communication; the various celestial aids to sea-going navigation, such as the North Star; the existence of rivers, lakes, and ponds; the manner in which both plant and animal life serve useful and purposeful objectives in support of other life and, in particular, those of man; and an almost endless list of physiological features of animal life which are well-adapted, fit, and suitable to the carrying out of various functions, and so on. In commenting on the marvels of the clouds and rain, as another specific example, Ray found an inference to design in their dispersement and distribution by the action of the winds, thinking it providential that rain descends down on the Earth gradually and by drops

47

because "if it should fall down in a continued stream like a river, it would gall the ground, wash away plants by the roots, overthrow houses, and greatly incommode if not suffocate animals. . . ."[7]

Paley found great significance in the provision of nature to provide things beforehand "which are not to be used until a considerable time afterwards; for this implies a contemplation of the future, which only belongs to intelligence." As examples of this, he referred to innumerable natural "contrivances" of living things, including the horns of animals, the milk of a female parent, wings of birds, and so on. But, to him, nothing else in the natural world showed more of the creative design of a higher intelligence than the eye. It is, Paley said, far too intricate and complex a contrivance to have been the product of any other cause. As a part of this, he was fascinated with light as complementary to the existence of sight. He said: "Its particles move with such velocity that, if it were not for the proportionate minuteness of which they are composed, the force would be destructive to the tenderest of animal substances, such as the eye."[8] On the cosmic side of things, he perceived design in the suitableness of the Earth and sea to its inhabitants, in the rotation of the Earth upon which the change of seasons depend, etc.

"No one could believe," said J. N. Shearman, in a later design argument that emphasized some of the points raised by Paley, "that any chance assemblage of wheels, bars, screws, and springs could produce a watch." By the same token, he said that no one could fail to conclude that "the workings of the eye in terms of imagery, optical lenses, etc. must have been guided and controlled by an intelligence which knew how to make a present arrangement of things with a view to the future . . . the end result had to be foreseen in order to bring such objects about and an intelligence directed them so as to produce the orderly arrangement of parts which . . . [are] . . . observed to exist."[9] Shearman then pointed to numerous instances of natural organisms fulfilling definite ends and producing a constant and useful result by means of machinery far more complicated and remarkable than that of any watch, not only in terms of design, order and regularity of arrangement, but also in orderly and regular performance of functions. This brings to mind a very early version of a design argument rendered by Aquinas in the 13th century who, in his so-called "Fifth Way," sought to show that the goal-seeking characteristics of living things have followed a path "as straight as the archer's arrow" toward purposive goals.[10]

One empirical point of weakness in the traditional old argument from design was that its proponents were mostly limited in knowledge to the things and events as related to an earlier era of scientific knowledge. Nevertheless, a great many of their observations are useful today from the cumulative standpoint, the importance of which was stressed by Heinecken in his book "God in the Space Age" where he noted that there is "no one thing in the chain that is adequate to carry the burden of conclusive conviction about the existence and nature of God."[11] Then, too, for our purposes here, there is significance to be attached to the "leap-forward" in knowledge—indicative of design in a progressive and comparative way over the course of nearly three centuries of design arguments.

The effect of Darwin's "Origin of Species" on the argument from design was substantial. Appearing in 1859, it was (and still is) viewed by many in science as offering a purely mechanistic accounting for the appearances of design and purposefulness in living organisms through natural selection. It was (and is today) simply argued that organic evolution "did not require" or "establish any need for" the appeal to a supernatural origin. By reason of this purely mechanistic explanation, according to Allan Broms, "it not only summarized the overwhelming evidence for evolution as against special creation, but also provided a single and convincingly obvious explanation of evolutionary adaptation by natural selection."[12] It was no longer thought necessary, according to Peter A. Bertocci, "to postulate specific actions of the Creator to account for the harmonious interplay between the abilities and needs of living things and their environment."[13] The force of the story of organic evolution, he noted, caused many to turn to other kinds of arguments to support a designed creation, such as to ontological and moral arguments, as well as to arguments based on religious experience. This, rather than to provide additional support for the argument from design.[14]

The assertion that natural selection could fully account for the appearance in living organisms of purposeful means-to-ends characteristics seemed to add a measure of credibility to the Epicurean idea that the non-living world of nature, as then less known, was also randomly evolved and developed without the need of a designer being involved in the process. Thus, the design arguments raised by Ray, Paley, and others—even those relating to inanimate nature and its many relationships to animate nature—were swept away by the tidal force of the Darwinian concept of evolution. The fact that the concept was (and is) limited in application alone to the animate side of the natural world did not seem to matter.

In retrospect and in the light of our vastly increased knowledge of inanimate nature to be herein considered, one may seriously raise the point that the two aspects of nature, the animate and inanimate, are much too perfectly harmonized, fit, and suitable to each other to reasonably look upon them as standing apart and independent from one another in an evolutionary sense. It is quite inadequate to attribute this to adaptation of the animate to the inanimate. The selective processes involved in the development of living systems, in accordance with the modern theory of organic evolution, had no influence on the circumstances that resulted in the design to be seen in inanimate phenomena that complements the animate on the broad scale. It would seem to follow that something more is needed to explain both worlds. But the point to make here is simply that the development of the theory of organic evolution in the post-Darwin era may be seen today as having over-reacted against the argument from design with respect to the phenomena it described that was not subject to the influence of selection in living systems.

Since, as indicated in the introductory chapter, an empirically-based design argument is of itself unable to provide absolute "certainty" in proof of a designed universe, it is unnecessary to elaborate in any detail on the philosophical arguments that require such proof. It is, however, relevant here to briefly consider the nature of these arguments and to make several important comments concerning the same.

In his "Dialogues,"[15] published posthumously in 1779, Hume essentially based his logical criticism on the argument that one may not prove the existence of an infinite Being merely from observed "effects" in a finite natural world that give the appearance of an intelligently designed universe. Although it does not detract significantly from the persuasive force of his principle of logic, it is to be noted that he related his argument mainly to the question of proof of an infinite, all-perfect, omnipotent, and omnipresent biblical God. The finite may not, he argued, be equated in any logical manner of proof with the infinite.

A majority of the philosophers of today express the view that Hume's argument is "unanswerable," according to McPherson in his recent book "The Argument From Design." "For us to say," said McPherson, "that A is the cause of B we must, in general, be able to identify both A and B."[16] Another recent criticism of design arguments in general, that of Hurlbutt in his book "Hume, Newton, and The Design Argument," is much the same effect. He noted, on the basis of Hume, that in order to demonstrate a cause for any effect it is necessary to have observed the cause and the effect in conjunction, as no one has seen the origin of one world "let alone worlds."[17]

The matter of positive and direct observation, as indicated in the introductory chapter, is the missing ingredient in this regard, but it does not leave us deficient in other proofs based on observation which, while indirect, are of strong and convincing probative value. Hume's logic, as previously mentioned, does not eliminate the inferences and presumptions of an intelligently designed universe to be considered herein, but only presents a problem with respect to proof that would support the matter of absolute certainty and the precise nature of the creative essence of a Designer of the universe. But

51

while some modern philosophical writers would disregard any form of proof less than that of certainty, it is clear from the writings of both Hume and Kant that they would not have done so. Each of them recognized the value of proof of the nature as found in the argument from design.

In his "Critique of Pure Reason," Kant said that the argument from design, being based on observation, is one that deserves to be considered with respect because it is "the oldest, the clearest and the most accordant with the common reason of mankind."[18] It is rather clear from other expressions of Kant that his chief difficulty with the argument, quite apart from the contingency of its certainty aspect, was simply that we do not have the empirical knowledge in its support. Thus, he said: "The utmost, therefore, that the argument can prove is an *architect* of the world who is always very much hampered by the adaptability of the material with which he works." This observation was made, of course, several centuries ago. As A E. Taylor observed some thirty years ago: ". . . The vast expansion of our knowledge in the last century or century and a half, so far from weakening the traditional 'argument from design,' have made it much stronger than it could have appeared in the days of Hume, Voltaire, and Kant."[19] In the case of Hume, his expression of respect for the old argument from design was coupled with the view that it is "a remote analogy to human intelligence."

The logic of Hume and Kant should now be viewed with far less rigidity, influence, and significance. Modern discovery and a vast explosion in acceptable knowledge over the centuries have significantly advanced the scope of our capability to identify "A" as cause from the observed effects of nature ("B"). This, in a highly reliable way that is now firmly implanted in the experience of man which was simply unavailing in earlier days.

During the time of Hume, and for several centuries thereafter, the effects ("B") in nature that were said to give the appearance of "intelligent design" were of a limited general scope and mainly related to analogies of the sort described above. The identity of "A" from "B" was also obscured by lack of an experience factor with which to relate the appearances of things in terms of design.

But in the chapters to come we will not only see "B" in a far broader aspect of design but, more importantly, see that "B" (as representative of the whole of phenomena that infers design) has become divisible into a triad of component empirical aspects (a "C," "D," and "E" of proof). Each of these serve as different kinds of base points of observation, inferential of design, which can relate to human experience in a way that assists our identification of "A" by a sort of triangulation. As a simple unrelated example of this, take the case of a mariner who is lost on the high seas with only one position "fix" (a star, land monument, etc.) from which he may calculate and seek to identify his precise present location, "A." The one fix alone is unreliable and insufficient, but if he can record as many as, say three "fixes," the positive identification of his position, while not certain in absolute terms (because of possible errors in his observation), is nevertheless of such high reliability in experience that he may confidently assume its correctness. As I mentioned in the introductory chapter, science itself frequently relies on a somewhat similar kind of procedure in the verification of its hypotheses in seeking to establish a theory of general acceptability. Where "actual" observation of a yet to be identified causative "A" is missing, the research scientist looks for different sorts of observable phenomena that point to the same "A" with such invariant regularity that he may assume the correctness of the identification. While not infallible, of course, the experience of science in the use of such a procedure has become recognized as highly reliable, more especially in the case where an unidentified "A" may only be one of two possible alternatives.

The problem in any case of inductive reasoning from effect to cause is to know that the observable evidence points to one final cause rather than to another. It is here that the observed facts derived from one kind of observational base may serve to verify others of a different base to the end that the pattern of invariance and regularity is such that a single conclusion may be obtained in achieving a reliable identification.

It is premature in the early stage of this work, of course, for the reader to see how the phenomena of nature, as enhanced by modern knowledge, falls into divisible patterns from which to "triangulate" the identity of "A," as cause, in an ultimate sense of either design or chance. In this chapter, we have been considering only the "C" of a possible triangulation —the old "argument from design" (i.e., mainly analogy) and, in the next chapter, the wider and distinctive kind of empirically-based argument to design which arose in this century (as "D") that relates the "fitness" and "harmony" of nature for the general support and existence of life to "innumerable" aspects of empirical observation. Later on, it is the broader and distinctive "E" (the phenomenon of man's mind and consciousness in a special and unique creative relationship alone with nature) that adds a broad new base of observation which serves to complete the picture in a directional way and in a manner of verification that most assuredly bespeaks intelligent design, rather than random chance, as the "A" cause of it all. While each of these bases of observation rely on probalities and overlap with the others in some ways, this also occurs in many of the scientific approaches to verification that rely on effect to cause.

During the first half of this century, the "wider" or restructured form of design argument as mentioned began to take shape and will be reviewed in the following chapter. While borrowing from the cumulative effect of the earlier arguments from design, this form branched more into the world of inanimate nature, and its relationship to animate nature. It posed a challenging question to science of the day which had tended to disregard the empirical basis of all design arguments on the strength of Darwinian explanations related to the animate side of things.

# 4

## Fitness of the Environment

Probably the most significant book of this century, relating to "intelligent design," was written in 1913 by the American biochemist, L. J. Henderson, and entitled "Fitness of the Environment."[1] When put into a modern empirical context, it may be seen retrospectively as having opened up (and, in a way, re-opened) a most important pathway in support of the view of an intelligently designed universe. It furnished the basic theme for the wider or so-called re-structured forms of design arguments which came along in this century. New emphasis was placed on fit and suitable inter-relationships between animate (living) nature, on the one hand, and the environment of inanimate nature on the other; this, as contributing to the existence and support of life on Earth. At the same time, interest continued to be shown in arguments based mostly on analogy, but with less emphasis, as in the case of the earlier arguments from design. Objections to this wider theme of design are the same in this day as in Henderson's time.

Henderson reached out to establish a closer linkage between the inanimate and animate aspects of nature than had been possible earlier. This is not to say that some of the earlier design arguments before Darwin in the 19th century had overlooked various points of linkage between the two aspects of nature, as mentioned in the preceding chapter. It is rather to say that the fervor of the post-Darwin thinking (related, as it was, to the animate side of things) blindly swept away the significance of these early known linkages (inanimate to animate) in terms of the view of intelligent design.

Henderson observed that it had been "the habit" of biologists since Darwin to consider only the adaptations of living organisms to the environment. "Yet," he said, "fitness in the environment must be as well as fitness in the organism. How, for example, could man adapt his civilization to water power if no water power existed within his reach?"[2] A few other questions offering similar examples serve to emphasize his point: How could animals and early man take shelter in caves if there were no caves? How could early man obtain heat from fire if there were no wood or other combustible substances? "The real and unique fitness of the environment," said Henderson, "is one part of a reciprocal relationship of which fitness of the organism is the other." He argued that the process of cosmic evolution is indivisibly linked with the fundamental characteristics of the organism and that "one fitness is not less important than the other."[3]

The main new contribution of Henderson to this line of thinking related to the physico-chemical characteristics of three chemical elements, carbon, hydrogen, and oxygen, and of the compounds, water and carbonic acid. He said:

> They constitute a unique ensemble of fitness, among all possible chemical substances, for a living organism which must be complex, regulated, and engaged in active metabolism; that there are no other compounds which share more than a small part of the qualities of fitness of water and carbonic acid, and no other elements which share those of carbon, hydrogen, and oxygen.[4]

As to chemical compounds containing the elements carbon, hydrogen, and oxygen, he called attention to their possession of unique properties which together result in maximum fitness in certain respects, e.g. as sources of matter and energy for the processes of metabolism, as sources of complex structures, as the means of satisfying complex life functions, and so on. As to the unique properties of water, he called attention to a

56

great number of unusual features which result in maximum fitness in certain respects, e.g. mobility, ubiquity, constancy of temperature and richness of the environment, richness of the organism in chemical constituents, variety of chemical processes, electrical phenomena, colloidal phenomena, etc. As to carbon dioxide, he noted that it possesses very unusual properties, e.g. magnitude of absorption coefficient and strength as acid, which provide maximum fitness in various ways. He noted that none of the characteristics of these substances are known to be unfit.

When we consider the existence of inter-relationships between cosmic phenomena (including inanimate matter) and the animated world of living things, we are concerning ourselves (except coincidentally in some cases) with something quite different and apart from analogies made to show design under the old argument from design. We are instead looking to another and additional dimension of empirical observation to design, one that enhances immeasurably the overall picture of a designed world. It is not an illusion on our part whenever we recognize something that naturally fits together and is suitable in relation to something else even though, to some extent, this may be a matter of degree. In this and in some of the chapters to follow, we will be considering the provision of the fitness and suitability of the phenomena of nature, untouched by the hand of man, to permit the existence and development of life. In this sense, a distinction should be drawn as against the fitness and suitability of nature with respect to man's capacity to convert the same to specialized uses and purposes. The latter kind of fitness and suitability, in relation to man and design, will be considered in Chapter 7. Taken on the whole, it shows how closely the natural world is tied together into a united and harmoniously functioning entity.

Although Henderson devoted the greater part of his attention to the elements and the compound substances as mentioned, he called attention to some of the other then known phenomena which he considered to be of great significance in favoring the existence of life on this planet, such as:

57

The size of the Earth, which enables it to retain its present atmosphere; the eccentricity of its orbit and the inclination of the eliptic; the relative amounts of land and sea and a host of other functions . . . (are) an extremely favorable abode for the living organism. The adjustment of the quantity of water and of its density, as compared with that of the Earth, afford some of the most marked and beautiful instances of design . . . (as shown by Laplace). The world would have been constantly liable to have been deluged from the slightest causes had the mean density of the ocean exceeded that of the Earth. . . . The relative gravity of water, as compared with Earth, keeps the ocean within its destined limits, notwithstanding its incessant motion.[5]

Recognizing, as he did, that all physico-chemical transformations consist of re-arrangements of the atoms of the chemical elements and that the universe is made up of a relatively small number of material ingredients, he found it difficult to reasonably attribute to chance the phenomena of the fit and suitable properties of inanimate matter to the existence of life, there being no known process or laws that would make it so.

In a brief commentary which appeared in 1951 in the British Association for Advancement of Science Report, the late C. F. A. Pantin, referring to Henderson's thesis, was very much impressed with his point that design appears in the inanimate world as in the animate world and that, on the inanimate side, this may not be attributed to the selective mechanisms of natural selection. He said:

Can we discern design in the properties of the units which make such a (living) organism possible? These properties of the units are not the result of selection in a Darwinian sense.[6]

The proposition of Henderson that life, as we know it on Earth, could not have appeared under conditions better suited to its nature, was referred to by Peter A. Bertocci in a design argument published in 1951.[7] He said there is "not one chance

58

in countless millions of millions that the peculiarly appropriate qualities of carbon, hydrogen, and oxygen, should simultaneously occur in the three elements otherwise than through the operation of a natural law which somehow connects them together."[8]

F. R. Tennant, as a part of his wider view of design first published in 1928, pointed to the existence of "innumerable" fit animate-inanimate inter-relationships. He said: ". . . It is rather when the essential part played by the environment, physical and organic, in the progressive development of the organic world, is appreciated, that non-teleological explanation ceases to be plausible in this sphere, and, conspiration being precluded, external design begins to be indicated or strongly suggested."[9]

He recalled to mind the vast array of inferences which had been presented by the earlier writers. This, together with the fitness argument of Henderson, led him to the view that there existed an empirical basis for a "reasonable belief" in an intelligent Designer. He explained that ". . . the inanimate processes appear to have been the means for the development of the fitness and survival of life in terms of the concept of natural selection; that such means involve the convergence of innumerable events toward a result" and that "neither science nor logic is able to abate the forcibleness of this appeal" to a higher intelligence. "The fitness of our world," he said, "to be the home of living things depends upon certain primary conditions, astronomical, thermal, chemical, etc., and on the coincidence of qualities apparently not casually connected with one another, the number of which would doubtless surprise anyone wholly unlearned in the sciences. . . ."[10]

In his book, Bertocci, to some extent like Tennant, constructed a wider design argument to take into account "the interconnectedness of physical nature, life, and human experience" rather than simply "specific restricted evidence of design and fruitful adaptation"[11] as in the case of the old design arguments. He broadened these aspects to cover, as well, such things as the relevance of thought to reality, the interrelation of moral effort and the order of nature, the inter-relation between value and nature, the significance of aesthetic experience, the world as good for Man, and religious experience as confirmatory of design. On the empirical side, he strongly supported the Henderson thesis by his own recurrent theme: "And the fact still remains that life's activities are situated in a world who supports them."[12]

Let us now turn to examine the criticism that has been made of the basic design concept of "fitness of the environment" as developed by Henderson and other writers of the wider or reconstructed design arguments of the nature as mentioned. Typical of the criticism is that of Wallace I. Matson who said:

> The arguments based on 'the fitness of the environment' resemble the probability argument in dwelling on the complex concatenation of 'probable' characteristics that matter in general, and the Earth in particular, must have in order to render life possible. . . . Such arguments, however, amount to regarding this world with the laws of nature operative in it, as only one of the infinite 'possible worlds.'[13]

David Lack considered it to be a weak argument to claim that life would not have been possible without the particular physical and chemical composition of the Earth and the universe because, as he said: "It assumes that there can be no life except in the forms in which we know it . . . (there is) no intrinsic reason why life of some sort should not exist in a world of very different physical and chemical make-up from our own."[14]

The nature of this criticism has not changed over the years. Other examples of similar criticism to that of Matson and Lack are found in the previously mentioned works of Hick, McPherson, and others. A typical elaboration of the criticism, as specifically related to the chemical elements mentioned by Henderson, is that found in the book "Intelligent Life in the Universe" by I. S. Shklovskii and Carl Sagan.[15] It is premature, they say, "to conclude that ours is the only, or even the best of all possible, biochemistries." It is then asked: "Might we be biased in our judgment that living systems must be carbon-based and aqueous?" The book then points to the possibility that some hydrocarbon solutions having wide liquid ranges and adequate temperature stabilities might be a substitute for water and that, at low temperatures, some silicon compounds have a high stability and can generate complexity in a manner similar to carbon compounds.[16] The point should be made, however, that there are other learned scientists who doubt that any other element could replace the unique fitness of carbon and, as concerns a substitute for water, one writer expressed the view of many scientists when he said: "It might be possible to conceive of life based on some other liquid but no substitute will have as useful a range of properties."

It should be first noted that Henderson himself recognized the possibility of the existence of life elsewhere, as he pointed out that the universe as a whole appears to be not unlike our part of it, with the same energy-matter interchanges and with the Earth being more or less typical in chemical constituency.[18] Because of this, it may not be assumed that Henderson sought to support the view that life on Earth is alone and unique throughout the universe. His argument was to say that the few chemical elements that are involved in life processes on our planet are not only "fit" but are the "fittest possible" from among all the natural chemical elements of the Periodic Table of elements. We do not, of course, have any observational means to verify other life biochemistries. But does it really matter in terms of a designed creation?

The above mentioned criticism of Matson and Lack suggests that, if it should turn out that life exists elsewhere in the universe of a somewhat different biochemistry (which may or may not be the case) the fitness of life biochemistry on Earth is somehow to be downgraded and lacking in significance from a design standpoint. This is most difficult to follow. If life indeed exists elsewhere, it is in consequence of the unique availability, rather than unavailability, of the essential and extremely limited chemistry for it. There is no reason why the narrower perspective of relating fitness for life on our planet may not be upgraded broadly to encompass the concept

61

of fitness for life in other regions of the universe as well. Whatever may be fit and suitable for life at one point of time and space may be completely different at another point of time and space. In any event, intelligent design is still the better inference. In a chance creation, there would be no need for elemental chemical matter that could be involved in life processes here or anywhere else. Generally speaking, the whole of phenomena (of limited diversity as we have considered) that has brought the indicia of design to our Earth exists throughout the vast reaches of the universe. The recent discovery that organic molecules exist elsewhere in our galaxy and perhaps throughout the universe adds to the growing evidence. The opportunities for design elsewhere should serve to upgrade the view of design in the whole of it, as well as in our part of it. In point of fact, this possibility (life elsewhere in the universe) may be seen as a new and significant inference to design for reasons to be outlined in Chapter 8 that are even different than those we are considering here.

Pantin, in his book "The Relations Between the Sciences," pointed out that there are certain pre-conditions which are fairly narrowly prescribed for life to exist anywhere under any circumstances. Referring to the DNA (deoxyribonucleic acid) molecule, the substance on which the hereditary code of life is based, he considered this to be the most remarkable example of "that particular fitness of properties of matter for the existence of living things to which Henderson drew attention so many years ago."[19] He noted that "the manner in which this can give a heritable code, the power of replication, the initiation of a sequence of events leading to an adult organism, the power of variation, and hence the power of adaptation, offers an extraordinary collection of unique features, the absence of any one of which would render such a system impossible."[20] He pointed out that life elsewhere would likely be a water-hydrogen-carbon compound system and that, in the light of present knowledge, "there seemed likely to be few, if any, alternatives to the evolution of the adaptive organisms to that based upon nucleic acids; the special properties of these rest too firmly on the unique geometrical structure in

62

electronic properties of certain few elements of the Periodic Table for us to see alternatives."[21]

In his book "We Are Not Alone," Walter Sullivan, the well known science writer, also gave consideration to the possible existence of life elsewhere throughout the universe. He, too, dealt with the limitation in alternatives with respect to the known chemical elements and raised the yet unsettled and most-perplexing question as to the exclusitivity for life in the universe of the DNA molecule when he said, ". . . Either life, disregarding all other paths of development, always involves the same chemical structure no matter where it arises, which he (J. D. Bernal) considered 'inherently improbable,' or life on Earth and all life elsewhere has a common ancestry, which, he said, 'strains the imagination' and added that 'Perhaps Haldane was right and our spark of life came from elsewhere in the galaxy, or indeed from other galaxies.' "[22] While questions of this nature involve speculation, it can be said that the molecular pathway to the origin of life is to be seen as very narrowly proscribed.

Pantin applied his observations with respect to the rigid limitations of the properties of matter which might very well apply to life here, as we know it, or elsewhere as we do not know it. He said: "We might have supposed in the history of organisms that some point might be reached where no further emergent properties in available configurations were possible to permit advance. . . . The standard parts available for the construction of organisms are the units of matter and energy which can exist only in certain possible configurations. Like the engineer, natural selection takes third place by giving reality to one or other of a series of possible structural solutions with materials available. . . ."[23]

As we shall see in the next chapter, the method of construction of the universe as a whole engages the limited kinds of elemental matter to achieve the necessary chemical transformations of substances to bring about the structural arrangements as are found and known to exist. Whenever we contemplate the existence of life elsewhere, there are some stark realities that need to be taken into account. In relation to life on Earth, for instance, there are only certain limited ways in which an eye (like a camera), or a voice box (like a resonant mechanism), or an ear drum (like a sound receiver) may be constructed, just like there are only certain narrowly prescribed ways in which a computing machine or television set may be put together.[24] In how many other ways may devices of this sort, possibly essential to advanced intelligent life elsewhere, be invented? This should not be taken to suggest that the existence of life elsewhere, with or without the same biochemistry, would need to resemble the same form, shape, and to possess the exact physical functions as life on Earth (that is, from a design standpoint), except in the event that the conditions elsewhere, including environmental conditions in their interaction with such life, were identical so as to produce the same adaptive results. In a later chapter, it should be mentioned here, the view will be rather strongly put forth that evolutionary changes in living organisms fill a purposeful result in a design context.

Today, the "fitness of the environment" argument may be seen in a far broader context. A great deal of the "fitness" phenomena that we will consider, inferring intelligent design, bears no direct relationship simply to the making of life possible on Earth (or elsewhere), biochemically. It goes far beyond that, as we shall see. Yet, we will continue in the next and subsequent chapters to emphasize the fitness and suitability role of cosmic, including inanimate, phenomena to the scheme of life, and to consider the manner in which modern knowledge, together with the cumulative knowledge of the past, has quite overwhelmed the materialistic claim of a non-designed world.

# 5

## The Amazing Atoms

### 1. *General*

When John Ray wrote his argument from design in the late seventeenth century, natural substances were still being looked upon, as by the ancient Greeks, to fall within one or the other of four "elements," i.e. fire, water, earth, and air. Consequently, neither he nor Paley a century after him were in a position to find inferential evidence of design in the atoms as we now know them. It was not until the early part of the nineteenth century that the idea of atomism gained an established credibility when the English chemist John Dalton and his colleagues first formulated an atomic theory. Even so, the atoms were still looked upon as being hard, simple, and solid invisible spheres.

Only in the earlier part of this century did we obtain a general picture of the internal structure of the atom in result of the work of Rutherford and others.[1] Atoms could thereafter be seen as comprising a system analogous (in some ways) to our solar system with negatively charged particles, called electrons, revolving around a positively charged nucleus, and with the positive charge balancing the negative charge so that the total atom is uncharged in a stable configuration. Unlike the solar system, however, it is the attractive force between these positive and negative charges that takes the place of the force of gravitation which, for example, the Sun exerts upon the planets.[2] Then, later on, came other discoveries, including the theory of quantum mechanics which governs the motions of material particles. More recent studies in nuclear physics have further enhanced our knowledge, but the continuing parade of newly discovered and incompletely understood particles associated with the nucleus of the atom is most perplexing. But notwithstanding the remaining mysteries, the knowledge already gained does furnish a basis for some interesting observations strongly suggesting that intelligent design was very much involved in the creation of these microcosmic entities.

We now know that "everything in nature," according to the theoretical physicist Victor Weisskopf, in his book *Knowledge and Wonder*,* "is made up of only ninety-two different kinds of atoms of different kinds of properties, each one belonging to a well-defined and specific chemical element."[3] Atoms of one element differ from those of the others only by the number of negatively charged electrons, a number which also determines how many positive-charged units there are in the nucleus. For instance, the simplest atom, the hydrogen atom, has one electron and one positive-charged unit in its nucleus, whereas the uranium atom, being the ninety-second and last of the natural elements, has ninety-two electrons and an equal number of positive-charged units in its nucleus.[4] Elements may combine with one another to form compounds of different substances of which the smallest unit is called a molecule; but the element, as the smallest unit of a chemical compound, may not be broken-down chemically beyond its fundamental atom unit. It is important to note, as did Weisskopf, that atoms comprising the elements will always have the same identical properties wherever found. Thus, the element helium will always be helium and the element gold will always be gold with the same unique properties and individuality. For this reason, they are sometimes referred to as "irreducible elementary substances" of which all the infinite variety of living and non-living materials in the world are composed.[5] Even so-called isotopes of the same element, while varying in atomic

---

* Excerpts from *Knowledge and Wonder: The Natural World as Man Knows It* by Victor F. Weisskopf. Copyright © 1962, 1966 by Doubleday & Co., Inc. Reprinted by permission of the publisher.

weight, are of such similiar chemical quality that they are not classified as separate elements.

Living organisms contain a number of the elements. The most prevalent of those in the human body are carbon, hydrogen, oxygen, nitrogen, phosphorous, and sulphur. There are many other elements that are almost household words, such as silver, iron, calcium, tin, gold, copper, aluminum, platinum, fluorine, iodine, lead, nickel, to name a few. To the chemist, of course, the elements make up the "tools of his trade," so to speak, in everything from theoretical research to practical application and this would surely include (other than those mentioned) the elements silicon, helium, mercury, boron, neon, argon, bromine, chlorine, manganese, bismuth, potassium, sodium, zinc, uranium, tungsten, lithium, cobalt, cadmium, vanadium, and others.

## 2. *Origin*

The origin of atoms, according to the late George Gamow, the American physicist, in his book "Matter, Earth, and Sky,"[*] is to be attributed to thermonuclear reactions that are thought to have taken place under conditions of very high temperature extremes when the universe was expanding at an early stage. The explosion of what has been called a "primeval fireball" (in keeping with the so-called "big bang" theory of the origin of the universe) caused matter to become disassociated into a mixture of the basic elementary constituent particles of the atoms. In a very short time, noted Gamow, the thermonuclear temperature is thought to have suddenly dropped thereby cooling the universe enough for these basic particles to have aggregated into complex nuclei. It is possible, he said, that the heavier natural elements were built-up at a later stage in the history of the universe in higher temperature extremities as in exploding supernovae of stars. It is well known today that stars convert hydrogen into helium and that at least some stars in various stages of their evolution, according to George Abell, must be building up helium into carbon and heavier elements. "Thus," he said, "inside stars, some of the lighter elements of the universe are gradually being converted into heavier ones."[7]*

### 3. *The Right Choice*

If one were to describe the atoms as being "amazing," he would simply be expressing what a great many physicists and chemists have been saying for decades about them. To think that these "invisible" building-blocks could, in their interactions with other phenomena, possess within themselves, or in their combinations, the latent potential capacity to construct the whole of the future development of both living and non-living matter in the universe is almost incomprehensible. A number of scientists who have looked upon the atoms and their structure in great bewilderment attribute the necessity of a higher intelligence as being involved. Osborne W. Greenwood, for instance, questioned the materialistic viewpoint that the atom could have been produced by reason of a sort of mechanical inherency in the void of space. He was especially intrigued with the type of atomic build-up that would bring about the ninety-two recurring elements in nature, particularly the resolution of the electrons with their capability of approaching the speed of light orbiting around a central core or nucleus and with their exact equal quantity of negative electrical charge to balance an equal positive charge.[8] "The more we learn about the laws that govern the distribution of the protons and electrons to produce the various elements," said John A. Buehler, "the more we become aware of the harmony and order that exists in nature. . . ."[9] As applied to the study of biology, Robert E. D. Clark said that many of the atoms had to be "so designed that they will be able of fulfilling the role which they will subsequently play in living organisms."[10]

This modern age has only served to confirm the early importance of the casual comment of the eminent nineteenth century Scottish physicist, James Clerk Maxwell, to the effect

* Excerpts here and on pp. 123-124 from *Exploration of the Universe,* updated brief edition by George Abell, © 1964, 1969, 1973 by Holt, Rinehart and Winston. Reprinted by permission of publisher.

that the atom has all the "earmarks of a manufactured article." This would seem to be far more in evidence today than at any time in the past if we look to the newly discovered complexity of the atom at the particle level, as well as to the remarkable end-results of the atoms which are quite well known to us today.

It is quite true that the atoms are designed in a way that is appropriate to what they in fact accomplish. No one can doubt that for a moment. The fact that they have produced an enormous web of interrelated substances that, it seems, logically correspond in terms of human intelligence to that which may be attributable to great foresight and planning does not in itself, of course, disprove the idea of a chance creation, nor prove the idea of a designed creation. Yet, it does place the fundamental issue in a proper perspective. And what they accomplish goes amazingly far beyond the ninety-two elements themselves into molecular compounds and material aggregations that are, as we shall see, most fit and suitable in a manner that displays remarkable creativity, order, differentiation, and purposiveness in respect to *both* the inanimate and the animate worlds of nature on a comprehensive scale.

## 4. *Approach to Design*

One of the approaches to design here will be to look for a conjunctiveness between the creativity and logic of the human mind and the overt creativity and the compelling logic that is to be found at the atomic level. How would the specifications for the construction of a universe, for example, as related specifically to the atoms and their elements, assure a logical design engineer of a successful completion of such a task? From a design standpoint alone one may rationalize by analogy, as well as by logic, ordinary common sense and intuition, on this question. The assumption of a designed universe requires that the Designer would not only have advance knowledge of what the atomic building-blocks would do in carrying out a project involving the construction of the universe, but in addition, would have so designed and programmed these basic units of matter in such a manner that, together with complementary forces and laws, they would have the requisite properties as would result in the fulfillment of purposeful objectives.

## 5. *The Right Size*

We have a universe consisting of the very small and the very large. This has been a puzzling phenomenon to philosophers for centuries. It is what Teilhard de Chardin referred to as the "infinitesimal" and the "immense."[11] We now have some good reasons, suggestive of design, for the very large and these will be considered in Chapter 8. *But why the very small?*

It has been estimated by Gamow that the size of the human head is about half-way in between the size of our sun and the size of the atom, or about half-way in between the size of an atomic nucleus and the diameter of our planetary system (on a logarithmic scale).[12] So minute are these tiny creations that even the most powerful of electron microscopes fall short of penetrating the innermost secrets of the nucleus of the atom. In fact, the observation of elementary particles within the nuclei of atoms, particularly newly discovered particles, has been delayed at least by an inadequacy in the equipment as requisite to better skill in observation.[13] The relative spacial distances within the atoms themselves are also immense and most difficult for us to conceive on the human scale of reckoning. The nucleus is very small in comparison with the diameter of the atom as represented by its outer orbiting electron waves. Thus, one comparison states that if the atom were expanded until the diameter of its outer electron shell equaled the distance between New York and San Francisco, the nucleus would be about the size of a city block.[14]

In the selection of elementary substances to be set in motion as basic "building-blocks" of matter, it shows both logic and wisdom that such a minute unit the size of the atom was employed rather than a larger unit which would have restricted the wider range (in terms of size) in what might be put together. Quite obviously, if the basic atomic building-blocks were to have been the size of an orange, and yet possess the remarkable propensities of the atoms to construct the world of nature, the scale of the molecular aggregations of matter would be significantly different and the energy consumptive requirements so vastly enlarged that a race of human beings, for example, would be comprised of enormous celestial giants. There would be no place for anything like the ordinary butterfly, the raindrop, the elephant, or the like. But, as it is, the infinitesimally small units, seemingly of great complexity by necessity, co-exist in a vast universe with immensity at the other end of the spacial scale where, there too, restrictions of a different dimension appear to be absent.

## 6. *Aggregating Propensities*

Further, what could be more ingenious and logical than the provision for atomic building-blocks that are essentially self-constructing into higher levels of material aggregations? This, apart from the suggestion made in the introductory chapter of an *atomos mentis* aspect, without any apparent external assistance other than from complementary cosmic forces as, for example, those which bring about an interplay of positive and negative charges in the atoms. Except for the atomic elements comprising the so-called inert noble gases and some of the heavier elements having little tendency to unite or combine with others (strongly suggesting an intent to preserve such elements in their natural state independently of others for specific purposes and uses), the atoms are so structured in their electronic configurations that they possess a bonding capability called *chemical valency*.

The reader should here recall to mind the quoted reference to Isaac Asimov, in Chapter 2, to the effect that the atoms come together only in certain limited ways, and that some ways are more probable than others. This, to appreciate the selectivity involved in the co-valency capabilities of the atoms. From their interactions with one another, involving either a transfer of electrons from one atom to another or a sharing of electrons between them, a neutralizing stabilization of positive and negative charge is achieved that results in aggrega-

71

tions that form a specific list of the properties of the elements of the nature described earlier in this chapter.

On their own, as independent entities, they seem to have no utility or purpose. If the universe were simply made up of atoms or other particle configurations, large or small, that were complete units of themselves then, quite obviously, nothing would have come together to produce anything of meaning in the universe. Gravitational attraction that could be expected to bring them together would lack any aspect of selectivity. They would simply be "ends" in and themselves. J. H. Reyner in his book "The Universe of Relationships"[15] finds a grand design, intelligence, and foreknowledge in the atoms as being "incomplete creations" seeking to obtain a state of completion which provides them with their distinctive chemical properties. Later on, in subsequent chapters, we will see how this principle of "goal-seeking" carries forward far beyond the microlevel of things toward purposeful and fit end results that are ultimately achieved in both inanimate and animate nature. The fact that the atoms, by reason of their characteristics, unite with only certain other atoms of the elements caused Reyner to comment that they have certain "likes" and "dislikes."[16] Everything around us, he said, "is produced by the ingenious blending of a few basic atoms, often not more than three or four at a time and that the same elements, slightly rearranged, can produce widely different substances."[17] He relates these discontinuities in terms of atomic "incompleteness" to explain why the elements differ as they do. If they simply had the power to come together into complete units in the formation of higher levels of elemental matter, without more, we would have "mere multiplicity which in itself is sterile."[18] Instead, we have a much greater variety of possibilities by reason of the fact that all of the elements do not have the same valency; that otherwise the possible combinations would be strictly limited in number and would conform "to a rigid and virtually invariable pattern."[19]

7. *Means to an End*

That the atoms basically are only a means to an end, rather

than an end in themselves, appears to be further expressed in the many different or specialized operative mechanisms and forces in nature that serve to perfectly complement their activities and remarkable end results. The forces and the constituents of the atoms, both as means, fully complement one another as though designed specifically to accomplish something else (as they do in fact). As one simple example of this, Reyner called attention to the fact that the atomic elements have the facility of transformation. Thus, certain of the elements have more than one valency (nitrogen, for example, can combine in five different ways) and he showed that these features allow for a greater number of compounds. This facility of transformation he considers "to be one of the fundamental characteristics of the universe, and one of the clearest indications of higher intelligence (for in a dead or accidental universe there would be no need for this possibility). . . ."[20]

## 8. Differentiation in Mechanics

I have previously noted that the attractive force between the positive and negative charge in atomic behavior differs from the force of gravitation as related to celestial mechanics involved with orbiting planetary systems. Science has no "natural" explanation as to the basic cause of these distinctively different forces.

It is beyond the scope of this work (and quite unnecessary as well) to elaborate in detail on the quantum theory which, in one aspect at least, has to do with selected energy states and orbital configurations of the electrons in relation to the nucleus of an atom. The electrical attraction between the nucleus and the orbiting electron waves, as mentioned, takes the place of the force of gravity. In the interior of atoms, the number of electron waves and the manner in which they are distributed, as in groups or "shells" in varying distances from the nucleus, determines the different characteristics of the atom and, hence, the different properties of the elements. If two atoms of the same kind were governed by planetary forces, however, they would not exhibit identical properties except very rarely.[21] According to Weisskopf, a series of confined electron wave "states" is related to their assigned quantum states of energy. This furnishes the patterns that are the basis of the orderly arrangement of molecules in crystals. "The simple beauty of a crystal reflects on a larger scale the fundamental shapes of its atomic patterns. Ultimately all the regularities of form and structure that we see in nature, ranging from the hexagonal shape of a snowflake to the intricate symmetries of living forms in flowers and animals, are based upon the symmetries of these atomic patterns."[22] What I have set forth is, of course, a vast oversimplification.

The important point to make here is that it is simply incredulous to believe that blind chance could have invented, drawn, and activated the essential distinction required as between the atomic level of particle activity, on the one hand, and the principles of gravitation and celestial mechanics which govern the motion and activities of planetary systems. Each of the separate governing principles is uniquely fit and suitable to its own maze of phenomena, but not as to the other. This, notwithstanding any development in the future of a unifying theory. In turn, each has been found to be fit and suitable to life here (and prospectively to projections of life elsewhere in the universe).

As we shall see in later chapters, a great number and variety of distinctions have been invented, drawn, and activated in both inanimate and animate nature with respect to still other remarkable phenomena complementary to life in general, and to the mind of man, in particular. This, in a manner that defies "chance" and infers the stongest empirical evidence of an intelligent, coherent, and logical method of construction and design in the universe. It suggests that, if there be a cosmic Mind, according to William Pollard, it is not at all unlike the mind of man.[23] It gives us some basic insight into the material basis for the construction of the universe and the processes through which design operates in guiding and directing the basic building-blocks of matter, together with universal laws and forces, into purposeful end-results. All of this adds up to a showing that there is a high degree of reliability that may

74

be counted upon whenever a "rational element" may be seen by the human mind in the manner in which the things of the universe have been put together.

## 9. *Stability, Identity, Regeneration*

It would also be expected of a Designer that sound engineering practices would require the atoms to be constructed in such a manner that, when subjected to a range of external conditions, they would have certain fundamental characteristics lying within certain behavioral limits of stable configuration which Weisskopf described as "remarkable," being:

(1) stability (maintenance of their specific properties in spite of other perturbations to which they are subjected); (2) indentity (all atoms of the same kind—same electron number Z—exhibit identical properties; they emit and absorb the same frequencies, they have exactly the same size, shape, and internal motion); (3) regeneration (if an atom is distorted and its electron orbits forced to change by high pressure or by close neighboring atoms, it regains its exact original shape and orbits when the cause of distortion is removed).[24]

## 10. *The Elements of the Atoms*

The most amazing thing of all about the atoms has to do with what they have created in our physical world as a derivative of their special propensities and remarkable activities. This is more important for our purposes here than seeking to understand, as in science, how they function, and what mechanisms and forces are involved in the process. It goes without saying that, from a design standpoint, one would expect that these basic building-blocks would fulfill a desired end toward basic objectives. We should first, however, consider some important facts concerning the elements of the atoms.

When arranged progressively in accordance with their atomic weights (as, for example, hydrogen is number one, being the simplest and lightest of the elements with only one electron and one proton; helium is next in line with two electrons and two protons, and so on), the ninety-two elements in nature may be classified into a Periodic Table of the elements which reflect remarkable regularities. When so arranged, the elements of similar properties occur at regular intervals and may, therefore, be divided into periods. The reliability of the relationships are such that, following the initial preparation of an incomplete Table by the Russian chemist, Mendeléef, in 1869, predictions could be made of new elements yet to be discovered in nature and their proper position with respect to the Table. Both the physical and chemical properties of the elements, said Mendeléef, vary as periodic functions of their atomic weights. There are two elements in the first period, eight elements in the second and third periods, eighteen elements in the fourth and fifth periods, and thirty-two elements in the sixth period. The periods are separated by a specific one of the six so-called inert gases (helium, neon, argon, krypton, xenon, and radon) which do not possess any appreciable tendency to form a chemical bond. The elements in a given family have similar electronic configurations and there is a regular and predictable variation in properties of the elements and their compounds.[25] Elmer W. Maurer, a chemist, argued that the periodic chart of the elements is not a matter of chance and said: "It is a beautifully designed scheme of law and order in the universe."[26] The regularity and relationship shown in the Periodic Table are sufficiently dependable that chemists have been able to make use of the Table in much the same fashion that mathematicians have made use of logarithmic tables.[27] John A. Buehler called attention to the definite pattern that is followed from hydrogen to uranium. "It may well be," he said, "that what we refer to as disordered chaos at the subatomic level is not that at all. . . ."[28]

We have come a long way indeed from the time that Henderson analyzed three of the ninety-two natural elements and several of their compounds to say they are highly fit and suitable to the existence of life. We may now see in the elements an enormous variety of fit and useful natural substances that relate not only to the existence of life but, more significantly, to man and his intelligence in a very special way. The amazing growth in knowledge relating to the utility of the elements was underscored recently by A. R. Battersby, Professor of Organic Chemistry at the University of Cambridge, when he said: "The natural products which were studied say fifty years ago were the readily isolated ones and it was rather by chance, in many instances, that the materials so obtained were of medicinal or other value."[29] The advance in human knowledge with respect to the utilization of the elements in recent times, however, caused Ewart Jones, Professor of Chemistry at Oxford University, to say: "Mankind now has at its disposal a bewildering range of products of chemist's discoveries and inventions."[30] The reader may apply his own experience to the world of nature in this modern day to envisage the "staggering zoo" of the things of the world, relating to the chemical elements, that serve in varying degrees and ways to complement life and man's activities. Is this not what one would expect in a designed universe? As basic building-blocks, the chemical elements have filled a particular niche in the precise and useful construction of the properties of matter, both in the inanimate as well as in the animate worlds of nature.

But our amazement of the atoms goes well beyond the basic elements themselves when we recognize that so many end-products, whether as chemical compounds (numbering in excess of a million) or as higher aggregations of matter, are constructed by them and have found their way to service and to benefit mankind. Interacting with all of this have been perfectly complementary and order-giving laws and forces that permit the necessary chemical reactions, transformations, etc. of the elements into meaningful realizations. In later chapters, we will see other interesting and remarkable phenomena that have come in consequence of the properties of the elements far up the ladder of both animate and inanimate evolution. The end-results show such advance knowledge and intelligent foresight in the design of things that the idea of chance as the causative factor is far more remote than it may have appeared some few decades ago. This, when one takes into account the remarkable purposive nature of molecular arrangements, their regularity in taking on specific assigned roles and functions, and the many unique and useful properties that have come in consequence.

A great many of the elements of the Periodic Table which were not considered to be useful to man have, in this modern age, been found to be most fit and useful. For example, the element helium, as an inert gas, was considered to be useless and flared as a waste product from natural gas wells not many years ago. Today we know that it is considered by many to be essential to medical research and space exploration. But what about argon, neon, krypton, and xenon, also elements of the Table that are inert gases? They, too, have found their way to the service of man. Who would have thought that the element uranium, the last and heaviest of the ninety-two natural elements in the Table, would today be a critical substance for nuclear energy? Much the same could be said with respect to presently known uses of many of the other specific elements, as well as to some other remarkable regularities and characteristics of the Periodic Table as a whole; however, we trust that the point has been sufficiently made with respect to the broad new implications to design that have arisen in consequence of our greater and modern knowledge of the elements.

But the elements of the Table and their beneficial uses to mankind are merely the "tip of the iceberg," as we shall see, when it comes to consider phenomena of the natural world that, in this day, relate in a most special and meaningful way to man and his conscious creativity.

Like the parts of a child's Erector Set where the most basic standard part is the simplest, lightest, and the most abundant, the hydrogen atom is the simplest, lightest, and most abundant standard part in making the construction of the universe a reality. The next in simplicity is the element helium which comprises approximately 10% of the make-up of the universe. From thermonuclear reactions, involving the hydrogen atom, comes helium and, from it in turn, many of the other elements.

Perhaps we should pause at this point to take note of the obvious intent to construct a universe of great and meaningful variety and diversity. Each of the ninety-two elements have distinctively different properties—shades of difference. This phenomenon of diversity and variety is found throughout nature and may also be seen, for examples, in the distinctive variety of colors that come from the spectrum of light, in the symmetries of great variety of form and shape traceable to the atoms, in the distinctive differences between the million or more plant and animal species, etc. Perhaps even our discriminating appreciation of musical notes might some day be traceable to the quantum wave states of electronic energy in the atom. Reyner, it should be noted, made an interesting comparison between the musical octaves and "octave" groupings of certain families of the chemical elements of the Periodic Table where similar elements appear at the same "note" in their respective octave grouping—all of this being traceable to the arrangement of the orbits of electron waves around the nucleus of an atom under the quantum theory which holds that the possible orbits for the electrons "are not infinite but are limited to certain specific positions corresponding to definite quantums of energy."[31] In terms of design, one may see a common origin of phenomena of this nature, i.e. the handiwork of an ingenious and discriminating craftsman. One might even wonder whether the atoms, and the activities of the mysterious particles associated with their nuclei, will not be fully understood until related to the functioning end-results of their amazing activities in much the same manner as scientists trace crystals and snowflakes to electronic configurations of the atoms. To an extent, we will consider this possibility in concluding chapters when we will turn to focus our attention on cosmic and inanimate phenomena as they inter-relate to animate (living) phenomena. Here is a fertile field for scientists to "think" design, as suggested that they should do in Chapter 2.

## 11. *Efficiency and Economy*

A further remarkable indicia of design is that one would expect a Designer, in the manner of construction of the universe, to achieve the efficiency and economy that comes from engaging a few elements to perform multiple functions. As mentioned above, Reyner pointed out that everything around us is produced by the ingenious blending of a few basic atoms and that the same elements, slightly rearranged, can produce widely different substances.[32] Of the elements, hydrogen, oxygen, carbon, and nitrogen are but a few examples of this phenomena. They are involved in a great variety of compounds and substances as though with a view to efficiency and economy. But the same principle holds true with respect to complex phenomena at the macrolevel where it is to be seen that certain phenomena perform a multitude of varied and diverse functions as, for one example, the Moon functionally relates to a multitude of such different things as the tides, the ocean currents, the reflection of light, and, even prospectively, to outer space exploration.

## 12. *The Element Carbon*

Because of the dominant role it plays in living organisms, special mention should be made of the element carbon. Greenwood called it "the most unique physical entity we know in the universe." [33] Others have said the same thing with respect to light, sight, gravity, water, the ozone layer, hydrogen, mind and consciousness, and the self-replicating DNA molecule. But, he, like Sir A. S. Eddington, was especially impressed by the fact that this element, which is number 6 in the scale of atomic weights of the Periodic Table, and the essential ingredient for life as we know it, does not have the same limitation of the other ninety-two elements. The compounds of carbon are almost limitless in variety and number. In his Swarthmore lectures, Eddington expressed the fact that animate life would not have begun if Nature's arithmetic had overlooked the number 6. "We can scarcely call it an accident," he said.[34] He noted that the general plan of the 92 elements "contemplates a material world of considerable but limited diversity; but the element carbon, embodying the number 6, and because of the peculiarity of the number 6, rebels against limits. . . ."[35] The significance of this is that the other elements are mysteriously surpassed by carbon in consequence of "its activity, its capacity, its potential leap into a significance possessed by no other element. . . ."[36] It is as though carbon had been specifically earmarked for the particular purpose of the production of life. In brief, the number 6 element "steps remarkably out of line" in its position in the Periodic Table to explode in a very special and meaningful way for the production of life, whereas the other elements carry out other material functions but in a vastly less diverse and quantitative sort of way. While this uniqueness may be traced to the innerstructure of carbon atoms, it is strange indeed that the one element which is the most important one involved in the chemistry of living things just so happens to be the only element with these unique and amazing propensities. While the element silicon has sometimes been considered as a possible substitute for carbon with respect to possible life elsewhere, it is generally recognized that its properties, while closely related to carbon in the families of properties of the elements, are too limited to play the same diverse role in nature as carbon.

## 13. *Simplicity to Complexity*

As we have seen, the idea of a "chance" creation has evolved on the theme that the inanimate world of nature is basically very simple, reflects disorder, and requires little explanation; that the animate world, on the other hand, is explicable by processes involved in organic evolution. A sort of "broad brush" mechanistic accounting for the whole of nature.

The discovery that the atoms are not simply sticky, solid spheres gave no reason of itself to alter the idea of basic simplicity. As humans, we have a way of considering things to be complex that we do not understand, and then, when understood, simplicity is the rule of the day. The basic "simplicity" attributed to the principle of the quantum theory as related to the internal structure of the atoms is a good example. So too, in reference to the genetic code in living organisms, it has been said that the operation of the genetic code is simple in principle. The fact, as mentioned, that there are

81

92 different kinds of atoms in nature, each belonging to the 92 different kinds of chemical elements could, as well, be reasonably assimilated into the idea of simplicity. Perhaps this will also be the theme whenever the story of the unseen mysterious particles deep in the interior of the atoms has been formulated into a complete theory of elementary particles.

But in recent years it has become clear that the atoms are far more complex and mysterious at the elementary particle level than earlier thought to be the case. Protons, neutrons, and four other "elementary" particles (photons, neutrinos, positrons, and mesons that were known to exist in the 1930's) are by no means the only elementary particles known to exist today in consequence of observation or theoretical assumption. A. W. Merrison, former Director of England's Daresbury Nuclear Physics Laboratory, refers to the new elementary particles discovered since 1948 as a "staggering zoo" of particles—"a Pandora's box."[37] Well over a hundred new sorts of elementary particles have been discovered in the past decade. Some of these have been classified into families of particles. Some of them have long lifetimes and others have lifetimes that are very short on the atomic scale. It is known that certain interactions that occur between particles and four basic forces have been identified. These are called the strong, the electromagnetic, the weak, and the gravitational forces.[38] Nuclear science has yet to develop an acceptable, let alone comprehensible, theory of elementary particles and there is, of course, a great deal yet to be understood with respect to the structure, nature, and purpose of many of these particles. The seemingly endless new stream of particles appears to have upset those who, according to Yoichiro Nambu, "hold the conviction, or at least the fond wish, that nature should be simple."[39] In their book "Revolutions in Physics," Barry M. Casper and Richard J. Noer, like Merrison, also referred to the dimensions of the elementary particle problem as a "Pandora's Box" in discussing the complex world of the 1970's that has involved the discovery of so many different particles. They said: "Just as ninety chemical elements seemed to be too many basic building blocks to nineteenth-century scientists, so today there is a feeling among physicists that one hundred 'elementary' particles is too large a number. There is a wide-spread expectation among physicists that man's understanding of the structure of matter is due for another historic conceptual change."[40]

But does it really make a difference with respect to the question of chance or design that the atoms are proving to be more intricate and complex in various ways and that we still do not fully understand them? In the view of Merrison, perhaps not. "So far as we know," he said, "the few first known elementary particles (comprising the electrons, neutrons, protons, photons, and neutrinos) are all that are necessary *to construct* the universe at anything above the atomic level," but knowledge of the "bewildering variety of elementary particles is fundamental to our *understanding* of the universe."[41]

## 14. *Linkages*

I wish to stress, in reference to the above mentioned view of Merrison, his words: *"So far as we know."* This, to make the point that science lacks the certainty to know what role, if any, the multitude of newly discovered elementary particles may play in the nature of things. "It would appear," said Sheldon L. Glashow, professor of physics at Harvard University, "that nature could have made do with half as many fundamental things."[42] "Surely," he also said, "the second group was not created simply for the entertainment or edification of physicists. . . ."[43] Could it be that they possessed within themselves, before the fact, the basis of origination for various unique qualities that find expression down the line in living things, such as the computer-like qualities of self-replication, including the first coded genetic information in DNA, the cognition aspect of the protein molecule, the basis for specie differentiation, or even the phenomenon of mind and consciousness?

There is no positive evidence in science that gives an answer. The origin of these qualities of life are beyond the reach of present-day observation and, therefore, still open to speculation. It will be recalled that, in the introductory chapter, I set forth the present empirical basis for an atom-mind (*atomos mentis*) inter-relationship that is difficult to ignore, even though speculative. It is also interesting to note that some keen minds in the sciences are today questioning whether pure randomness and the selective processes that are now recognized under the modern theory of organic evolution are sufficient to fully explain the phenomenon of the origin of some of the qualities of life as mentioned. There is a nagging tendency to search for a closer linkage to the atoms on the inanimate side of things to better account for such phenomena than to simply say that the atoms provided only the basic architecture and chemical transformations that produced the precisely correct properties of living and non-living matter.

In any event, it would seem that an ultimate answer would have to resolve the basic question as to how and why the atoms had the latent potential capacity in the first place to accomplish such a remarkable result. This takes us back, does it not, to the origin of the atoms as discussed earlier in this chapter. A remote point of time in the past, indeed, and the usual time-scale of sixteen billion years or so, as reflective of the estimated age of the universe, multiplied by enormous opportunities which would permit "anything" to happen in keeping with the idea of chance, simply would not seem applicable.

In the next chapter we will consider some of the intermediate and more final results of inanimate phenomena. To be sure, the amazing atoms will be seen as very much in the picture, although sometimes remotely and indirectly, and at higher levels of transformed substance and activity than we have found at the microcosmic level. Some of the forces in nature that interact with the elements will also be seen to have spun off into other channels of specialized activity, Further, the idea of materialism, based on mechanisms comprising "ordinary" elemental substances and "simple" forces, will not seem adequate—in any explanatory way—to cover the vast multitude of highly fit, suitable, and harmonious relationships to be considered that are of both a material and intangible character.

# 6

## Earth and Environs

A broad spectrum of cosmic phenomena both permits and complements the existence and development of life on this planet. It would be an almost impossible task to enumerate it all, and this would certainly be impractical here. The focus of attention in this chapter, therefore, will be to set forth what might be regarded as the major phenomena which serve the purpose mentioned. Some of this will comprise that which has been referred to in past design arguments and, in addition, will include much of that which has more recently come to light. Significantly, relatively new discovery has provided the means for the complete picture that may now be presented. In some cases, specific major phenomena are suggestive of intelligent design on their own, but the overall picture of a well-coordinated whole is perhaps the more important thing to grasp here. And, of course, any phenomena that relate to the support and development of life necessarily include mankind as a beneficiary. This, however, is to be taken here in the broad sense rather than in the special manner to be considered in Chapter 7.

It may be that certain of the phenomena to be described herein with respect to the Earth and its environment could have been somewhat differently arranged or constituted and still allow for the existence and development of life as we do, or do not, know it. The same may be said as concerns the possibility of life elsewhere throughout the vastness of the universe. But it is quite inconceivable to think of any set of conditions and operating mechanisms, here or anywhere else, that would be more fit and suitable, more harmonious, inter-related and unified for the function and support of life than those which relate to Earth and its immediate environment. Of one thing the reader may be sure—that, in relation to the purposes as mentioned (i.e. the existence and development of life), the phenomena to be considered is real, rather than illusory, very deterministic in terms of means-to-ends objectives, and there is not one single inference of "non-design" to it.

## 1. *Introduction*

On the basis of using an estimated age of the Earth as 4.5 billion years, Don L. Eicher in his book "Geologic Time" simplified one's understanding of the length of the Earth's geologic history by compressing events into a single hypothetical year. Although Eicher was more descriptive of events which occurred during the passage of time involved, for our limited needs here, I shall describe only a few of these in order to acquaint the reader with the enormous amount of time involved. Assuming the Earth came into existence on the first of January in such a hypothetical year, Eicher pointed out that the oldest rocks we know on Earth date from about mid-March and the first living things appeared in the ocean in May; land plants and animals emerged in late November, and early man-like creatures appeared sometime during the evening of December 31st. Rome, he said, ruled the western world for five seconds less than one minute before the end of the year, and Columbus discovered America barely three seconds before midnight.[1]

To many, this seems a long, long time to sustain the idea of a designed creation. Man, it is thought, came along too late to be as significant as we would make him out to be. What could a Designer have been doing all that time? Perhaps this is a purely subjective question and, if pursued, one might ask what a Designer had been doing in all of eternity. Here we could lapse into metaphysics and the meaning of time and space which, most assuredly, is entirely unrelated to our finite conception of it in terms of significance. In any event, within the time frame of the age of the Earth with which we are more immediately interested, design becomes very much alive when we view the progressive means-to-ends aspects of the dynamic cosmic activities that have been taking place during the whole of this seemingly enormous period of time on the human scale of reckoning.

Geologic history is filled with the story of an Earth which has undergone great chaos and upheaval during successive time-scale epochs. In the process of this change, however, an order of the greatest magnitude has emerged even though, in the process, it would have given the appearance to us of random disorder and confusion. To be sure, we have helped to fashion to some extent a degree of orderliness, yet if this is not itself indicative of design, it does not account for the simple fact that nature is perfectly fit and suitable to both our existence and development whether or not we had applied our "ordered" minds to it.

Like a theatrical drama, a long period of preparation was required to present a performance which, for man, has been of relatively short duration so far. The dynamic activities which have transpired over prehuman history have made possible the organization and accessibility of both mechanisms for survival and useful materials upon which both animal and human existence and development depends. It would seem that the emergence of man, at an earlier period in geologic history, would have been quite premature. Coming along, however, as a relative newcomer at the far end of Eicher's hypothetical year, the basic elements, the natural laws and other related phenomena had linked together into suitable form, substance, and fitness as though in preparation for his arrival on the scene. Significant changes had occurred in terms of Earth and its environment over geologic history physico-chemically, geologically, etc., in a progressive pattern. Each stage was built onto preceding stages in a manner that has contributed to the present state of affairs to which we are able to ascribe meaning. In the ordinary popular story of biological evolution one simply does not get the picture of sense and

87

purpose, in the logical way that points toward intelligent design, in the early cosmic occurrences and events that transpired over the course of geologic time. In retrospect, we can see a perfectly good reason for all these early occurrences.

More than a hundred years ago, in 1866, G. Hartwig in his book "The Harmonics of Nature" described some of the events that were involved in the preparation of the Earth for pre-life in the then limited knowledge of science of his day. He observed that long before organic life appeared on earth, fire, air, and water had been "busy preparing for its future residents." His description is interesting and, in general, is still appropriate even though modern knowledge has enhanced our understanding of the basic mechanisms and processes involved. He said:

> The subterranean fires have never ceased to react against the solid Earth rind to pile up mountain chains, to heave up continents, to pour forth torrents of liquid stone from volcanoes, or to shake whole continents (earthquakes). The waters, in alliance with the disintegrating influences of the atmosphere, have constantly been active in destroying the igneous formations, in splitting and dissolving mountain peaks, in reducing crumbled rocks into smaller and smaller fragments, and in washing them down to a lower level, destined to be again and again upheaved, and then again and again swept into the ocean. . . . Conflicting powers of fire water and air . . . whether in blind confusion with fortuitous anarchy or whether . . . directed by a higher hand, and rendered subservient to the establishment and progressive development of organic life? . . . The answer cannot for an instant be doubted. . . .[2]

## 2. *The Earth's Crust and Continental Drift*

The activities which have taken place on and within the outer crust of the Earth during the course of geologic time provide us with a reasonable starting point to describe the long preparatory aspects as mentioned. A British geologist of the early nineteenth century, William Buckland, pointed out how devoid the Earth would have been for life potential if it had presented only one unvaried mass of granite or lava or had its nucleus been surrounded by entire concentric coverings of stratified rocks like the coats of an onion.[3] But this was not the Earth's destiny. There was aloof in this part of the universe, in any event, all the necessary causative agencies to make the Earth something special in a manner that strongly implies an advance awareness of the results to be accomplished.

The widely accepted new theory of continental drift has given us an amazing new insight into the manner of the construction and differentiation of the Earth's crust in a way in which life (especially human life and intelligence) could arise and be best accommodated.

The theory holds that the crust of the Earth is quite mobile, rather than fixed, and has been moving about on plates[4] with all sorts of diverse and meaningful results as related to life. There are some who believe that this is what gave rise to the continental land masses from an earlier Earth-encompassing primordial ocean. Its origin and processes, although subject to several conflicting views among geologists, are believed to have been continuous for some billions of years. One view is that the volume of continental crust has been mostly the same from early geologic times and worked over and over again. The view of Stephen Moorbath, of the University of Oxford's Department of Geology, in a recent article entitled "The Oldest Rocks and the Growth of Continents,"[5] is that the volume and extent of the earliest continental crust (aged at least 3.8 billion years) and very small (not more than 5 or 10 per cent of the present continental landward areas) has grown through geologic time by an irreversible chemical differentiation of the upper mantle of the Earth, followed by accretion of the newly differentiated material to the pre-existing continents, particularly at or near their margins. In this view, for example, only about 50% of the present area of the North American continent was in existence a little more than half the geologic age of the Earth.[6]

Most recently, some two hundred million years ago, this plate movement activity, called global plate tectonics, commenced the lateral separation of the continents as we now know them from a single large land mass (a "supercontinent") called "Pangaea."[7] One has to thus picture a long formulative era of the Earth's geologic history as including physico-chemical changes accompanied by violent earthquakes, vulcanism, creation of ocean basins and mountain ranges, ocean floor-spreading, collision of continents, etc. The uplifting of landward areas in this manner and the subsequent degradations that occurred, in result of erosive and other physical processes, played a significant role in the formulative make-up of the present topographical and internal composition of the Earth's crust and in the sedimentation and substrafication of the upper crustal formations.[8] At times, and from time to time, land masses have been covered by shallow seas which permitted the deposition of marine fossils and other sediments of diverse classifications.

The machine-like apparatus which made possible the movement of crustal plates on a global basis and, therefore, provided for the suitable conditions on the Earth's surface and in the substrata of the crust for interaction with other phenomena to permit the existence and development of land inhabitation has been called the "nuclear machine" by the eminent English scientist Fred Hoyle. It is powered, he says, by a source of stored energy in the interior of the Earth which comprises radioactive decay.[9] Gamow stated the present view expressed by Hoyle that all the planets in our solar system were formed by the aggregation of cool interstellar gas and dust particles from around the Sun.[10] It had earlier been assumed in science that the interior heat of the Earth was simply the result of a now discarded hypothesis that the entire Earth was initially in a molten viscous state, having been rejected as a planet from the Sun, and that the Earth's crust has gradually been cooling down. This included the thought that the internal heat of the Earth was due to the gravitational compression of such material, rather than from heat generated "by the decay of the long-lived radioactive isotopes of such elements as uranium, thorium, potassium and rubidium present in minute concentrations in its mantle."[11]

The result of all this mobile activity (of which the above oversimplified version is all that is needed here) is remarkable, to say the least, and shows a great ingenuity implicit in its very conception. The dynamic processes involved rebuked Buckland's view of a possible crust of the Earth with an un-varied mass of granitic rock "like the coats of an onion" into something quite different and highly beneficial for the exist-ence of life. As indicated above, the dynamic processes which brought all of this about occurred over a large period of time and, to an extent, are continuing into the present. According to Hoyle, there would probably be no mineral deposits on the Earth's surface in the absence of this continuous turning over of the Earth's crust.[12] "The nuclear engine inside the Earth," said Hoyle, "does much more than provide us with interesting scenery; it provides the environment for life as we know it." [13] He points out, in this connection, that without the system of plate movements, the gradual wearing down of the continents "might well smooth out the Earth so much that, instead of the continents sticking out of the ocean, water would entirely cover the whole surface of the Earth." [14] It is quite easy to see the need for the on-going character of this dynamic activity—earthquakes, vulcanism and all that necessarily goes with it. Then too, the uplift of mountain formations permits a host of useful and beneficial activities that are essential to the support of life as to be mentioned. As a remarkable illustration of design, in terms of pre-conceived perfection, it is to be noted that mountain ranges exist on every major continent and pro-vide the origin of the principal river systems on each of them that are essential to the support of life. All of this is to say nothing of the fact that the division of land mass into divided segments has no doubt provided a better circulation and dis-tribution of ocean currents in the operation of weather systems than would have been possible with respect to a single land mass. It is not difficult to visualize, too, that if the land mass of the Earth comprised only a single supercontinent, the climates, and the range of climatic conditions, would have been completely different from that which we experience, and quite possibly, immense areas would be reduced to arid deserts.

91

It is also apparent that a division of a single land mass into divided segments has resulted in greater diversity for the fulfilling of ecological roles and fitness in living organisms. Bjorn Kurtén, in an article entitled "Continental Drift and Evolution," suggests that land separation may account for the fact that mammals diversified into half again as many orders as the reptiles in a third of the time.[15]

Proceeding from this somewhat initiating phenomena as concerns the outer crust of the Earth, we can now move on to see how other complicated and quite different mechanisms and systems have interacted with the movement of the crustal plates in a most harmonious manner to participate in the preparations for the development of life. Inferences to design are to be seen in both the highly coordinated and perfectly fit relationships as well as in certain remarkable features of the mechanisms and systems themselves.

### 3. *Rocks and Soil*

On the surface of the Earth, billions of years transpired to disintegrate igneous and sedimentary rocks to build the soil upon which all agriculture and so much else depends. But disintegration of surface rock alone did not make the soil. It also required decomposition or chemical change. The soil physicist Dale Swarzendruber pointed out that scientific studies show that the soil "is a world of wonder" with a "network of design." He explained how the soluble bases (such as calcium, magnesium and potassium) are preferentially removed in the weathering of igneous rocks, thus leaving behind the oxides of silicon, aluminum, and iron to comprise the bulk, i.e., the soil material.[16]

Some of the other forces involved in the making of the soil were described by Jean, Harrah, Herman, and Powers in "Man and His Physical Universe,"[17] as follows:

"In this transition there are many forces involved. The oxygen of the air is an extremely important agent. It unites with the metals in rock to form oxides. Water too combines with minerals to change their constitution. But perhaps the most potent agent of all in promoting rock

92

decay is the carbonic acid derived from the carbon dioxide of the air combined with water. Because of its weight, carbon dioxide tends to settle down next to the Earth, which places it in the best position to unite with moisture to form dilute acid. . . . Small quantities of other acids, such as nitric and sulphuric acids are brought down from the air by the falling rain, and humic acids of all sorts form as products of decaying vegetation. These agents all attack the surface of rock particles from the tiniest grain of sand to massive boulders, and gradually transform them into chemical substances necessary to soil."[18]*

Hundreds of thousands to millions of unicellular plants (bacteria) to the gram of soil are needed in order for the soil to become fertile and productive. According to the above authors,[19] decaying organic matter comprising leaves, roots, stubble, and the excretia of animals add to the fertility of the soil. Bacteria are indispensable to work this over and make it a necessary component of fertile soil. The actions of earthworms, burrowing animals, insects and other "denizens" of the soil provide their contribution by loosening up the soil, providing a grinding action, admitting air, and water, and making possible the soil as a suitable medium for the roots of plants.[20] So impressive are these forces and activities in soil-making that the authors said: "What important stuff it is! What innumerable forces have done their bit in its formation! The most valuable of all our natural resources, how men ought to treasure and conserve it!"[21]

In order for plants to grow, according to Lester J. Zimmerman, also a soil scientist, it is not enough to have light, chemicals, air, and water. "There is," he said, "a power within the seed which becomes active in the proper environment. Many intricate and harmonious reactions begin to appear."[22]

## 4. *Fossil Fuels and Minerals*

The natural manufacture of fossil fuels, as well as of minerals, required more than specific properties of various ele-

---

* Excerpt used with permission of Ginn & Co. © 1949.

ments of the atoms and their compounds. For instance, it required thermal and hydraulic activity below the surface of the Earth to provide the physico-chemical reactions to transform the decadent remains of plant and animal life into useful energy (in the case of the fossil fuels), and to make possible the development of useful minerals (in the case of mineralization). As noted by Pollard, the processes which have, over long stretches of Earth's geologic history, concentrated ores of iron, copper, uranium, and other vital metals have, by now, well stocked the Earth with them for man's requirements. Later on in the Earth's history coal-beds and oil-fields were laid down slowly over a hundred million years "to provide vast reserves of fossilized fuels for man's utilization, primarily in the twentieth century and after."[23]

Had it not been for the abundance on Earth of organic plant and animal life in the earlier periods of its history, fossil fuels would not be available to us. According to M. King Hubbert, in an article entitled "The Energy Resources of the Earth," the "chemical energy stored up from the sunshine of the past six hundred million years has resulted in the existence of these fossil fuels."[24] It should also be noted, in a preparatory sense of development, that the oldest minerals on Earth are estimated to be at least three-fourths of the age of the Earth, according to an essay of Adolf Knoph.[25]

As by design, oil for fuel was accessible to early man on the surface of the Earth through seepages from the Earth's interior. In this day, natural drive mechanisms within the outer crust of the Earth, in the form of subterranean water or gas pressure, are the sole means of permitting the production of oil and gas from depths below the surface. Then, too, the occurrence below the surface of the Earth of underground "traps" for the accumulation of reservoirs of oil and gas is the coincident result of crustal faulting or fracturing, or occasionally in result of stratigraphical causes. It is further remarkable to consider that events over geologic time made it possible for these important substances to be accumulated, rather than to be widely or thinly dispersed and, for all practical purposes, rendered useless and unrecoverable.

Adrian Berry says that it almost raises "the suspicion of some cosmic design that coal, oil, fissionable uranium, and countless other precious raw materials are found in the Earth's crust and in the oceans."[26] It is astonishing, he noted, that these commodities have been able to survive perhaps one hundred million years of violent geographical and atmospheric change. The fact, he said, that coal and oil were buried at shallow depths beneath the surface saved them from oxidation and, in almost the same manner of expression as by Buckland more than a century earlier, he called attention to the easy accessibility of these materials in the eighteenth and nineteenth centuries. Buckland called attention to the convenience of coal and mineral deposits for the sinking of mines. This, in result of the location of irregular depressions or basins on the surface of the Earth. This was a time when our technology was primitive. Freeman J. Dyson, whose remarkable essay "Energy in the Universe" will be considered more fully later on, noted that fissionable uranium and thorium have been able to survive in the Earth's crust until ready for man's use. "Not more than one in a million of the earth's uranium nuclei has disappeared . . . during the whole of geological history."[27]

It would also seem that design is indicated in the provision made for a sort of reasonable distribution around the globe of both minerals and fossil fuels. In the case of mineralization, sea-floor spreading in consequence of the drift of the Earth's crustal plates has contributed to this. In a preparatory sense, minerals are still being manufactured by natural processes but, as the processes involved are slower than in the natural manufacture of fossil fuels, their initial creations, in a sense of design, came about much earlier than the latter.

In the case of the fossil fuels, it is to be noted that the oceans have covered land areas over geologic history—thus contributing on a vast scale to the occurrence of depositions and the reasonable distribution of organic materials from marine life around the whole of the globe. To this should be added the modern knowledge that the crustal plates of the Earth have shifted and changed a number of times over geologic history. These shifts have permitted tropical vegetation, plants, and other forms of life to have inhabited vast areas that now lie within the arctic and antarctic circles, deserts, etc. It was unintended in the design of things that vast areas of the globe be left to waste, but rather to be useful for storage of fossilized fuel energy.

## 5. *Water*

Ordinary water of the inanimate world of nature has often been referred to as showing great intelligent design in much the same manner as the eye of living organisms has been referred to in the animate world. I have already furnished Henderson's somewhat technical comments with respect to some of the properties of water. As it is a most unique substance, as well as one of the most abundant compounds on the Earth (serving many useful and diverse purposes in addition to being an important constituent of living organisms), it is perhaps well to further elaborate on its amazing properties.

Life on Earth, and quite possibly anywhere else in the universe, would be impossible without it. Other compounds do not perform in the same manner, in either the liquid or solid state, even though liquid ammonia or some other liquid might be put forth as a less viable substitute in some limited ways at different temperature ranges. Water is found in the Earth's crust, in the soil, in the rivers, lakes, oceans, and in the atmsophere. Wherever it is found, it is most fit and useful.

One of its many remarkable properties is that of expanding when it freezes and becoming less dense in the solid than in the liquid state. This permits ice to float on top of a lake or river, for example, and not settle to the bottom. If it were to freeze solid throughout, the lakes and rivers would be solid blocks of ice and there would be no life in the water. The frozen ice on the top of a lake or river insulates the water below while the freezing point of the water provides a release of sufficient heat to keep the temperature of the remainder of the water at or below about 32°F.

It has a great many other unique qualities as well. It is the best solvent.[28] It is the chief cause of the proper functioning of some of the phenomena explained earlier in this chapter, including the erosion of mountains and transportation of rocks and sediments, etc. Thomas D. Parke, a research chemist, writing an essay entitled "Plain Water Will Tell You The Story,"[29] included some of these points about water and added some additional ones. He noted that its formula weight is 18 and that one would predict it would be a gas at ordinary temperature and pressures. Ammonia, with a formula weight of 17, is a gas at temperatures as low as -33°C at atmospheric pressure. Hydro-sulphide, closely related to water by position in the Periodic Table and with a formula weight of 34, is a gas at temperatures down to -59°C. The fact that water exists as a liquid at all, at ordinary temperatures, is something he thought most unusual and should cause us to stop and think.

Parke further said: "Water has many other properties—strong evidence of design—covers three-fourths of the earth with a tremendous influence on the temperatures and weather conditions which prevail. There would be a catastrophic variation in temperature if water did not have a unique combination of properties. A high heat of melting, a long period of liquidity, and a very high heat of vaporization. As such it is a wonderful shock absorber to changes in temperature . . . built-in resistance to temperature."[30] He also noted that it has a high surface tension which aids in plant growth (as the best known solvent) and as such plays a vital role in the life processes of our bodies as a principle constituent of our blood. It has a high vapor pressure over a wide range of temperatures and still remains liquid throughout the whole range needed for life. It should also be noted that its surface tension is such that it is not prevented from percolating into the soil so as to give nourishment to the roots of plants or to help replenish the supplies of subterranean water so vital to geothermal and hydraulic processes, artesian wells, etc.

In his book "Supernature,"[31] Lyall Watson made reference to water as being one way in which all living things can be directly controlled by cosmic activity and, in addition, pointed out some other anomalies not mentioned above. He noted that it is an "ideal go-between" in triggering biological reactions very quickly and with very little expenditure of energy.[32]

The importance of this cannot be under-estimated since, as he said, all living processes take place in an aqueous medium.[33]

The oceans comprise nearly three-fourths of the surface of the Earth and it has been said that they are in due proportion to the necessities of a proper ocean circulatory system and a proper functioning weather machine. The actual distribution of sea and land over the surface of the Earth is likewise of the highest importance to the present condition of marine and land organic life. As noted by Hartwig: "If the oceans were considerably smaller or if Asia and America were concentrated within the tropics, the tides, the ocean currents, and the mutual phenomenon on which the existence of the vegetable and animal kingdoms depend, would be so profoundly modified, that it is extremely doubtful whether man could have existed."[34]

## 6. *The Sun, Earth, and Life*

Our Sun and its many complex functions have been highly and uniquely coordinated to interact with the epochal activities on the Earth. It is, of course, our basic source of life-giving energy. In an article entitled "The Energy Cycle of the Earth,"[35] Abraham H. Oort described, among other things, the cycle of solar energy from the time it enters the atmosphere as sunlight and the effect this has on the circulation of atmosphere and the oceans in distributing the solar energy in the matter of determining climatic conditions at varying latitudes. He notes the importance of the circulatory system to the existence of life and the fact that life could not exist if incoming solar radiation to a particular climatic zone were in balance with outgoing terrestrial radiation from the same zone.[36] So interwoven are the ocean currents which are driven by the winds (for the most part) to the redistribution of solar heat with the atmosphere that, according to Oort, the two systems, the oceans and the atmosphere, must be considered together. The final circulation pattern, he noted, is determined by the interaction of the two systems with each system influencing the other "in a complicated cycle of events."[37]

The complexity and harmony of circulatory systems may

98

readily be seen in the well-known mechanism as described in a television production several years ago entitled "The Weather Machine,"[38] (on a grant from Champion International Corporation) as follows:

> The Weather Machine has five major working parts. Just like a machine, the weather runs on energy—energy from the Sun. Energy, in the form of heat, churns the earth's atmosphere, causing heated air to rise and cool air to flow in and under it to take its place. Because of the earth's spherical shape, the Sun heats the atmosphere unevenly —cold at the poles and hot at the equator, which sets the massive machinery of heat transfer in motion. The earth's motion in space—its spin and its yearly journey around the Sun—set the atmosphere to swirling, and change the seasons. And the earth's irregular surfaces—land and sea masses, mountains and plains—further mix and modify the ever changing weather.

The manner of coordination of all this phenomena found expression in Oort's comment, as mentioned, that the oceans and the atmosphere must be considered together because the ocean currents, which are driven by the winds for the most part, redistribute the solar heat with the atmosphere.

But the benefits which are derived from the Sun are by no means at all limited to this particular cyclical phenomenon as described. The cosmic or electromagnetic energy interactions with the amazing properties of the chemical elements bring about a great many of the remarkable transformations in nature which we discussed in the last chapter. Then again, other interactions are equally remarkable. The Sun has spawned and plays a predominant role in the various other machine-like cyclical processes as, for example, the oxygen cycle (whereby the air is maintained with constancy because a balance has been struck between plant and animal life), the amazing process of photosynthesis (whereby plant carbohydrates are stored in the form of life support energy to animal life), the nitrogen cycle (whereby various processes maintain an approximate constancy of nitrogen in the air), the hydrogen cycle (whereby hydrogen combines with other elements to form many substances as, for example, plant and animal tissues, petroleum, and water in a functional way, etc.).[39]

No less remarkable than the above intricately coordinated phenomena is the foresight which is fully evident in the provision for a number of energy storage systems on the Earth itself to meet future needs in a manner that direct light and heat from the Sun (by its nature and remoteness) are unable to provide. Life simply must depend on more than a direct flow of energy from the Sun. The amazing thing from a design standpoint is that this need was remarkably anticipated and, hence, we find energy stored within the local Earth environment in different specialized ways for specialized purposes to be served. This required different types of unique natural machinery for this purpose. As though by positive assignment, rather than by limited-time randomness, elemental matter and interacting forces had to fall into well-defined, coordinated, and determined arrangements in order to bring about the variety of storage systems to be found.

In addition to the energy storage available from fossil fuels, I have already referred to the "nuclear machine" that, from energy derived from radioactive material stored in the interior of the Earth, drives the movements of the crustal plates of the Earth. Reference has also been made to the thermal and hydraulic machinery within the crust itself which is powered by internal heat and pressure to operate a host of life-important dynamic activities (including the operation of subterranean water systems, artesian wells, the movement of petroleum hydrocarbons to the surface of the Earth, and so on). Other sources of available energy on Earth include nuclear energy derived from the atom, the heat energy of fire from combustible products on the surface of the Earth, geothermal energy stored within the Earth's crust and available in result of the thermal and hydraulic activity as mentioned, energy derived from water that gives us hydroelectric power, thermal differential energy as a potential source of energy from the oceans, tidal energy from the Moon, etc. But more important

100

than all of these sources of energy for the existence and general maintenance of life is the process of photosynthesis which enables plants to chemically store solar energy, by reason of an exchange with the environment. Brief mention has already been made of this process and it is not felt necessary to elaborate more fully on it other than to say that it is a major source of energy supply that is essential to the existence of both plants and animals on the Earth. Perhaps equally important, as related to all forms of animal life, is the energy storage capacity associated with animal metabolism that operates by virtue of a different sort of mechanism and which enables animals to set aside energy until broken-down as needed.

Basically, the differing storage mechanisms do the same thing—provide energy—but yet accommodate quite different sorts of needs and requirements. David M. Gates, for instance, in an article entitled "The Flow of Energy in the Biosphere" discussed the manner in which some of these energy sources are utilized in different ways by living systems.[40] In a way, the differentiation required in energy storage systems, although less complex in some ways, recalls to mind the keen and ingenious differentiation that had to be made between quantum mechanics in the interior of atoms and the force mechanisms involved in the celestial mechanics of planetary systems. All of these basic differentiations were made, as far as we know, within narrow time-frames—far too much to expect of blind chance. In another way, they reflect the complexity—rather than simplicity—of cosmic and inanimate phenomena.

The distance and inclination of the Earth from the Sun has frequently been pointed to in terms of design. For instance, William Paley, nearly two centuries ago, called attention to the shape of the Earth which, like an orange, is an oblate spheroid. As such, he noted that in a state of rotary motion it gets upon a permanent axis and keeps there and "its poles preserve their direction with respect to the plane and to the center of its orbit. . . ."[41] He pointed out that if the axis of rotation were as many as could be drawn through the center

101

of an object that is not shaped like the Earth to opposite points upon its whole surface, then none of these axes would be permanent. But with an oblate spheroid like the Earth, either its shorter diameter or its longest diameters, at right angles with the former, "must all terminate in the single circumference which goes round the thickest part of the object." This general observation was more scientifically refined by other writers in more recent times. Frank Allen, for example, described the daily rotation of the Earth on its polar axis (giving both day and night) and the yearly rotation around the Sun as giving "stability to its orientation in space and, coupled with the inclination (23°) of the polar axis to the plane of its revolution (the eliptic), affords regularity to the seasons, thus doubling the habitable area of the Earth and providing a greater diversity of plant life than a static globe could sustain."[42] A point made earlier by Hartwig is interesting. He said that, if the Earth were farther removed from the Sun, the seas would be frozen as solid material and the circulation of fluids for life would be arrested or impossible. If much nearer the Sun, the water would constantly be volatized and then again precipitated in great showers and floods.[43]

The size of the Earth, as well, contributes significantly to the matter of life-sustaining suitability. I have previously called attention to Henderson's comment on size as related to the ability of the Earth to hold its atmosphere. It is generally recognized in science today that the physico-chemical conditions which existed in the early stages of Earth's history underwent great change. As a part of this, its hydrogen escaped into space as a prelude to the occurrence of conditions which were productive of an oxygen atmosphere. In his book "We Are Not Alone," Walter Sullivan called attention to the calculations of Fu Shu Haung,[44] the astrophysicist, to show that "for a planet to be large enough to hold its oxygen, yet small enough to get rid of its hydrogen in time for advanced life to evolve, its radius should lie between one thousand and twenty thousand kilos. The radius of the Earth is some six thousand three hundred eighty kilos." Sullivan further referred to the conclusion of Harrison Brown of the California Institute of Technology that for an oxygen atmosphere to appear "a planet must be small enough (as is the Earth) so that, over an extended period of time, its hydrogen will escape into space."[45]

## 7. Ozone Layer

During the early formulative stages of the Earth's history, a rare event occurred in the formation of an ozone layer comprising triatomic oxygen ($O_3$) at the upper level of the Earth's atmosphere. It is unique not only in that it screens harmful ultraviolet rays from the Sun and higher energy radiations from outer space but, as noted by Pollard it is, as well, an ideal radiation shield that is transparent to light.[46] It makes life, as we know it, possible on Earth. In his book "Is God Evident?"[47] Gerald Heard said that we have a transparent blanket to give us just what we can stand—light but very little ultraviolet, heat but very little infrared. He recalled a conversation which he had with Sir George Simpson, then head of the British Meteorological Service, which was quite descriptive of this phenomenon. Simpson called the ozone phenomenon "a very complex and efficient thermostat" in observing that: ". . . Because as the Sun has been found to be a . . . variable, a pulsing star—its output of heat therefore varies. As we can't shift out or into another orbit as heat rises or falls, we have to have a screen . . . for when the heat increases this draws aqueous vapor from the sea and stores it as a haze-screen high up and when the Sun's heat falls the aqueous vapor falls down to the sea, the sky is clear and more heat comes in. . . ."[48] It is of just the right thickness and composition to have the unusual life-saving benefit. If it were slightly narrower in band or of any other known possible composition, it would not serve its purpose. Here again, one of the elements, oxygen, was released from early plant life, during its life cycle, to build up the atmosphere that gave rise to the ozone layer. H. N. V. Temperley described how this cleared the way for the evolution of higher forms of life that breathe and that the sunlight gradually toned down to an intensity at which such higher forms of life were viable and, at the same time, the spontaneous appearance of new life would stop.[49]

## 8. *Moon*

From the time of the ancients, the Moon has been looked upon as purposeful in the sense that it provides a night light for the inhabitants of the Earth and that its size and light intensity are just right for this purpose. Its influence on ocean tides is well known, just as well as the effect which such tides have on the creation of tidal energy and on the circulatory systems which relate to ocean currents and the climatic conditions on Earth. It is also seen in a relationship aspect to the plate tectonics involved in the above described new theory of continental drift. Then again, man's venture into space and his inspection of the Moon has revealed additional inferences to design. Many of the moon rocks found exhibit "a glazing in concentration toward high points and edges"[50] according to a display sign at the NASA Center in Houston, Texas. This is said to have been an "unexpected" discovery. The NASA explanation is simply that the geologic origin of these effects are not known. But the coincidence of this in relation to the reflective power of the Moon is quite surprising. This is especially so when it is also realized, as independently reported in a publication of *Awake!*[51] that about fifty-percent of the lunar soil facing the Earth consists of tiny glass particles of different sizes and shapes which are extremely lustrous when the light of the Sun shines on them. In contrast, it is said, very little glass is found naturally in the soil of Earth nor, for that matter, on any of the planets that have been explored in our solar system. The tiny glass beads in Moon soil are characterized as similar to the glass beads in roadside reflectors which catch an automobile headlight and shine brightly.[52] Thus, from the standpoint of the inhabitants of Earth, the moonlight reflection capability could not have been better planned.

Still other observations have been made with respect to the Moon in connection with its potential use in space exploration as a launching platform and for other purposes. Adrian Berry, for instance, considers it to be a curious coincidence that the Earth, the one inhabited planet in our Solar System, should have a huge Moon out of all proportion to its size in relation to other larger "Moons" in our Solar System.[53] I have previously called attention to his "suspicion" of intelligent design by reason of the Moon's soft maria basins for landing space vehicles; that is, on the side that permanently faces the Earth. The "back" side of the Moon, in contrast, is made up of much rougher terrain and without the marias found on "our" side. Fred Hoyle thinks both of these differences present a "very queer situation."[54] Then, too, according to Berry, oxygen is available, presently in the form of oxides and, if water is not beneath the surface of the Moon (as many postulate), it may be made available on the moon with human ingenuity.[55]

## 9. *Clouds*

I have previously referred to William Paley's fascination for the clouds and their movement across the surface of the Earth. Professor Bruce C. Parker of the Virginia Polytechnic Institute has indicated that, in result of research, the clouds are living ecosystems where minute, multi-celled organisms come to life, multiply, and shower chemical products like vitamins on the Earth, thus playing a significant role in the dispersal of micro-organisms and chemicals.[56] It should be noted, as well, that thunderstorms over the entire Earth are a significant factor in maintaining soil fertility. According to Asimov, they daily form some 250,000 tons of nitrates.[57]

## 10. *Clean-Up*

Life on Earth in any form has not been given the destiny of permanency as a substitute for renewal by reproduction processes. Unless the means of decay of living things had been provided to cleanse and continually renew the platform of the Earth in order to make way for new living organisms to take their place, life as we know it would not be possible. The action of predatory creatures, rather than being viewed as a point to make against the idea of design, should be viewed from the standpoint of the important ecological role which they (together with the activity of the weather machine, chemical activity, etc.) play in maintaining both a natural balance and a fit environment for the existence of life.

## 11. *Summary*

We have thus seen how the major phenomena of a cosmic nature tie together in a most perfectly fit and suitable manner to complement the existence and development of life on this planet. None of it may be faulted. In a word, the Earth and its environs are remarkably well-designed. Those who may say that any part of it is "imperfect" or "unfit" have absolutely nothing to suggest that would improve the system overall or in its component parts. This will be even more evident when we consider still other phenomena in the remaining chapters. It all speaks overwhelmingly in favor of a designed and deterministic inanimate or cosmic world, contrary to the present view of indeterminism in science. "There is no vagueness, looseness, or ambiguity," in the world, said Richard Taylor.[58] ". . . Everything in nature is and always has been determinate, with no loose edges at all, and she was forever destined to bring forth just what she has produced, however slight may be our understanding of the origins of these works. . . ."[59]

All of the foregoing reflects that complex engineering problems were involved (from our point of view) with respect to both the phenomena mentioned and the matter of its timely coordination in reference to life. The fact that the best solutions were taken as related to the objective of fitness, suitability, and compatibility to animate systems on Earth brings us again to the suggestion that both inanimate and animate worlds of nature should be considered together as though the consequence of a single creative evolutionary process. Even though Henderson, at a much earlier time in this century, related the inanimate aspects of nature mostly to the few elements and compounds as mentioned, his comment on this subject is indeed appropriate. As quoted by Eric C. Rust, Henderson said: "The way in which cosmic evolution works step by step with biological evolution suggests that the two streams of evolution are in some sense one, and that what appears to be contingent happenings really constitute an orderly development yielding results not merely contingent, but

106

resembling those which in human action we recognize as purposeful."[60] Certainly, the manner in which the natural substances and machinery of the non-animate world have been tailor-made to serve functions and purposes for the animate world of nature are comparable to the way in which the processes of biological evolution have participated in relating living organisms to purposive end-functions.

Is it not a bit too coincidental that when man arrived on the scene, the continents had divided, mountain chains had been thrown up, major river systems and their tributaries were flowing on each of the continents, lakes, streams, and ponds had developed, the oceans had become distributed, temperate climatic regions and conditions had been established, soil had been made ready for agriculture, the machinery and mechanisms described above had been geared up and were rolling, minerals of a wide variety of useful types had come into existence, fuel and other energy sources had been made available, and so on? Upon man's arrival, to be considered in the next chapter, the Earth had transformed into a fit and suitable habitat for his uses and purposes. The dynamic activities which transpired over pre-human history made possible the organization and accessibility of both mechanisms for survival and useful materials upon which both human existence and development depends.

R. Buckminster Fuller (as reported in an article by Harold Taylor in the Saturday Review) said that the universe with the Earth planet in it "has been arranging its resources in its own way over endless stretches of time and space, and by whatever happy accident the Earth has been honored by a mixture of benevolent energy radiations from the Sun and gravitational pulls by the Moon, the combination of these energies, along with the accumulated energies within the mineral stockpiles deposited below the Earth's surface, has given the Earth's inhabitants an extraordinary favorable environment in which to pursue a full and rich life. . . ."[61]

The words of one of the leading innovative scientists in space and energy, Freeman J. Dyson, provide us with the sort of enthusiasm that is appropriate to the next chapter:

Nature has been kinder to us than we had any right to expect. As we look out into the universe and identify the many accidents of physics and astronomy that have worked together to our benefit, it almost seems as if the universe must in some sense have known that we were coming.[62]

# 7

# Mind and the Environment

There has been an increasing tendency in recent years for the materialists to depict man as simply another biological creature with remarkable qualities that may be explained totally in terms of evolutionary processes; that is, in conjunction with "ordinary" laws of physics and chemistry. It is claimed that his characteristic features of mind and consciousness (including the capacity for original thought, memory, expression of values, emotions, sentiments, etc.) are merely advanced stages of evolution that may be found, incipiently or in rudimentary form at least, in other forms of living beings at lower levels of the evolutionary ladder. His uniqueness, if not fully denied, is considered to be of far less importance than what had been thought to be the case not so long ago. Nothing is thought to have been planned with the aim envisaged by Karl Heim of endowing one unique creature (man) with dominion over the Earth in whom the creation of the world is perfected in "the last act of the drama, the finale of the composition, at the apex of the pyramid."[1]

The fact is that man is indeed unique among the more than a million living animal species on Earth. None other have been shown to possess the high-level development of the characteristic features of the nature mentioned, much less in combination with the physical characteristics that permit the beneficial use of the environment as a whole. Even so, this remarkable aspect of man's existence does not of itself suggest to those of a materialistic view that design is to be inferred. It is, to them, a phenomenon of nature that just happened by chance. But rather than let the matter simply rest at that, an empirical basis for a fresh challenge to such a concept has become increasingly evident in this late 20th century.

Man is empirically unique from all other life on Earth in still another highly significant way that should be regarded as one of the most remarkable realizations to come forth in our time. A very special relationship exists alone between man and the natural world. It is, as previously mentioned, a mutually reciprocal relationship that goes far beyond mere compatibility, and one that has become increasingly evident in recent times by reason of man's greatly enhanced understanding of the substances and processes of nature. Man's rational thought, as we shall consider below, has linked up with a most fit, suitable, and affirmatively contributing environment that has given a special meaning to the phenomena that we have been considering in earlier chapters. Other than by design, there is no rational explanation as to why the environment is so well equipped and prepared for the uses and purposes of man nor, for that matter, for man to be reciprocally equipped and prepared mentally to take advantage of the bounties of the environment. Such an harmonious state of affairs is precisely what one would expect to find in a designed rather than in a non-designed world.

The environment has furthered the development and advancement of man in almost countless ways. In the early days following his arrival on the evolutionary scene, man's needs were met at first from nature with the more simple and basic raw materials for his development that were roughly attuned to his then limited, yet developing, knowledge. His progressive anthropological story reflects the use or availability of materials for fire and shelter, tools for hunting, soil for agriculture, cooking and storage devices, textiles, beasts of burden for transportation, and so on. Later on, came new discoveries which brought along the wheel, the drill, the cart and wagon, the wind and sail for marine transportation, metal working, irrigation, the art of writing and mathematics, the construction of buildings from suitable natural materials, the making of glass, works of art and literature, astronomy and the calendar, the

110

alphabet, water power, mechanical power, paper and printing, compasses and ships, steam power, electricity, and so on.

The above-described inter-relationships between man and nature were only the "tip of the iceberg." A seemingly endless stream of new and different inter-relationships has come to be revealed in step with man's creative advancement. The only limitation, it seems, is the limitation of the environment itself. These new linkages have enabled man, for example, to: (1) move about on sea, land, and in the air with great facility thus bringing the Earth, the solar system, the galaxy, and indeed perhaps distant galaxies much closer together in present or projected meaningful ways, (2) communicate, as well as to see, at great distances incredibly far beyond normal range of ordinary hearing and sight, (3) escape gravity with yet untold promising future consequences, (4) harness a host of diverse energy sources to a variety of needed and purposeful uses, including the power and energy of the Sun, the atom, fossil fuels, wind, water, geothermal steam, etc., (5) transform elemental matter into an almost countless and "bewildering" array of useful materials and substances, (6) convert, increasingly, so-called inhospitable areas of the Earth, such as deserts, jungles, polar areas, and the like, to present and potential use—an exercise of man's dominion not unlike that over plant and animal matter, (7) modify life processes in the physical and chemical sense, and (8) make almost countless practical and useful applications of discoveries arising from a great many of the applied fields of science. The latter would certainly include such things as the creation of artificial light and the harnessing of tremendous energy in the form of laser beams, as well as to use the mysterious substance of light in a variety of other beneficial ways; the penetration of opaque objects through the discovery of X-rays and other more recent and sophisticated scanning mechanisms; the preservation of food through the use of refrigeration and the stimulation of food production by the use of fertilizers and by other means; the development of technologies to survey the Earth's potential for new resources, including agricultural, mineral and the like, as well as to locate soils of adequate fertility, the existence of

111

crop diseases, etc.; the enlargement of the scope of mental retention capacities through computerized mechanisms; the modification of climatic temperature ranges as related to immediate environmental conditions; and such a variety of additional discoveries that are actually quite overwhelming.

The sort of picture one may get from the foregoing, taken in conjunction with the whole of other natural phenomena considered elsewhere herein, not only reflects a fit, suitable, and harmonious interplay between man and nature but, additionally, serves to challenge in no uncertain terms the view of an indeterministic, imperfect, and disordered world. There seems to be no end to it. It is a real world, as described by Richard Taylor, that has no "loose edges" or parts, and is quite deterministic. Those who would say that the world of man's environment merely represents a manufactured by-product of man's ordered imagination, overlook that his original thought has been led along by a receptive and benign environment. This is obvious from the empirical evidence as we have seen. As indicated in the introductory chapter, man had no control over the environment as it was presented to him. What shows "design" is thus significantly enlarged in this day by relating the whole of inanimate and animate nature to man, his mind and consciousness, rather than limiting such a showing to either the "appearances" of things or to the fitness of the environment to the existence and support of life in general.

Having made almost insatiable and beneficial applications of nature so far, are there any further "design" environmental pathways to be opened by man with respect to the future? Will his gift and capacity for original and creative thought be turned inward toward stagnation? It is today "perfectly reasonable," says Adrian Berry, "to extrapolate the line of man's history of ever-improving technology" into the remote future."[2] It is impractical here, of course, to set forth the various concepts of an empirical nature on which Berry's remarkable book "The Next Ten Thousand Years" is based. In Berry's view:

Useful things will continue to be invented. And the very continuation of such inventions is a justification for faith

112

in some great design. The treasures lying in our path, and our human capacity to use them, may for all we know have been prepared by some cosmic intelligence with an interest in our advancement. . . .[3]

Much of the phenomena mentioned above, involving inventiveness, reflect a sort of a "progress" in the civilization of mankind. To many, it is felt that we could do without certain kinds of progress; that a number of the activities of man have served only to his detriment and have opened up problems. Such criticisms are not without merit, of course, and one should not underestimate the damage or harm that man, in the exercise of his inventiveness in relation to an abundant natural environment, is capable of producing. But these are the sorts of problems that are man-made, are they not? As William Pollard observed in his book "Man on a Spaceship," man may use his inventiveness "either as a blessing or as a curse."[4] As we have seen, man has the means to work out his existence in countless ways that may serve him well. It would seem that the only condition attached to man's unique relationship with nature, as mentioned, is that his intelligence, creativity, and wisdom achieve an appropriate level of understanding so as to exercise wise constraint in shaping the natural world to his own best practical needs and reasonable uses. One of the marks of design in man has been his unique personal freedom and this would seem to require a constructive use of the resources of nature and to avoid a destructive pattern. It is most encouraging that, providentially, a rapidly growing awareness of this need has become apparent only in the last decade or so. The point should be emphasized, however, that any failure on the part of man to exercise a wisdom that is appropriate to the preservation of his environment is not to be considered a result of any fundamental error in the design of fit, suitable, and compatible natural phenomena. This, notwithstanding the possiblity of its use as "either a blessing or a curse."

Is is germane to the above consideration of man's civilization in relation to the future that we should briefly consider the concern being expressed today about the exhaustion of

113

nature's bounty. The Earth, by reason of its limited size, is finite, yet, in the last chapter, we noted that its size is, from a design standpoint, optimum for the existence and development of life. If we had a choice to live on a much larger or much smaller Earth, we would find it in our best interest to keep this one. We have already seen how well the Earth was prepared and stocked with vital life-sustaining resources. The growth of populations and the increased use of our resources has, nevertheless, caused many to project a future of impending disaster for the human race. In so doing, they have little faith in the design of things and in man's capacity for original thought. Perhaps they should "think" design since Nature has shown a sort of timeliness in the past to meet the on-coming needs and requirements of man. As we shall see, the future is highly promising in this regard if one takes a broad view of the available potential for both energy and mineral supplies with respect to the Earth (to be considered here) and to the planets of our solar system (to be considered in the next chapter).

In the early days of man's history, he tapped wood, peat, oil seeps, and coal sources found on the surface of the Earth for fuel and, as his needs increased, made discovery of oil, gas, and other petroleum supplies. It was not long ago that great concern was expressed about the exhaustion of future energy needs simply on the basis of this form of energy. Today, as these are dwindling in supply from presently known reservoirs, man is beginning to make use of various other alternative energy sources that will be fully capable of providing an adequate substitute for the future. There are few scientists today, knowledgeable in energy matters, who do not feel that this problem is answerable to the point of solution for a great many years to come, if not indefinitely. The introduction of energy from ordinary natural sources are now within practical application, such as geothermal energy, solar radiation, energy from wind, water (including the prospect of thermal differential energy from the oceans), waste materials, to say nothing of the potential large-scale use of nuclear energy (as to which a new step in the potential breakthrough for fusion has only recently been announced). For the most part, these sources are no longer considered experimental. They provide the means to obtain energy from the environment with only minimal damage.[5] Gerard Morgan-Grenville, head of the National Centre for the Development of Alternate Technology, in Wales, has been involved in protracted experimentation on this subject and confirms (as have so many others) that "mankind can live in reasonable harmony with his environment—and live comfortably."[6]

The discovery of these new energy sources has apparently occurred so as to keep man's requirements ahead of need. In specific reference to nuclear energy, for example, Pollard said it is providential that the key discoveries which made it possible for man to use nuclear energy were made at the critical time that they were.[7] At various times Dr. Glenn T. Seaborg, former Chairman of the U.S. Atomic Energy Commission, and Edward Teller, the famous physicist, have made similar remarks to the effect that the discovery of nuclear energy opened up vast new resources at a most opportune time in our energy consumption history. Pollard further pointed out that until only a dozen years ago or so, man was exclusively dependent on chemical energy (except for hydro-electric power) derived from fossilized fuels. He noted that nuclear energy is extremely common and present throughout all of the universe (giving the example of our Sun and other millions of stars in the galaxies as constituting natural hydrogen sources) and called attention to the fact that discussions of nuclear energy today completely miss the point of its natural character. "The amazing thing," he said, "is that man should have stumbled on nuclear energy and the possibility of its controlled utilization less than thirty years ago."[8] Its use provides an adequate source of energy and he gave examples of providing for an adequate food supply or means of producing food for an enlarged population, the means of providing abundant water from nuclear-powered desalinization plants which could be constructed along the oceans of the world, for purposes of irrigation of desert areas and of areas not previously required for agriculture, and so on. According to Pollard, by the end of the century nuclear power and sea water desalting plants "will be commonplace in every country of the world," saying, "This is an essential requirement for the maintenance of the population which the Earth will be then sustaining."[9] Since the time these comments and projections were made, a decade or so ago, it should be noted that technology has advanced rapidly toward the wide-scale use of several of the other alternate energy sources as above mentioned, such as solar energy.

Then, too, it was also not long ago that scientists were concerned about future mineral resources on Earth. Today the present concern appears to be more related to distribution, economics, and the geographical situation. Once again, it seems quite timely that vast areas of the Earth formerly thought to be "inhospitable" to man, such as desert, arctic, and offshore ocean areas, are revealing still new potential sources of useful minerals in much the same manner that new areas are continually opening up, technologically, for the discovery and development of new sources of fossil fuels. Further, in terms of additional supplies, an important linkage has been discovered between mineral outcroppings in or near continents and the new theory of continental drift and plate tectonics around the globe. This is considered a great help to exploration geologists. For instance, "sea-floor spreading" associated with the plate tectonics has resulted in the deposition of nodules, about the size of grapefruits, on the floor of the oceans which contain a variety of minerals for harvesting. Man has already started the research and development to convert these nodules to his mineral supply, which will serve his needs for a number of vital minerals for many years to come. As noted by Claiborne Pell in an article in the Saturday Review,[10] even the most conservative estimates of resources in the sea-bed overwhelms those who are accustomed to making dire predictions of exhausted mineral resources. The potential, he said, in manganese, aluminum, nickel, cobalt, and other metal nodules on the sea-bed will enable the supply of staggering quantities for man's future requirements. For instance, the metal content of manganese nodules, according to one study of reserves in the Pacific Ocean alone, came up with the esti-

116

mate that the nodules contain three hundred fifty-eight billion tons of manganese, the equivalent, at present rates of consumption, to reserves for 400,000 years, compared to known land reserves of only one hundred years[11]—a sort of analogy to the biblical miracle of the loaves and fishes.

Let us now turn to yet another aspect of man, his mind and consciousness.

Is there a correspondence or a kindredship between the mind of man and the cosmic mind of a Designer? There are some keen minds who think so. William Pollard is one of these and I am indebted to him for first bringing to my attention, in his previously mentioned book,[12] an essay written by a Nobel Prize winner in physics, Eugene Wigner, entitled "The Unreasonable Effectiveness of Mathematics in the Natural Sciences."[13] Wigner observed that the "enormous usefulness of mathematics in the natural sciences is something bordering on the mysterious and that there is no rational explanation for it." Further, he said, "the miracle of the appropriateness of the language of mathematics for the formulation of the laws of physics is a wonderful gift which we neither understand nor deserve. . . ."[14] Elaborating on Wigner's thesis, Pollard said there have been a number of occasions in the history of physics since Newton "in which a mathematical system, originally a pure product of the human mind, has subsequent to its development proved remarkably applicable to an accurate description of nature." Pollard further said that nature itself is certainly not "a product of the human mind, and the correspondence between a mathematical system and the structure of things in the natural world has a kind of miraculous quality about it."[15] One of the three examples given by Wigner of these sorts of "miracles," and which he said could be multiplied almost infinitely, was experienced by Albert Einstein in the development of his General Theory of Relativity and related to his effort to define a four-dimensional space-time geometry. There was only one possibility and the correct solution, as expressed in his gravitational field equations and abstractly conceived, precisely corresponded with nature to show the manner in which bodies in nature move under the influence of each other's

117

gravity. It is reported that Einstein was lastingly impressed with the correspondence he had achieved with nature. The second example of this kind of amazing phenomenon related to Newton's formulation of the law of universal gravitation and the motion of bodies with respect to it. Newton's concept was formulated on very scant observation, and yet, the law which he established has been verified in accuracy to less than a ten thousandth of a percent. The third example given by Wigner of a remarkable correspondence between human imagination and reason and the phenomena of nature had to do with the mathematician David Hilburt, who, early in this century, developed a mathematical theory of spaces where all lengths are complex numbers and which, as Wigner pointed out, are neither natural nor simple and are never seen in any direct observation of nature.[16]

Summarizing this amazing phenomenon of correspondence between the realism of nature and the human mind, Pollard said:

> . . . Yet now we have discovered that systems spun out by the brain, for no other purpose than our sheer delight with their beauty, correspond precisely with the intricate design of the natural order which pre-dated man and his brain. That surely is to make the discovery that man is amazingly like the designer of that order.[17]

The foregoing observations are not unlike that made by the English theologian J. S. Habgood, when he said that the more science makes sense in things "the more firmly we ought to believe that the reality behind nature is a mind not unlike our own."[18] And Eric C. Rust, as well, expressed the view that the emergence of the human mind, following an evolutionary process, which is itself able to understand the process, implies that the mind was there all the time. He asked: "How can a purely fortuitous process throw up a mind which can give it meaning and control it? Mathematical thought and statistical probability shudder at the thought."[19]

All of this gives cause for serious reflecton on the countless inferences in the natural world which appeal to us as having the appearance of being the product and logic of a higher intelligence. If the human mind demonstratively interconnects in mathematical systems with the order in nature, why should it not also interconnect in other ways as well? It simply requires recognition that an intelligence is behind the order of nature, does it not? One should ask whether the countless analogies to intelligence of Ray, Paley, and others (Chapters 3 and 4), the logic implicit in the manner of construction and utility of the atoms (Chapter 5), the logic of the harmony, fitness, and compatibility of natural phenomena for the existence of life on Earth (Chapter 6), the logic in the special relationship that man and his mind holds to his environment (as shown in this chapter), and the design that is becoming evident in cosmology (in the next chapter), does not serve to verify the nature and existence of a cosmic mind of the Designer of the universe. The analogies and inter-relationships referred to in design arguments seem to touch the kindredship between two intellects and, in so doing, serve to substantially upgrade the general quality and nature of all inferences to show design.

I should like to add here another amazing example of that marvelous correspondence between the human mind and a cosmic Mind which, in origin, is to be attributed to the studies of Leonardo Fibboniaci in the early thirteenth century and "re-discovered" at St. Mary's College in California in 1960. This has reference to the Fibboniaci mathematical sequence of numbers which appear to pervade, although not universally, both the cosmic and animate worlds of nature with such frequency that the science writer Eric Hoffer[20] said that the numbers appear far too often to be discounted "as mere chance." It seems that the amazing features of the numerical sequence of Fibboniaci numbers makes one think that he has come across a long-lost fragment of a Designer's notebook. Adrian Berry, in an article appearing in the London Daily Telegraph,[21] said there are beginning to appear so many applications of Fibboniaci numbers in science, psychology, astronomy, art, oceanography, and in a number of other fields of scientific endeavor, that many scientists "are beginning to wonder whether it may be linked with some mysterious law governing events throughout the universe." There is now a Fibboniaci Quarterly published at St. Mary's College near San Francisco and, in addition, a book on the subject has been written entitled "Fibboniaci and Lucas Numbers"[22] by a co-editor of the Quarterly, Verner E. Hoggart, Jr. The sequence of numbers is: 1, 1, 2, 3, 5, 8, 13, 21, 34, 55, 89, 144, 233, 377, and so on ad infinitum. Each Fibboniaci number is the sum of the two preceding numbers, so that one plus one equals two; one plus two equals three; two plus three equals five, and so on to infinity. Every third number is divisible by two, every fourth number by three, every fifth number by five, every sixth number by eight, and so on. The divisors themselves form a sequence in which each is the sum of its two preceding numbers.[23]

Many interesting observations here come to light when one contemplates the above mathematical sequence. As noted by Berry, the ratio between any Fibboniaci number beyond three and its successor is always the irrational number 1.61803, obtained by halving the sum of one and the square root of five. It is, said Hoffer, a magic ratio that recurs throughout art and nature.[24] This numbers relationship, without man having consciously known of it earlier, comprises the so-called Golden Mean which is the mathematical basis for such things as the Parthenon, the shape of ordinary playing cards, Greek vases, classical architecture of the Greeks, the spirals of galaxies, the curves of snail shells, etc. It also provides the same numbers relationship with respect to the branches of trees, leaves of palm trees, scales of fir-cones, the shape of sunflower seeds, and so on. As an illustration, in the application of the sequence of numbers to the spiral seed formations of sunflowers, it is to be noted that ordinary-size sunflowers have 34 or 55 spirals growing in opposite directions. Giant sunflowers usually have 89 and 144 of such spirals. Even the common musical chords contain a portion of the numbers, 3, 5, and 8.

Berry pointed out that the ratio of Fibboniaci numbers has been found to improve on Bode's Law (which is a scheme, in effect, for remembering the distances of the planets from the Sun).[25] The application of Bode's Law, according to Berry,[26] is that when four is subtracted from each distance of a planet from the Sun they climb in a simple doubling sequence of three, six, twelve, twenty-four, and so on. The Fibboniaci system eliminates the complication of subtracting four. Pluto and the planet Neptune break the sequence under Bode's Law, yet it has been discovered, he said, that the Fibboniaci system conforms with Neptune, whereas it disobeys Bode's Law, and while Pluto does not seem to fall into place under the Fibboniaci system, it is a source of argument that Pluto is not a proper planet anyway but merely an escaped Moon.

Of further interest from the standpoint of this work, is that the Fibboniaci sequence of numbers appears to transcend and cross-over both the cosmic and the animate worlds of phenomena, showing not only a definite mathematical relationship existing in certain phenomena with respect to each, but also showing a direct abstraction and linkage between the mind of man and a cosmic mind. We see both the "A" and the "B" in conjunction more visibly than in the earlier examples given. Then, too, the cross-over aspect as mentioned implies that something else is needed to explain the origin and evolution of the animate world of nature than simply events and selective processes said to be peculiar and random to that world.

Before moving ahead to the next chapter, where we will consider still other aspects of cosmic design, I should like to close this one by returning again to its main theme, i.e., that the uniqueness of the mind of man, as well as its development and advancement, is solely dependent on the uniqueness and availability in the natural world of marvelously compatible supporting phenomena, forces, and materials. No purely mechanistic explanation for this exists and the probabilities of chance are best expressed as zero. From the "stage" of the natural world, man may be creative—not only in the sense of improving his quality of life—but in expressing values that may well bring him toward a sense of significance and realization of his ultimate purpose and destiny.

# 8

## Design in Cosmology

"The astronomical universe is a beauty to behold, a wonder to contemplate, and a challenge to understand." These words of Ivan R. King of the University of California in the Preface to his book "The Universe Unfolding"[1] are drawn into special relevance here by his further words: "Surely, when we contemplate Man and the Universe, one of the greatest wonders is that we have come to know what we know about it."[2]

Do we really know enough about the universe, however, to project meaning and significance in relation to man, his mind and consciousness? One may well ask whether or not science has advanced our knowledge sufficiently so as to allow us to venture upon meaningful inferences to intelligent design with respect to "outer space." In many ways the scope and quality of some, but by no means all, present-day inferences of this sort are not too unlike those which prevailed in early-day design arguments relating to "earth, fire, water, and air." And space science writers who might be prone to regard the inferences to design in this direction as being entirely too speculative, premature, or who might simply attribute it all to blind chance, should long hesitate before drawing any such conclusion. For one thing, astronomical indicia of design should be seen cumulatively rather than in isolation of past and new inferences to design of the nature we have been considering in other fields of observation. Even before man developed the present sophisticated means of investigating the mysteries of space, the idea of an accidental creation was already to be seen as an overwhelmingly improbable alternative. Then again, it

122

should be noted that any overt appearances of imperfection in space may turn out to be illusory, rather than real, in much the same manner as we have experienced in our planetary sphere.

The one definite thing we can now say is that there are a great many more substantive inferences to intelligent design with respect to cosmology than were primitively conceived by the early writers. We may now say that these inferences have grown immeasurably during the past three or four decades. That we may now point to an enlarging vista of celestial "design" only serves to enhance the fundamental credibility of design arguments formerly much more limited to the Earth environs. Then, too, our view of the known universe has been deeply enriched with the empirically-based prospect of the existence of mind and consciousness elsewhere—a possible scheme or system overall—to say nothing of the significance as may be attached to the very fact of space exploration and discovery, together with all the potential this holds for the future of man and the greater distribution of mind and consciousness, values, etc.

As in the case of our approach to design with respect to the atoms and other cosmic phenomena, we will be looking here primarily to the end-products or results of outer space knowledge, rather than be more concerned, as in science, with the specific mechanisms and processes of universal phenomena as now known or theorized.

The most widely-accepted theory in science on the origin of our universe, based on present-day evidence from observation and astronomical data, is that it had a special "beginning" some 16 to 20 billion years ago. Because we cannot expect to discover today what occurred before then, said George Abell of the University of California in his authoritative book "Exploration of the Universe," the theory is lacking of course in terms of absolute certainty.[3] It is called the "big bang" theory and was originally proposed by the Belgian astronomer Abbe Lemaitre in 1920. Gamow described how the universe had its origin in this manner by paraphrasing Lemaitre's concept as follows: ". . . Our universe started its evolutionary history from a highly compressed, extremely hot, and completely homogeneous state which he called 'the primeval atom.' . . . As the result of progressive expansion, the masses of the universe have been gradually thinning out, cooling down, and differentiating, giving rise to the highly complex structure of the universe as we know it today."[4] The originating "explosion" ("big bang") of this gigantic primeval atom caused a widespread dispersal of its substance in all directions through space. By reason of the unifying forces of attraction, masses of the primeval material, interstellar dust, gases, etc. clustered together into stellar systems called galaxies that are today continuing to recede away from the initial point of dispersal at enormous velocities. The particular galaxy in which our Earth is only a tiny object is merely one of the billions of galaxies in the vastness of space. According to Abell, Edwin Hubble found that (when allowances are made for interstellar absorption) "the distribution of galaxies, on the large scale, is the same in all directions, and that the mean density of galaxies in space seems to be about the same at all distances. On the small scale, however, galaxies tend to be grouped into clusters of galaxies."[5]

In addition to scientific evidence of the big bang theory of the origin of the universe, and well-considered by Abell in his book (but which will not be repeated here because of its highly technical nature), special mention should be made of the fact that an application of the second law of thermodynamics has been frequently made in support of the theory to show that the energy of the universe is running down. The law is sometimes called the law of entropy. Rather than to detail here a description of the law, the consequence of its application to our discussion should suffice. Edward L. Kessel, for instance, stated this consequence as follows: ". . . [it] . . . is evident that our universe could not have existed from eternity, else it would have long since run out of useful energy and ground to a halt."[6]

While this application of the second law is conceptually (although not necessarily) tied to the initial big bang theory of the origin of the universe, it has not yet been definitely established in science, as noted by Bernardine Bonansea, that the law is valid for the entire universe.[7] Wallace I. Matson, while questioning the validity of the law in our universe, pointed to two common inferences that seem to arise from the view that the universe is running down: "First, nature must have been 'wound up' in the first place by some outside force; second, these processes within nature that show increase of organization cannot be 'merely natural' but must be somehow under the guidance of an extraorganizing force."[8]

In any event, it appears that science is today quite confident with respect to the big bang theory on cosmological grounds quite independent of the application of the second law of thermodynamics. This, notwithstanding the Steady State Theory (that the universe has been in a state of continuous creation), a proponent of which has been Fred Hoyle, among others. In relation to the big bang theory, the question has arisen as to whether or not there has been an oscillating succession of big bangs. This has introduced the idea that our present universe may be a more recent rendition of a succession of universes in an eternity of time. The doubt which appears to be prevalent at present on this is whether the galaxies will decelerate to reverse the expansion process in the course of future time by gravitational attraction or, on the other hand, will never so decelerate. If the latter, according to a director of the Hale Observatories, as quoted in an article by Sterling Seagrave: "Then the expansion is irreversible and the Universe has apparently happened only once."[9] The views on this have themselves oscillated back and forth several times over the past year. For instance, recent evidence of a confirmatory nature that the universe will forever expand is from the photography of a rocket telescope showing details of a bright quasar thought to be at the "edge" of the universe. As reported in April, 1977, Dr. Arthur F. Davidsen, the American astronomer, deduced from the sharp details of the quasar that there appeared to be insufficient matter between the galaxies for the universe to ever be pulled into contraction.[10] But then, in July, 1977, astronomers at the Harvard Smithsonian Center for Astronomy independently detected and

125

corroborated photographic findings from a new British telescope in Australia that far more galaxies exist than previously thought.[11] So, at this writing, there are those who think this extra mass of material may gravitationally bring about an eventual contraction. The possible existence of earlier universes to that of the present sheds no light on the design of things except one might say that a universal God would be expected to have been "busy" long before the dawn of this finite universe some 16 or more billion years ago. In a different universe, if that be possible, we are unable to say what design or non-design, would be in evidence. As noted earlier, this speculation does not detract from the design that is increasingly evident in this one.

C. P. Snow, in a British television interview, said that the prevailing scientific theory that the universe had a beginning is as strong an argument as can be made for a theistic creation.[12] In discussing the big bang theory of the origin of the universe, the following relevant comment appeared in a cover story—"STARS—Where Life Begins," in Time Magazine: Most cosmologists—scientists who study the structure and evolution of the universe—agree that the biblical account of creation, in imagining an initial void, may be uncannily close to the truth."[13]

Even the evidence today to support the view of a "timeless Superspace" existing "outside" of what we now view as our universe, and assumed to contain matter that seems to be unaccounted for from the event of the "big bang," is not seen as conflicting with the basic theory, according to Adrian Berry in reference to an article by J. A. Wheeler, "Our Universe: The Known and the Unknown."[14]

If we now turn our attention from scientific explanations as to "how" the physical universe came into existence and, instead, reflect on some of the "end-results" in space as are evident today, there are some very distinctive regularities and orderly arrangements that are recognized as having come about in consequence of it all.

One could fill the pages of this chapter with the conceptions of elaborate celestial systems envisaged by the ancient civiliza-

126

tions of Earth—a sort of forerunner to modern astronomy. Yet we are not particularly concerned here with the historical aspects of things. To earlier writers on "design," distant galaxies were unknown and "outer space" cosmology was regional with respect to a limited fringe area of our own galaxy. "Only half a century ago, within our lifetimes," according to Seagrave, "many astronomers assumed that there was only one galaxy in the universe."[15]

Perhaps it will suffice, historically, to note that Paley, in writing his comprehensive design argument nearly two centuries ago on the marvels of our planet, expressed an apology for the then "inadequacy in knowledge of astronomy" and not being able to pursue his subject very far in that direction.[16] It is interesting to note, however, what Paley did have to say on this as a sort of comparison with present-day knowledge. In brief paraphrase and summary, he found design:

1) "In the motions, relations, attitudes, and correspondence of parts within the solar system, including the centripetal forces which sustain heavenly motions . . . making possible [the] construction of planetary systems; . . . [in] . . . the law in which attraction, incessantly drawing a body toward the centre, never brings, nor ever will bring, the body to that centre, but keep it in eternal circulation around it";[17]

2) In the permanency of the elliptical orbit of the planets around the Sun, noting that the attraction varies reciprocally as the square of the distance rather than varying according to any direct law of the distance saying "that, while it is true the direct central proportion of the distance would have produced an ellipse, yet the perturbing forces would have acted with so much advantavge as to be continually changing the dimension of the ellipse." He then noted that "the permanency of our ellipse, founded on the most beneficial of narrow limits, is vital, out of an infinite number of possible laws that could have been admissable for the supporting of the heavenly bodies";[18]

127

3) In the existence of a single Sun "being central to a revolving system with its radiant heat and luminosity being fairly distributed among the orbiting planets (none of which have these characteristics and which, without the Sun in the center, would otherwise be cold and opaque)." He contrasted this arrangement to what a system would be like where a cold mass were at the center and one of its orbiting planets were in fact a star or Sun; that, in such a case, there would be no fair distribution. He said: "There . . . [is] . . . no antecedent necessity . . . that would require the stationary body [relatively] to alone give heat and light";[19] and,

4) In the shape of the Earth as an oblate spheroid for the reasons as previously mentioned in Chapter 6.

There have been those who, while recognizing the existence of order in the known universe, have described it as comprising a great deal of apparent disorder and confusion. Whether or not this is apparent, rather than real, is presently unknown and could be a reflection of our ignorance. Many refer to the activity of the atoms as reflecting great disorder and confusion but, from the phenomena we have described in earlier chapters, the end-results of atomic activity show quite the opposite. This leads one to wonder whether we could be in for the same sorts of surprises on the large macroscale of universal phenomena and activity. In any event, no one is prepared even today to challenge F. R. Tennant, who said that even though there may appear to be an irrational or unregulated element in the universe, scientific investigations show "that the universe contains an infinite variety of objects and actions, and yet operates according to principles which are so fixed and stable that they are exactly definable."[20] The special relationships that are found to exist in the universe, definable in mathematical terms, no doubt caused Sir James Jeans to say that "the universe appears to have been designed by a pure mathematician." He said, "Our efforts to interpret nature in terms of the concepts of pure mathematics have, so far, proved brillantly successful."[21]

One may envisage, in a sense of design, an architectural plan being carried out within an organizational framework that permits a means of harmonious regulation and control. For instance, the phenomenon of gravitation which, for all of our exposure to it, still escapes us as to its cause. This, notwithstanding our precise laws that define its characteristic features. Without this controlling regulatory phenomenon, total disorder and disorganization would have been the rule of the universe. Its most remarkable feature is that it cannot be screened out. According to Paul R. Heyl: "Many substances are partially or wholly opaque to light, heat, sound; electric and magnetic forces can be greatly reduced by interposing a suitable screen; but there is no known screen for gravitation."[22] If, in origin and subsequent development, there had simply been a random concourse of aimlessly drifting interstellar dust and energy in the universe, existing in some totally incohesive manner, it is not difficult to visualize the endless chaos and incoherency that would have been expected.

It is a source of some wonder that the universe exhibits such highly contrasting features comprising the "immensity" of space in the universe and the "infinitesimally small" realm of the atoms. In a design context, I have suggested a good and "logical" reason (Chapter 5), for the small microcosmic entities of matter, the atoms. On the large scale of size, Freemen J. Dyson of the Institute for Advanced Study at Princeton seems to have given a very sound reason for the great distances between celestial objects with respect to which Adrian Berry finds at least a "suspicion" of intelligent design.[23] According to Dyson, the matter of size of the universe, while giving one the impression of irrelevant extravagance in largeness, is "our primary protection against a variety of catastrophies." He describes this in relation to what he calls an important "hangup" which enables the survival of the universe as we know it. Citing the formula $Gdt^2=1$ (where $G$ is the constant in Newton's law of gravitation; $d$ is an average density in a volume of space filled with matter, and $t$ is "free-fall" time which is the time it would take matter to collapse gravitationally in the absence of other "hangups"), Dyson said the effect is that "when we have an extravagantly small density $d$, and therefore an extravagantly big volume of space, the free-fall time $t$ can become so long that gravitational collapse is postponed to a remote future."[24] In applying the formula to some pertinent facts on the average density of our universe (about one atom per cubic meter) he reached the following conclusion:

> If the matter in the universe were not spread out with such an exceedingly low density, the free-fall time would already have ended and our remote ancestors would long ago have been engulfed and incinerated in a universal cosmic collapse.[25]

Now, Dyson makes the point that our own galaxy is of a density "a million times higher than that of the universe as a whole" and, while the distances between the stars in our galaxy are also extravagantly large, this is not enough for our preservation without the introduction of another important hangup which he calls "the spin hangup" that preserves our galaxy as a whole, as well as preserving the planets from collapsing into the Sun. It is explained that "an extended object cannot collapse gravitationally if it is spinning rapidly. Instead of collapsing, the outer parts of the object settle into stationary orbits revolving around the inner parts." Although not infinitely permanent, the combination of the two basic hangups give a long-term longevity.[26]

A third hangup is what Dyson calls the "thermonuclear hangup." It is a universal phenomenon by implication of the discovery that the universe originally comprised pure hydrogen that burns to form helium in stars. When it is heated and compressed, the burning releases energy which "opposes further compression." As a result, he says, a star containing a large proportion of hydrogen "is unable to collapse gravitationally beyond a certain point until the hydrogen is all burned up." Although Dyson goes into greater detail than is practical here, his following comment helps to summarize the end results of this dynamic activity:

The preponderance of hydrogen in the universe ensures that our night sky is filled with well-behaved stars like our own sun, placidly pouring out their energy for the benefit of any attendant life-forms and giving to the celestial sphere its historic attribute of serene immobility.[27]

Still other amazing "hangups" are noted by Dyson which, when combined with those mentioned, reflect a delicate balance among gravitation, nuclear reactions, and radiation that keeps the energy in the universe from flowing too rapidly.

But let us return now to the matter of the immensity of the size of the universe in relation to the protection of life, here or elsewhere, as against catastrophies. It should be here noted that the materialists are keen to pointing out that man is an insignificant biological creature existing on a tiny planet revolving around a minor star in an ordinary galaxy in an immense universe of countless billions of planets, stars, and galaxies. But Dyson has pointed out that "if sheer distance had not effectively isolated the quiet regions of the universe from the noisy ones, no type of biological evolution would have been possible."[28] As explained by Berry, in reference to Dyson's concepts, not only do the interstellar distances, measured in light-years, make it extremely remote that collisions will occur between solar systems, but also it is necessary that the great distances be maintained to avoid the dangerous effects from nova and super-nova explosions which occur from time to time and involve the destruction of stars, in whole or in part. "We should not," said Berry, "be too dismayed by the scale of interstellar distances. Life could be impossible in all but the most remote solar systems if stars were too densely packed together."[29] He also noted that the vast distances between galaxies is also essential to our safety and, in this connection, cited the absolute necessity for life to maintain a very substantial distance from such space objects as quasars, radial galaxies, Seyfert galaxies, etc. that would be most inhospitable to the existence of life. Objects such as these are little known in their effects on surroundings, noted Dyson, yet he said, "It would be strange indeed if their effects did not turn out to be

131

of major importance, both for science and for the history of life in the universe."[30] What Dyson is saying with respect to phenomena on the broad universal scale is fully supported as a projection of our experience with respect to the phenomena described in earlier chapters that presented to us a remarkable picture of design.

Another mysterious phenomenon has to do with cosmic rays and electro-magnetic wave activity from vibrating energy sources. The effect is not yet defined in a broad cosmic sense, but some scientists have viewed their existence and activity as functional in relation to life processes as, for example in relation to the Earth environment, by the biologist Lyall Watson in his book "Supernature," referred to in the last chapter.[31] Gerald Heard, although not expressed in the same sense or context as Watson, sees evidence of design in the influence of the invisible, rhythmic cosmic activity of waves and wavelengths—both long and short, of varying intensities, etc.[32] Even bolts of lightning in storm clouds around the Earth are now seen to be the result of interacting collisions between cosmic rays and atoms in the upper atmosphere. Such is the new theory of James W. Follin, Ernest Gray, and Kwang Yu of Johns Hopkins University.

Many aspects of cosmic phenomena are being intently surveyed today and our overall knowledge is increasing with observation. This may, for example, be seen in the technical papers contributed to the recent book entitled "The Dusty Universe,"[33] by leading astrophysicists who are engaged in the study of the properties of interstellar and interplanetary dust and exploring possible cosmogonic relationships between the two. The present theory of the origin of the planets in our solar system from processes involving a condensation of a large cloud of gas and dust, if correct, is suggestive of design. One would expect, in accord with the theory, that the central cloud of dust would have had a far greater measure of homogeneity than has been found to be the case from planetary explorations and other observations of man so far which reflect a considerable diversity in planetary composition. A most recent hypothesis to account for the differences is that an outside "injection" of materials into the mass could have occurred at a most critical and opportune time. Are we to attribute any such event (or events) to chance? Paul A. Zimmerman, as early as the year 1959, in his book "Darwin, Evolution, and Creation" made a rather strong argument for design in relation to the then known differences in planetary composition.[34]

Today we are besieged with space-science fiction depicting life in various forms and shapes, intelligent and otherwise, on far distant galaxies and planets. This has, no doubt, been the outgrowth of space exploration and our greatly extended knowledge of universal phenomena of the past quarter-century or so. But it is also due no doubt to the prevailing empirically-based view of science that favors the "probable" or "inevitable" existence of life (including intelligent life) elsewhere throughout the universe. Here, we are likely to contradict Monod's view that man is "alone in the universe's own feeling of immensity."[35]

When one considers: 1) the enormity of space and time; 2) the common identification throughout the universe of the few kinds of "genetically-related" elements of the Periodic Table; 3) the material aggregations of the universe and the continuous flow of energy and light as related to all aspects of it; 4) the many galaxies that are spiral structured like our own and likely possessing the characteristics of the survival, spin, and thermonuclear "hangups" to which Dyson referred, together with the estimated billions of opportunities for planetary systems; 5) the apparent immutability and uniformity of cosmic laws, such as those relating to celestial mechanics, relativity, and quantum mechanics; 6) the continual activity in stars for the creation of the life and mind-useful atomic elements—together with the related significance to be attached to the recent discovery of the presence of organic molecules elsewhere in our galaxy and perhaps beyond; 7) the very existence of life, including mind and consciousness in the universe, even though now known to definitely occur only in our small part of it, it is quite proper to conceive that the Earth is by no means unique as the only life-sustaining oasis. We do have, in this sense, a broad threshold picture of "what other

133

worlds are like," at least on the basis of comparisons of an empirical nature to relate to our own experience, and the very existence of the requisite general conditions for the potential for life elsewhere strongly infers that the design we have found in our localized environment is not to be viewed as an isolated circumstance. Those who might frown on the concept of the existence of life elsewhere on religious grounds should not do so on account of any biblical constraint. As Heinecken noted, for instance, there is nothing in the Biblical witness to deny the possibility of other creatures of God.[36]

In an address before a Centennial celebration of the National Academy of Science in 1963,[37] George Wald expressed the growing scientific view when he said that the origin of life is an event which must happen, given enough time, whenever conditions exist that make it possible. He noted, on the basis of a conservative estimate at the time, that there are a minimum of one million planets in our galaxy alone and that billions or more planets many be found elsewhere in our known universe where life can occur. Since then, a recent estimate indicates there could be more than a billion such planets in our own galaxy of nearly two billion stars. This, taken together with the other conditions of uniformity known to exist throughout the universe, presents us with countless possibilities for life as we may, or may not, know it, to have arisen.

But if life, including intelligent life, does indeed exist elsewhere throughout the universe, how does this relate to the view of a designed and purposeful creation? So far, it seems that many leading space scientists and science writers in general—including those who have assisted in the development of the hypothesis that life exists elsewhere—have at least publicly adhered to the previously noted constraint that "a scientist should attempt to explain the pertinent phenomena of nature in terms of natural laws" and not to resort to "unprovable" hypotheses of "supernatural origins."[38] It will serve no useful purpose to repeat the criticism I made earlier in Chapter 2 against such a view as applied to the search for ultimate knowledge. The point to make here is simply that the manner of construction of the universe, coupled with the factors that make it operative for "other" life, call for an explanation. Must we again listen to explanations based on the idea of pure chance?

The similarity throughout the universe of the phenomena as above mentioned, as well as the similarity, if not the identity, of preconditions for the emergence of life anywhere as mentioned in an earlier chapter, reasonably implies that similar results were contemplated. Rather than life in a remote part of the universe as an isolated event, the likelihood of life on a broader scale suggests an overall plan. A growing number of writers seem to think so. For example, Cecil H. Douglas Clark has expressed the view that the possibility of life elsewhere rules out "what might otherwise be regarded as the uselessness and lack of purpose of such an immense universe."[39] James Miller, in an article entitled "New Quest for Life In Space," suggests: "Man may not be insignificant after all . . . he may be part of a universal scheme of things."[40] I have previously referred to criticism of design arguments for their lack of empirical and logical conclusiveness. But the real possibility that life exists elsewhere throughout the vastness of the universe now suggests to one such critic, John Hick, a new strong inference favoring the idea of design. In a recent comment, he said: ". . . . it is not, in that case, so implausible to consider the universe as a system designed to produce personal life. For apparently it is a system, rather than a random collection of matter, and apparently it is producing intelligent life at innumerable points throughout its vast complex."[41]

It is quite possible that one of the outstanding experts on sources and flow of energy in the universe, Freeman J. Dyson, may well have had the idea of intelligent design in mind in his essay "Energy in the Universe."[42] He noted that the local energy resources in our solar system seemed to fit into a larger cosmic scheme of things and expressed the view that we should not be surprised if it should turn out "that the origin and destiny of the energy in the universe cannot be completely understood in isolation from the phenomena of life and consciousness." He sees that life has intervened on our planet at least to reverse the process of energy dissipation in

135

the universe and speculates, therefore, that life might have a greater role to play than imagined previously and that life may have some success "in molding the universe to its own purposes." In accordance with this, he has further speculated that "design of the inanimate universe may not be as detached from the potentialities of life and intelligence as scientists of the 20th century have tended to suppose."[43] If there be such a reality, in my own view, it would not seem to suggest an end of itself (and this may, or may not, be what Dyson had in mind in his reference to mind and consciousness in terms of purpose).

In a purely random-chance universe, there would be no need for aggregations of matter and energy into the billions of fairly evenly spaced and distributed galactical systems that symbolize an "order" throughout the vast universe. The great majority of them have been observed and "mapped" as so-called "island universes." Mechanistically, of course, we could simply attribute this to the propulsion of material from the "explosion" of the primeval fireball and the subsequent collecting powers of gravity. But, "why" the coincidence of the existence of perhaps billions of them that are thought to harbor all the ingredients that make life possible and supportable? There are, to be sure, different kinds of galaxies, and there are some indications that a majority of them do not have the potential for life. Less than half are pinwheel-shaped "spirals," like our own, with curved extended arms that are thought to contain the potential for the heavier elements and other conditions needed for the formation of stars, planetary systems, and the existence of life. Mention has already been made of some of the irregular galaxies and, recently, the life-harboring potentialities of the elliptical galaxies have been drawn into question. Together with the spirals, they make up perhaps more than three-fourths of all the galaxies. The British astronomer, Dr. John Gribbin, writing in the May, 1977, issue of the United States journal *Astronomy,* sets forth a case against the existence of the heavier elements beyond hydrogen and helium in the ellipticals.[44] If this be so and if the universe has a harmony, asks Adrian Berry, then what is the function of the ellipticals?[45] Why do they, together with the spirals, predominate? The possibilities are open that they could serve some present or future purpose or function of which we are ignorant in keeping with the earlier comment of Dyson. If we should assume a harmony of all things in the universe, says Berry, the ellipticals could exist as *ballast* whose weight or mass could dictate the ultimate fate of a universe that will eventually contract by gravitation to enable the universe to start over again.[45] Perhaps, for the present, they may preserve a certain and yet non-defined balance to an ongoing universe. At any rate, this once again raises the empirically suggestive speculation of this writer, as discussed in the introductory chapter, of a possible *atomos mentis* correspondence on a universal scale. Could it be that a great deal of seemingly superfluous material in the universe is yet "unselected" in the intended design of things by the conscious activation of a higher creative intelligence, i.e., God? If future discoveries were to add support to such a presently obscure (yet empirically implied on a threshold basis) concept, they could serve to help explain the means and manner of creation.

When space scientists project the idea of life elsewhere in the universe they apparently do so by relating possible life-sustaining planetary systems as previously mentioned with other complementary life-sustaining celestial phenomena, such as neighboring stars, thermonuclear reactions, energy supply, and so on. It would seem perfectly reasonable that the components which make-up life-potential galaxies may be affected beneficially by the parts of the whole. This, even though some of the parts themselves may not display a meaning or purpose of their own. This is not simply an exercise in metaphysical thinking, for the principle appears to be established empirically with respect to the Earth environment (to be discussed in Chapters 10 and 12) that the component parts of both inanimate and animate matter (atoms, cells, etc.), and related systems or phenomena, rather than being meaningful on their own, are indeed meaningful to life only with respect to their ultimate composition. As components alone, they appear to serve no useful function. It simply requires an extension of this principle to nature as a whole throughout the universe. In a sense of design, the existence of "life-possible" galaxies, and no doubt the component parts within them, may reflect a need for the continuation of local regional environments that would maintain, notwithstanding the separation from their common and original primeval source, the integrity of matter, energy, and other cosmic phenomena that could produce and sustain meaningful aggregations, such as living systems. Each life-productive galaxy, or planetary areas within each, could thereby become bases for the spread of intelligent life. A broad extention in concept of the biblical command to go forth and to multiply. Do we obtain some insight on the basis of projections now being made by present-day scientists who point to the feasibility of human inhabitation of planets within our solar system and in the galaxy beyond? When this is considered in the context that the estimated remaining life-span of our solar system is approximately five billion years, we can conceive that the seed of mind and consciousness may have extended itself by that time into younger and what Berry calls "safer regions" in the cosmos within our galaxy and perhaps beyond.

If life does exist in countless galactical systems, what reasons could there be in the design of things for the multiplicity? Do they each exist as experimental systems? Is there a competition in the mind of the Creator? Assuming a biblical kind of spiritual world, would there be need for the development of values that could come only from a materialized existence and experience—a world of the good and "fallen" angels? Is it any one or a combination of these aspects, or something else? These are, of course, interesting questions and speculations to which I shall return momentarily.

If life is found to exist elsewhere in the universe, we have no way of knowing whether the conditions would be as fit and suitable as on Earth. In a design context, one could be led to expect that the conditions would be as fit and suitable in the course of an evolved period of time. Perhaps the best supposition we can make on this relates to the fact that the same ingredients of energy and matter are to be found elsewhere throughout the universe, as well as the universal laws to be applied, and it would seem logical to expect that an intelligent being elsewhere would need the ability to see, hear, and the other senses, and have the same penchant for intelligent discovery and inventiveness as found to be the case with respect to man on Earth with his intelligence.

If intelligent beings are to be found elsewhere throughout the universe, there is every reason to expect, from our own experience, that there would exist the freedom of thought and expression in some form or another that would likely relate to the same moral values of good and evil with which we are quite familiar. The physical form and the knowledge-level of other intelligent beings might be different, but those implanted with original and abstract thought would be likely candidates for quite similar values to our own. The basic rigid coded structure of the DNA molecule does not deny the tolerance, as we shall consider in Chapter 11, that allows for individually —hence, in man, free choice of values—assuming, as do many in science, that DNA may be the only molecular gateway to life anywhere. It should also be noted, as a matter of interest, that Fred Hoyle, in his contemplation of the existence of intelligent life elsewhere, in an unrelated context, contends that an intelligent being "anywhere" would be faced at some stage with the same kind of social situation as that which now confronts the human specie.[47]

It may thus be that intelligent creatures elsewhere may be linked into this aspect of good and evil as above-mentioned and that evil, rather than being a point of non-design in the universe, may be regarded as a measurable attribute of indeterminate freedom, and that its moral counterpart, good, may be seen as the ultimate purposive goal as so well expressed in biblical scriptures. If one were to ask what is the most unique occurrence as we know it, the answer would likely be that of human mind and consciousness and its freedom in the expression of values, and, if this be an "end" of itself in terms of man's existence, could it not also be said that it would be an end to be achieved in living systems elsewhere? Whether or not all of my readers will agree with this, they will have to admit on reflection that nothing is more interesting in terms of our contemplation of the universe than what this discussion implies.

I will now turn to an additional "new" inference to cosmic design, one that bears a positive relation to the thesis developed in the last chapter, that the mind and consciousness of man is the principal intended beneficiary of a fit and suitable world of cosmic and inanimate phenomena.

Life on Earth has moved about from sea to land, and vice versa, and into the air, with such facility that some are inclined to view this as directional in terms of design, and others simply regard these phenomena as accidental occurrences arising from physico-chemical and natural selective processes measurable over several billion years or so of geologic time.

But how are we to view man's leap beyond the Earth's gravity into outer space? Is it simply another improbable event achieved by chance? To many of those closely connected to space science, it represents the culmination of years of arduous scientific speculation, study, research and development. It further represents the pyramiding of countless discoveries, both new and old, toward a single-minded objective. This is to say nothing of the individual and collective intelligence involved. We should not, however, mark down such an achievement for posterity as simply another "successful accidental project" of man. The achievement may be seen as opening up a vast new picture favoring the intelligent design of things. We should pause to reflect on the fact that no natural or physical law intervened to suppress the accomplishment as one would expect to have been the case in an accidental world. Equally significant, in a different and still broader sense of design, is the fact that the whole of the phenomena of nature—in its myriad forms—was adequate to the challenge and did not prove deficient in providing all the necessary causative actions, forces, elements, materials, and conditions, both critical and essential, severally and in combination, to the meeting of such an objective. What is the odds-radio in relation to so many countless pieces of the puzzle that had to fit together just right for such an achievement? It well

140

demonstrates, empirically, the very special relationship between man, his mind and consciousness, and the phenomena of nature.

As has so often been the case with countless other discoveries of natural phenomena by man, we come to ask whether the law of chance and probabilities could carry forward so as to allow for the realities of space exploration. The materialists have, so far, accounted for the billions of individual events or changes that have surely occurred from the dawn of the universe down to man's present state of affairs on the basis of odds ranging from fifty-fifty to lesser ratios applicable to each such event or change. It would be unfortunate indeed in terms of man's meaning and significance to seek to extend space-travel phenomena to the incredulously improbable.

No doubt Kant, Hume, and Darwin would have considered it to be a masterful piece of science fiction for one to have suggested to them that leading men in science in the late twentieth century would be laying down blue-prints for the manner in which some of the planets within our solar system and perhaps beyond may be made inhabitable with life. After all, an almost innumerable list of pre-conditions have to be met for this to even be considered as a mere remote possibility, the absence of any one of which would serve to completely frustrate and render scientifically unsound any such venturesome thinking. And yet, as we now know, the pre-conditions may be met out of a combination of fit and suitable properties of matter and energy that are available to man. "The planets beckon," said Carl Sagan, the well-know space scientist, "we have put our ships into the cosmic ocean. The waters are benign and we have learned to sail. No longer are we bound to our solitary island Earth."[48]

A 1976 publication by NASA entitled "Space Colonization: A Design Study," is a proposal of a group of some thirty engineers, social and physical scientists on this subject. Isaac Asimov, in an article entitled "The Next Frontier?" also speaks of permanent colonies in space which would be involved in "supermarket" farming, the construction of greenhouses, commercial and residential areas, monorails, and a host of other earthbound technologies, all as related to space inhabitation by man.[49] Not to be outdone in the slightest in terms of serious space imagination, Arthur C. Clarke, a leading writer and thinker on space matters, has traced the course of evolution to depict man leaping out of the ocean of air to make possible "new sensations, experiences, and technologies."[50] It is said that interplanetary travel will be very commonplace in another several centuries almost to the same extent that trans-Atlantic travel has become today. Quoting again from Carl Sagan: "It may be that the voyages of Viking are of greater ultimate importance to the human race than even the voyages of Christopher Columbus almost five centuries ago."[51]

It may well be that man may someday break through what have been thought to be impossible distance-time barriers to reach galaxies in space that are billions of light years away from the Earth. To Adrian Berry, the potential for the unravelling of this travel accommodation for man in centuries to come is to be found in the potential of black holes in space. In his fascinating new book, "The Iron Sun: Crossing the Universe in Black Holes,"[52] he explores the feasibility of *instantaneous* travel through time and space to remote galactic regions of the universe. This is, of course, based upon projections of continued technological developments in centuries to come. Those who might think his views to be fiction would be surprised to know that the entrances to passages or "bridges" leading to other parts of the universe were first predicted by Einstein and a colleague in 1935 and, today, an impressive list of space scientists would join with Berry in this kind of speculation that finds support in empirical trends.

The effect of all of this is to enlarge our perspective into a much larger sphere of thought and this, of course, could open up the dawn of a vast new day for the utilization of mind and consciousness. We have now learned that Henderson's theme of "fitness of the environment" for life is not earthbound (either life as we do, or do not, know it), and the reality of space exploration and inhabitation, as a next frontier—a "stage"—for the further implementation of the values of man stretches the empirical basis for the concept of design into entire new dimensions. Essentially, it would seem we are at the bow-and-arrow stage with respect to this new vista, but seem to be headed in the direction where the whole of our solar system (and beyond) may well be incorporated into our way of thinking in much the same manner that we presently regard the Earth itself; that is, celestial objects may carry in the future a connotation simliar to that which distant lands carried to the early explorers. This new perspective may seem remote and far-fetched to many—but, notes Sagan, so did the voyages of Columbus and Marco Polo.

As in the case of a number of other critical discoveries during the course of human history at a most opportune time, this new perspective with respect to interplanetary, or even possibly future inter-galactical, travel and inhabitation comes at a time when the Earth is faced with a population explosion and a realization that its resources, while presently adequate, are diminishing and ultimately finite. There are few planetary scientists who have not recognized as entirely feasible the supplementation of the Earth's energy and mineral resources from planetary sources of supply within our solar system. Professor Dyson, for instance, recognizes that local energy resources in our solar system seem to fit into a larger cosmic scheme of things.[53] His scientific model of how this may be accomplished is generally accepted as feasible in the scientific community. He has shown how man might harness the power and energy of our Sun using already existing natural objects in space revolving around the Sun. Considering that only a minute fraction of the Sun's energy strikes the Earth, and that the remainder is apparently wasted into space, Dyson has calculated a means by which the use of the Sun may be engineered to capture "a much greater part of the Sun's radiation by building hundreds of thousands of new worlds to orbit the Sun at the same distance as the Earth."[54]

It would seem that modern discovery and knowledge of cosmic activity continue to confirm the view of Jeans that the Universe resembles the work of a great mathematician. It would also appear that Newtonian determinism is showing up in ways that were earlier limited in description to more general outlines. The view that order is inter-mixed with disorder and chaos in the universe as a whole is increasingly suspect. To this writer at least, the universe is beginning to look like a giant factory machine with "works in process" at different stages of completion, re-cycling, etc.—like an assembly line—and with life, especially intelligent life (already known in one part of it) as its most unique and distinguishable product. There are many signs of the continual working of processes that bring about change in a seemingly creative and controlled manner as, for instance, the continual burning of stars of varying ages and characteristics to produce different elements of the remarkable Periodic Table, energy flows, cosmic rays, etc. In end result, our own galaxy may well be representative of a great deal of activity that had earlier seemed chaotic. "We now have firm evidence," said Dyson, "that a locally violent environment existed in our galaxy immediately before the birth of the solar system."[55] The universe is friendly, he believes, and our Earth is not a unique oasis in a hostile universe. The cosmic "accidents" that have provided abundantly for us here will do the same elsewhere.[56] Such a view is, in my view, not so imaginative, speculatively, as one might think when it is taken in conjunction with other "fitness and suitability" phenomena considered herein that relate to both animate and inanimate matter and which comprise the "standard parts" everywhere available to attainable ends.

# 9

## What Happened to the Imperfections?

In an earlier chapter, I called attention to an empirical criticism of design arguments founded on the idea that a Designer of the universe "skilled in the art of world making" would not have allowed for the occurrence of earthquakes, volcanic activity, cyclones, tornadoes, floods, droughts, mountains, deserts, arctic areas, tropical jungles, the extinction of species (such as the dinosaurs), human evil, wickedness, cruelty, suffering, controversy, war, and so on. Somewhat representative of this kind of criticism is that of Basil Willey who said: "Nature of course includes lovely, grand and ideal things: sun, moon and stars, flowers, the beauty of the seasons, perhaps the music of the spheres; but it also includes jungles, deserts, disease-germs, drought, famine, blizzard and earthquake."[1]

While this enumeration of what are claimed to be "imperfections" in nature is not exclusive, it does set forth those most frequently mentioned by the critics of design arguments.

Various answers, mostly of a general nature, have been advanced to explain away these so-called imperfections in nature. Aquinas, for instance, expressed the view that the Creator may have willed some things to be done necessarily, and some things contingently.[2] Tennant observed that a designed interpretation of Nature does not require that every by-product or detail was purposed beforehand, but rather that they are the necessary outcome of processes which will fill the purpose themselves.[3] Teilhard de Chardin expressed the view that they should be looked upon in an "overall" context.[4]

145

Bertocci suggested that a creative intelligence may not succeed in all his undertaking and that there is no need to think that a Designer would be unlike ourselves in many ways. If there were "no other evidence and no other factors to be considered," said Bertocci, he would still find it "more coherent to believe in a universe largely governed by intelligence than in a universe in which mind-less purpose-less units of energy *somehow* fathered and protected living things and their evolution. . . ."[5]

While these expressions could be said to make sense on their own, modern knowledge has furnished us with some answers of an empirical nature; that is, we have come to better understand the nature and significance of many of the "flaws" of Nature and we may now regard them, as will be shown, in a much different light than before.

First of all, we should entertain a few pertinent observations.

The so-called imperfections appear to relate to matters that were known at the time of the earliest of human civilizations. With the exception perhaps of the extinction of species question, they do not comprise any new claims to "imperfection" as one should expect of a purely chance creation. After all, the growth in knowledge since the early days of man is remarkable. As we have seen, there has been a substantial growth in strong new inferences to design. At the same time, as this chapter will show, the trend in modern discovery has been to significantly reduce, rather than to increase, the importance of this entire form of empirical argument against design. This can only strengthen the quality of the inferential proofs of an intelligently designed universe.

Further, when measured against the inferences to design which could arguably comprise the sum total of all phenomena on which our existence, survival, and forward development depend, it should be rather clear to us by now that what have been claimed to constitute imperfections are, if indeed there be any, strikingly disproportionate and far outweighed by the overwhelming proofs of a purposeful design of things.

When we come to direct our attention to specifics, the

claimed imperfections appear to fall into several different broad categories. In one category, there are phenomena that today infer design, rather than imperfection, on the basis of modern knowledge. A second category would include phenomena which man, in the exercise of his mind and consciousness—itself of meaning in a design context as we have seen—has been able to overcome or to remedy, in whole or in part. Generally, these two categories do not involve the human condition, yet affect it directly or indirectly. A third category involves the human condition in a direct relationship (such as the existence of evil, controversy, war, and the like) which seems to be a non-remedial, yet personal sort of phenomenon on the basis of the historical record—a by-product of man's freedom of choice in many ways. It is not inconceivable that, in time, all claimed imperfections under the first two of the three mentioned categories may be empirically explained in terms of design, and the manner in which this has or could occur will be included somewhat in our consideration here. Interestingly, the substantial elimination or reduction of those events long considered to comprise imperfections and disorders in nature seems to isolate the remaining third category relating specifically to the human condition as mentioned.

Let us now turn our attention to specific instances of claimed imperfections and disorders in the natural world.

In Chapter 6, we considered the present-day beneficial results from an Earth that has undergone great environmental change in the course of geologic history. This has involved events such as earthquakes and volcanic activity. One can imagine a long period in the Earth's history when these activities were in far greater measure than at present. Yet they still have an important role to play as a part of the natural processes that are continually taking place to make the Earth an inhabitable and self-sustaining planet. We have long known of the stabilizing adjustments made internally within the Earth's crust, although our understanding of the beneficial results in a creative sense is rather recent. The new theory of continental drift and the movement of crustal plates around the globe, for one thing, has enhanced our understanding of this phenomenon. We have seen how this activity has provided us with the present environment that is most favorable to the existence of life as we know it. I have previously referred to Fred Hoyle's explanation of the processes involved. Should we look upon earthquakes and vulcanism as imperfections in nature? In Hoyle's view:

> We tend to think of earthquakes and of the outbursts of volcanoes as disasters, and we tend to regard mountain ranges as barren regions. . . . Yet on a broader view, we would be quite incorrect. Without this continuous turning over of the Earth's crust, there would probably be no mineral deposits on the Earth's surface . . . we can see that, without the system of plate movements, the surface of the Earth would almost certainly be far more inhospitable to man. Indeed, the gradual wearing down of the continents might well smooth out the Earth so much that, instead of the continents sticking out of the ocean, water would entirely cover the whole surface of the Earth. . . .[6]

Fortunately, the occurrence of earthquakes and volcanic activity are more usually confined to regions of the Earth where there is a coming together of the crustal plates and, while no one would belittle the harmful and sometimes lethal consequences that accompany their occurrence, the point to make here is that they should be seen in a different light than the critics of design have made them out. In the broad aspect, life depends on such activities. The critics should strike these phenomena from their list of imperfections unless and until they are prepared to suggest a "more" perfect construction of a world than that which engages crustal mobility and topographical change for reasons that are everywhere evident. And certainly, as we have seen, the mind of man accounts for a great deal in the scheme of things and, as a new science is developing to enable the prediction of these occurrences, we may look forward to less harmful and destructive consequences to life in the future. Speaking in Denver to the annual meeting of the American Association for the Advancement of Science on February 24, 1977, Professor Peter J.

Willie of the University of Chicago, said: "While earthquake prediction isn't yet infallible, it is 'within our reach.' "[7]

The observations would seem also to have application to other natural occurrences, such as tornadoes, cyclones, typhoons, floods, and the like. We have come to realize that these too normally occur as a part of, or in consequence of, the natural and critical life-giving processes from which they arise. They accompany the beneficial activities of the remarkably designed weather machine that is constantly undergoing change on an hourly basis. Supposedly, the critics would require, in a designed world, that an almost hourly intervention be made in the working of these processes to correct and make adjustments that would be completely free of their possible adverse consequences. That is, even if one could suggest that such adjustments would in fact always achieve a more perfect operation of the activities of the mechanisms to which they relate. We know of no other alternative means by which basic design objectives could be satisfactorily met if the basic processes operated differently. For instance, what could naturally replenish the subterranean fresh waters in the Earth's crust on the continental land masses if it were not the occasional flood? The kind of light rainfall from time to time that would be just perfect for the critics would not help that much. In a recent article in Scientific American entitled "Underground Reservoirs to Control the Water Cycle,"[8] Robert P. Ambroggi, an expert on the improved management of water resources, called attention to the fact that, at any one time, perhaps two-thirds of the fresh water of the Earth is held in underground reservoirs which require "recharging." He pointed to experience of the past three decades to note that, in a year of unusually heavy rainfall which may be expected at least once in 15 years, an aquifer that has been drawn down during the intervening years will be replenished. Although Ambroggi's main theme pointed to significant new opportunities by which man may regulate, manage, and control these aquifers when water is plentiful so as to substantially reduce water shortages that accompany drought, the importance of periods of heavy rainfall was emphasized in several of his examples, as follows:

149

For instance, the floods of 1969 in Tunisia replenished all the reservoirs that up to then had been described as overexploited. Similarly, a shallow aquifer in the Souss Valley of Morocco had supported a flourishing production of citrus fruit since 1946 but by 1957 was a source of great concern because the water table had declined at a rate of a meter per year. The rains of 1957 were well above normal; they recharged the aquifer by about 10 meters, almost restoring the initial situation. . . . Nature is therefore already operating a long-term storage system with some 10 or 15 years of residence time. . . .[9]

Now, in the tropical jungles, there are prolonged intervals of heavy rainfall but we have seen how this feeds moisture at a temperature range that is rather optimal for the operation of the weather machine. Then, too, who would want to take away the life-sustaining moisture that comes from the cyclonic activity of the monsoon seasons in the subcontinent of India, or the beneficial rainfalls which accompany increasingly predictable occurrences of tornadoes?

It bears repeating here that a Designer could be expected to have acted by and through natural laws and processes of his own design and choosing rather than in some other manner. It there were a better way that the mechanisms and processes that favor the existence and survival of life could have been more perfectly put together, science has absolutely nothing to offer. At most, the specific objections as mentioned may not be said to be substantial in a context of the overall beneficial working of the very intricate and complex mechanisms and processes involved.

Critical arguments of the type that point to imperfection in the existence of deserts, arctic areas, tropical jungles, mountains, and other seemingly "inhospitable" wastelands may no longer be taken seriously as an argument against design. To an extent, this has already been considered in Chapter 6. The topography and character of the Earth's surface has (and still is) undergone change from time to time, but this is interlaced with meaning and purpose in reference to life. Somehow it seems quite inconsistent in this day to talk

150

about colonization of less hospitable areas or "wastelands" on distant planets or on the seabed of the oceans when the same technological advances of man may be seen as potentially applicable here, as well as there. That is, if the need be such. In many cases, deserts have fertile soil and, if water be made available for irrigation, they can become extremely productive as valuable agricultural regions. To Ambroggi, the problem facing mankind on a global scale is not a lack of fresh water (if properly managed) but a lack of efficient regulation, naturally and artificially, of surface and particularly ground-water reservoirs.[10] Manipulating the exploitation of water in reference to the water cycle is but one of the methods mentioned by Ambroggi. Other means of making water available include the use of nuclear desalinization plants along the oceans bordering desert areas, the construction of dams, and even the current proposal of the Arabs to transport icebergs is not without merit. Then too, we should be coming to realize that the idea of "wasteland" should be viewed vertically, as well as horizontally. Some of the world's greatest deposits of minerals and petroleum for the potential use and benefit of mankind lie beneath the surface of many of these areas. This is to say nothing of the startling consequences we would suffer from the standpoint of the operative processes of the global weather machine if man were to suddenly decimate tropical jungles, polar regions, and mountain chains and convert them into something different. Further, in this day, no one should suggest to those concerned with the global environment that "wastelands" do not serve useful ecological functions and purposes in an overall sense. The engagement of the seemingly barren and remote stretches of Alaska as a site for the location of an oil pipeline furnishes us with a very recent example.

To point to causes leading to the death of living things, such as the occurrence of diseases or whatever, runs into difficulty if claimed to be an imperfection in design. For very good reasons to be considered in a later chapter, living things were designed in the first place to be reproductive (rather than not to be reproductive) and to exist on Earth in accord with life cycles—rather than having been designed to be one-time

151

enduring things. For every death that ends a life, there must naturally be a cause in relation to such a scheme of things.

Even so, we see design in the built-in microscopic organisms called anti-bodies which furnish a formidable form of protection against harmful bacteria. A great deal of research has been done on anti-bodies, particularly on the human body, and the results thus far show that specific anti-bodies exist for specific disease strains. If a particular disease is encountered, only the relevant specific anti-body comes forward to take up the challenge.[11] How this remarkable process of recognition works or how anti-bodies came into existence in the first place is a mystery in science and medicine. The fact they exist at all is inconceivable in terms of random accident. Then too, the advancements in medicine, acting together with elements derived from nature, have resulted in the containment of many diseases, if not in their elimination, and there is no reason to expect that further progress will not continue in this direction in the future. Much the same may be said with respect to birth defects or physical and mental disorders. Here again, we see that improvements have been made by the exercise of human intelligence in a remedial way toward at least a partial resolution of these problems. When this phenomenon becomes even better understood, these occurrences might be seen in a quite different light than today. For all we know, the occurrence of many of the "mistakes" or "deviations" from the norm, genetically, may well be unavoidable consequences of the processes and changes that have resulted in an overall improvement in basic design for the greater benefit of the whole.

Another criticism against design is that the fossil records show that some living species have followed certain "blind evolutionary alleys" to extinction. It is said that far more species have become extinct than are alive today in keeping with the modern theory of selection. Perhaps, if this be so, it has achieved a useful purpose in an overall sense of design and evolutionary progress. But perhaps, as well, the criticism may otherwise prove somewhat illusory, as in the case of the dinosaurs. A very recent and empirically well-grounded theory is that the dinosaurs did not become extinct after all. Many of their lines changed into birds and have carried on. Robert T. Bakker, in an article entitled "Dinosaur Renaissance,"[12] pointed out that even though the dinosaurs were a novelty, recent research shows they never died out completely as had been believed. It had been thought, he noted, that dinosaurs were obsolescent "cold-blooded" reptiles rather than warm-blooded creatures bioenergetically related to birds and mammals as is now clearly shown by the evidence. In consequence of recent research and studies, their evolutionary story is having to be re-written and this will require giving to them a new classification as land vertebrates, according to Bakker in a joint article with Peter M. Galton entitled "Dinosaur Morphyly and a New Class of Vertebrates in Nature."[13]

A related criticism argues that the idea of design is inconsistent with the deviations or branching-out of some living species in order to better adapt to their environment. Design, it is thought, would rather have sanctioned a "straight line" evolutionary course of direction. This was mentioned by Alfred Romer in an essay contributed to a book entitled "Genetics, Paleontology and Evolution."[14] Romer does say that the doctrine of "straight line" evolution is based upon a considerable body of evidence; that is, that phyletic lines generally proceed in one direction in an essentially undeviating fashion throughout their course, even though he argued that this phenomenon is "probably much less common than they were thought to be" and that there are probably few long-continued phyletic lines that are unbranched and do not change their direction.[15] If living things had come upon the scene in the beginning with the structural rigidity as evidenced in inorganic matter, and without the tolerance that allowed for flexibility and change, would this not be the strongest kind of an inference of imperfection? The living things of earlier evolutionary stages could be seen today as inept to our present environmental surroundings. Exceptions are to be found as in certain plant species that have survived the processes over geologic time as though intended to remain forever inviolate and distinctly identical from the beginning. Adaptations to meet changing

153

conditions of various kinds is an integral part of the story of organic evolution and the processes that are said to have brought about these changes are to be further considered later on in a design, rather than in a chance, context. The entire course of organic evolution has been one of "becoming." The point to make here is that the best solutions, generally at least, seem to have been worked out (over time) that would enable the filling of purposive and fit ecological niches which, at the same time, have given us the great diversity and variety we have come to find. It is not so important, in terms of design, to understand how this gradual improvement came about in terms of selective processes and mechanisms as the fact that it did so and that living things possessed the means required for such purpose. We have seen in earlier chapters that environmental changes (over geologic history) have prepared the way for a remarkable and eventual inter-connecting relationship with man and, as previously mentioned, there is no good reason we should not see both aspects of evolution, inorganic and organic, as simply a single preparatory evolution. The question of more importance to this subject, to be considered in the next chapter, relates to the question of directionality in the workings of organic evolutionary processes.

Nor is there a design problem with respect to changes affecting specie differentiation. Indeed, the existence of a million or more separate species has long been an argument favoring design for otherwise there would not only be a lack of diversity and variety in living things, but also a lack of inter-related and quite fit ecological roles that are in great evidence today. If there were only one specie, according to Ernst Mayr, all of life in our world would belong to a single inter-breeding community.[16] Specie differentiation is to be distinguished (in the sense used here) from the "branching-out" of phyletic lines of species to meet changing environment conditions which, of itself, may be seen as suggestive of design that it would be so. It is thought by the materialists that a break-down of a particular specie into some new specie somehow weakens the idea of a special creative design. But an actual change-over from a specie to a different specie is a rarity, rather than a common thing, and brought about only where circumstances seem to call for a basic alteration to be made. It should be noted, in this connection, that there is a natural built-in protection in the mechanisms of all living species to maintain their differential from one another.[17] It reminds one of the same care taken to protect living organisms from disease in the provision of anti-bodies. It shows an "intent" to maintain diversity of life forms among species to fulfill separate ecological functions.

There may have been a curious blending of design along with randomness in respect to the progression of living things in order to insure their greatest degree of adaptability, variability, improvement in form and function, etc., and it would seem that this is what the evolution of living things has been all about. Even the competitiveness among living things with respect to survival has assisted the plan of nature in this regard. The freedom allowed in the self-replicating structural mechanisms of living organisms to adapt to changing conditions does not appear to have been intended to be a guarantee of success in all cases, but why should it be?

We turn now to several other physical aspects of nature that, at first, may be seen as imperfections but, when taken in a broader view, do not seem to be that at all. As mentioned previously, the self-operating and continuous weather machine around the globe is in a constant state of motion and change. The manner in which it functions, as we have seen, makes possible the existence of life as we know it. It is a marvel of many components that interacts in an extremely coordinated fashion, yet undergoes frequent adjustments that make for stabilizations here and there. The fact that this assists the bringing about of cyclical droughts that, in turn, produce famine and suffering from time to time in certain areas, should not cause us to lose the sense of the remarkable design and beneficial effects from the overall system. Where famines occur one may usually find elsewhere an abundance in terms of an overall global balance, If mankind conducted its affairs with more wisdom and cooperation there would be far less reason for him to blame nature for his own unnecessary shortcomings.

155

Once again we come back to the point made in Chapter 7 that the intellect and values of man, if properly and wisely exercised, stand to count for a great deal in the overall scheme of things.

We may view the "finite" character of our natural resources in a similar way. I have previously called attention to the evidence that the size of the Earth fits into an optimal range of sizes, of all possible sizes, for the existence and development of life as we know it. Eventually, an Earth of any size could be looked upon as being finite, but it so happens that we are more immediately concerned with our own. When we first appreciate the "optimum" size that we enjoy and, second, the manner in which our Earth is well-stocked—even within and below areas that are not presently inhabited—then it can readily be seen in a broad context of design as a most remarkable phenomenon. Even though man has no guarantee with respect to his duration on this Earth, I have previously noted that solutions to problems as energy, minerals, and the like, have appeared at a time when there is growing concern over an "inadequacy" of our presently discovered and known resources.

Even if we have succeeded so far in contesting the view of imperfection in a world that shows great design, how do we account for the dual existence of good and evil, with evil being a significant causative factor in the occurrence of so much suffering, misery, wars, and the like? How does evil fit into a designed scheme of things, if at all? It is a characteristic that goes beyond mere survival and seems mostly peculiar to man as a by-product of his remarkable consciousness and freedom of choice. But is it not highly significant that evil and its consequences stand out uniquely in man within the framework of what otherwise appears to be a remarkably designed world in all other important respects, as we have seen so far? Have we not also seen that man, his mind and consciousness, is special in relation to the whole of both animate and inanimate phenomena within his reach? The convergence of these special features in man alone is hardly to be attributed to the implausibility of mere chance. Here we see the ingredients for

156

trial, error and accountability in the choice between good and evil. A ready, if not complete, answer to this enigma may be found in biblical sources. The strong implication of both design and purpose is there if one is willing to so recognize it. It would be most difficult not to do so if one concludes that, for the empirical reasons advanced in this work, the universe is designed and that man, his mind and consciousness, are special. For—in such a case—there must have been a purpose, and the one mentioned above stands out because of the very enigma it presents to what may otherwise be seen as a well-designed world.

We should now move along to consider design or chance in specific reference to the animate side of nature. As we shall see, common sense may rebel in disbelief to the materialistic view that random chance, having already claimed to be the cause of the countless cosmic and inanimate phenomena we have been considering, could yet account for the millions upon millions of individual events which have transpired on the animate side of things. One might ask at this stage: Is there anything left to chance?

# 10

## Direction in Organic Evolution

An early design argument of the thirteenth century, the so-called "Fifth Way" of St. Thomas Aquinas, presented the following concept:

> We see that things which lack knowledge, such as natural bodies, act for an end, and this is evident from their acting always, or nearly always, in the same way, so as to obtain the best result. Hence it is plain that they achieve their end, not fortuitously, but designedly. Now whatever lacks knowledge cannot move towards an end, unless it be directed by some being endowed with knowledge and intelligence; as the arrow is directed by the archer. . . .[1]

The controversy today is not whether living things appear to have been designed. The materialists admit to this, but deny that intelligent foreknowledge and direction is the cause of this phenomenon. Instead, they see random chance alone as involved with the processes of organic evolution that are said to have interacted with living organisms to produce the effects that are found.

There are more than a million species in the plant and animal world which demonstrate today the principle that living things have evolved into organized entities in a manner which satisfies the needs of their respective modes of existence. In the animal kingdom, for instance, physiological needs of one specie or another appear to have been fulfilled on a requirements and suitability basis, more or less, as befitting the tolerable genetic constraints of the particular specie. It bears repeating here the observation of Hilde S. Hein that "organisms, both structurally and functionally, appear to be designed for a purpose; that the parts are so organized as to suggest that there is a goal or end to which they are subordinate."[2]

The quality in living things to advance toward purposeful end-results in terms of fitness, function, utility, etc.—the so-called "goal-seeking" aspects of living things—has long been regarded by many as a strong inference in favor of an intelligently planned, designed, and directed world. Whatever may be said for some retrogressions or non-uniformity along the ascending evolutionary ladder of life, the results of today show great adaptation of life for the existing environmental situation. Even the story of organic evolution, with its description of certain selective processes which seek to explain much of this phenomenon, has not fully abated the appeal and strength of the inference to a great many who look at a broad picture of design. For instance, Lecomte du Noüy, in his view of an intelligent direction in evolution, made the point that nature has solved fantastic problems by means of various solutions and "chose the best—the ones best adapted to the ends."[3] John and Merle Coulter are among many equally impressed with the view of progressive evolution in their observation "that through all the stretch of earth's history, in spite of all imaginable changes in external conditions, certain structures in plants and animals have changed steadily in one direction. These steady changes have carried forward the group as a whole."[4]

The view of modern biology with respect to these goal-seeking qualities of living things, as interpreted at least in materialistic thinking, attributes the whole of this phenomenon simply to a series of millions upon millions of intermediate events selected by evolutionary processes that are said to have commenced to randomly interact with first bacterial life some 3.5 billion years ago. And this, without any independent source of cause. All structures and steps preceding the activity of selection in organic evolution simply belong to "chemistry and physics," in this view. The same chemistry and physics,

159

that is, which we have dwelt on through many chapters in this book and have found to be anything but "ordinary."

Such an explanation, as a total explanation, is incongruous with our earlier observations of the cosmic, including inanimate, phenomena of nature which, as we have seen, have worked themselves around in a sort of evolutionary process of their own, similarly selective and goal-seeking, resulting in remarkable means-to-ends relationships that suitably inter-connect most appropriately with the world of living things. We observed this first in atomic behaviour, then in the macrocosmic level as related to the Earth and, to an extent of knowledge, in the cosmos beyond, and from all of that we have seen how both aspects of nature have converged in a unique and special meaningful way to man, his mind and consciousness. These are facts that may not be ignored and they are as much a part of the end-results of the broad picture of universal evolutionary processes as anything else.

It would seem that any attempt to explain the means-to-ends relationships existing in the animate world should, at the same time, give meaningful recognition to this parallel and interconnecting aspect of selectivity and direction in the inanimate world. After all, both worlds owe their immediate origin and substance at least to the same chemical elements which comprise the limited "standard parts" available which, together with universal laws, have solved the problems involved in goal-seeking. These standard parts have been functional, although in different ways, in the phenomena of both the animate and inanimate worlds of nature and to say that there is a total randomness governing design-results in the animate world (because of random processes said to be active alone on that side of things) does not seem to be a very reasonable or plausible explanation when design-results on the inanimate side are without the availability of such processes. Overlooked is the fact that both aspects of nature have something very much in common in a relational sense when applied, especially, to the mind and consciousness of man. It bears repeating here that Darwinian concepts, born in an era of relative ignorance of the knowledge of inanimate nature, have simply not caught up with the growth of knowledge on that side of things as it affects the question of design or chance. A narrowness of view of the ultimate origin of things may be seen as the result. When the inanimate and animate aspects of nature are considered together, objectively in relation to the whole of natural phenomena, they bespeak forethought, direction, coordination, and advance knowledge.

In no way do the foregoing views take away from processes that may have been found to be operable in organic evolution; it simply calls into question the exclusivity of such processes (already an issue in modern biology) as well as the matter of the appeal of random chance in preference to "intended" or directed results in the evolution of living things.

We should next briefly consider, in relation to the above, the modern theory of the evolution of living things which is based primarily on limited observations from the fossil record, and which holds that the many different kinds of plants and animals alive today have all developed from earlier ones by reason of certain selective processes. The reader should understand that there have been a number of changes in the theory as concerns the active processes. For instance, Darwin knew nothing of heredity. Mendel's Law was not "re-discovered" until 1900. Our concern here is the present prevailing view. In his book "Processes of Organic Evolution," G. Ledyard Stebbins outlined five basic types of processes considered applicable to the modern synthetic theory of evolution. These are set forth as being "gene mutation, changes in chromosome structure and number, genetic re-combination, natural selection, and reproductive isolation."[5] The last two named basic types, i.e. natural selection and reproductive isolation, are those which, according to Stebbins, guide populations of organisms into adaptive channels. The physical environment (and all that this implies) is the important factor involved in these two. According to Ernst Mayr, in his book "Population, Species, and Evolution," there are reasons to assign a role of greater importance to natural selection as the environment has come to be considered "as one of the most important factors in evolution."[6] The first three processes mentioned by Stebbins may be seen as providing an almost endless opportunity for variation on which natural selection may act, subject to the genetically controlled limits of the particular specie. In the next chapter some further consideration will be given to these processes of evolutionary change, particularly as related to the DNA molecule and self-replication. Here, however, another aspect is of special interest.

It is to be noted that none of the basic selective processes of evolution, as mentioned, seems to suggest a conscious directional aspect in any form, or degree, or manner..

Interestingly, though, there are some (if not a growing number) evolutionists of today who express the view that conscious behavior (more identifiable or associated with higher life forms) may interplay functionally with recognized selective processes to produce change; that a change in an animal's habits brought about by its conscious behavioral activity may affect selection results within the Darwinian system. Now, while such a view does not go so far as to fall in with a concept of Lamarck that a change in the animal's behavior may itself actually guide or produce change in selective results, it is thought that behavior, nevertheless, functionally inter-relates with Darwinian selection processes in a manner (as to be discussed below) that is productive of change. And, of course, the very speculative idea of an *atomos mentis* aspect of guidance in evolutionary change, suggested in the introductory chapter, would be deemed revolutionary and unsupportable even to those who advance views on conscious behaviorism as an important factor in results achieved through selection. As mentioned, however, it is at least something to contemplate, as within the possible, if one first acknowledges that such an interplay has occurred in evolution and that this has helped to produce the remarkable and fit end-results in nature we have considered throughout earlier chapters. Once the idea of a mental relationship to change in evolution enters the picture, directly or indirectly, or even in the most rudimentary sense, one cannot help (in my view) but to think of this in a linkage sense and to search for a governing cause that is of a different and higher order than that of the organism itself as a physical entity.

Sir Alister Hardy, the eminent English zoologist, is today one of the leading proponents in support of evolution being brought about in the higher animals by conscious behavior acting as a selective force within the Darwinian system. He calls it "behavioural selection" and says it is a development of the ideas originally put forth by Mark Baldwin and Lloyd Morgan under the name of "organic selection." This view was expressed earlier in his book *The Living Stream*[7] and more recently in his book *The Biology of God*.[8] It is, he believes, a selection process that has been overlooked in the story of evolution.[9] Although he emphasizes that it is a form of selection within the Darwinian system, he points out that it is not brought about by agents outside the organism, i.e., the action of the physical environment or of predators or competitors, but by changes in the behavior of the organisms themselves. An example of this proposed additional selective process in evolution helps to clarify its significance. Hardy asks: "Does a terrestrial animal by chance get webbed-feet and then take to the water to use them? Of course not."[10] In Hardy's view, if an animal's inquisitive, exploratory activity leads it to change its behavior to one of hunting in the water, then when by chance variation (i.e., DNA mutation) some members of the population become so better equipped for swimming, they will tend to survive in larger numbers than those not so well adapted. This, of course, is Darwinian selection, *but* the primary cause of the selection was that of behavioral change; without this the chance mutation would *not* have been selected. In support of his view he quotes from R. F. Ewer's contributed article to Volume Thirteen of *New Biology* wherein she said that "behaviour will tend to be always one jump ahead of structure, and so play a decisive role in the evolutionary process."[11] In the example given by Hardy, the ordinary modern explanation in biology would simply be that the idea of consciousness in some manner of expression is inadmissible as a selective feature of evolutionary processes and that structural change would be ahead of behavior.

163

Richard Taylor pointed out that the powers and construction of living organisms are perfectly adapted to their mode of life in a seemingly purposeful or goal-directed manner, and that the supposition of modern biology that this is only apparent instead of real is not obviously the case. He noted that every creature has the anatomy, powers, and instincts "perfectly suited to its goal or mode of life" citing, for example, the hawk which has sharp talons, a rapacious beak, keen eyes, strength, and a digestive system all perfectly suited to a predatory mode of life and is so equipped *"in order"* to pursue its goals and that it is less artificial to say this than to claim that it is only *"because"* such beings are so equiped that they pursue their goals.[12]

In an interesting and different vein from what we have so far been considering in reference to consciousness, Taylor suggests that it would be irrational to attribute to an accidental occurrence the existence of our sense organs (such as our brains and central nervous systems) and, at the same time, to suppose that such faculties reveal some truth about things external to themselves; that we in fact consider them to be reliable guides in our pursuit of truth rather than to consider them as limited to what alone might be inferred from their own structure and arrangement and as not being able to tell us anything else outside of themselves.[13]

Hardy carried the behavior concept into human consciousness to suggest that Darwinian evolution "need no longer be considered an entirely materialistic doctrine. It can only be so regarded if we either deny the part played by conscious behaviour or deem consciousness itself to be no more than an illusory by-product of an entirely mechanistic system."[14]

Hardy observed that there are a number of other biologists who have independently been coming to the conclusion that behavior is an important selective tool in evolutionary processes. In addition to Ewer, he mentions C. H. Waddington and Ernst Mayr.

Hardy does not appear to pursue the mysterious element of rudimentary consciousness to its source other than to raise a question concerning the same in the mind-body aspect. He does, however, find most attractive the views expressed by Whitehead, Hartshorne, and Birch who, he said, conceptually believe there to be "an element of mind, not necessarily consciousness, but feeling, in everything including even the electron." He calls this the "Whitehead-Hartshorne-Birch line of reasoning" which presents a possibility which should not be overlooked.[15] In this connection, he refers to Sewall Wright, the American geneticist who, in his essay "Process and Divinity," expressed the view that mind may be present universally in molecules, atoms and elementary particles, as well as in all organisms and in their cells.[16] He (Hardy) also noted that J. B. S. Haldane expressed the same idea in his "The Inequality of Man."[17] In addition, it should be noted that Hardy is himself firmly convinced that organic evolution is linked with a God of the universe.* The unresolved question, in his view, is "how?" He asks: "Are we to regard God himself as part of the evolving process?" In his view, a creative element must be linked with the mental or psychic side of life and "playing its part within the Darwinian system of selection."[18] He expressed concurrence with both John Eccles and the late Charles Sherrington that mental events belong to a different order, although linked with the physical system.[19] Is this not another way of saying that once the substance of mind came forth it shared some affinity with a cosmic Mind that provided the linkage necessary to move life forward, directionally, toward ultimate purposive goals? As shown in Chapter 7, there are many examples of such a linkage between the mind of man and what seems to be attributed to a cosmic Mind in mathematical and perhaps even in more general logical abstractions.

In terms of intelligent design, an alternative supposition to the above might be that the few chemical elements of the atoms that are involved in life processes were programmed in

---

* Hardy, on page 14 of his *Biology of God*, writes as follows: "I must make it clear at the outset that by God I do not mean a deity in human form, although I readily grant that those who are conscious of this element may have a feeling towards it of a personal relationship indeed a devotional love-relationship; this, however, may be for good biological or psychological reasons linked with the emotions of an early child-parent affection, but none the worse for that—and no less real."

advance, in some yet unknown manner, to bring about in time the end results that are evident in an interplay with evolutionary processes. Certainly, the atoms possessed the latent potential capacity as requisite to such ends. This, in effect, would be consistent with an early concept known as the Cartesian Hypothesis which, in one aspect at least, was described by an early 18th century writer as "presupposing that God has only created matter, divided it into a certain number of parts, and put it into motion, according to a few laws . . . (so that) it would of itself have produced the world without anymore ado."[20] But the view of a linkage on the mental side as above suggested, involving a further linking-up with the latent potential capacities of the relevant kinds of atoms that are found to exist in life processes, as a means to achieve meaningful end-results in conjunction with other active processes would seem to be the more appealing supposition in a design context. It is not likely that anyone would suggest that living organisms, by themselves, would have the kind of advance knowledge or analytical capability that would enable them on their own to realize that the movement along an evolutionary pathway would provide a functional end-result. Take the above example of the first of a line of webbed-footed animals that took to water in the use of such an advantage, i.e. webbed-feet. To develop this advantage would only be of benefit to very remote descendants at that. It is only reasonable to suppose that the attainment of such a goal required foresight which the animal itself would be incapable of having on its own. Further, as another example, take the complex machinery of the eye as a mechanism for sight, or the ear as a mechanism for hearing; the living organisms that first acquired these faculties may not reasonably be seen on their own as being capable of summoning-up and maintaining, behaviorally, instrumentalities of such high intricacy and complexity.

The materialists may then ask why the course of evolution, in the attainment of goals, has included the trial and error aspect in a changing environmental situation during the course of time. Science, as well as the view of design, provided a fairly good answer for this, as will be considered in the next chapter. It is more important to ask, if behavior has a "steering" effect in helping to organize the goals of evolution, how biology is to reasonably account for the cause-to-effect aspect of such a phenomenon unless a basic intent and plan for such a result (rather than a haphazard arrangement) pre-existed in the first place. "In what sense can the whole process be called blind," asked John Habgood, "if consciousness plays a real part in the process and if the end products are conscious creatures capable of understanding their own development?"[21]

The idea that conscious behavior may be one of several guiding factors in evolution has a relevance to present-day views on the question of the mind-body relation. When the great French mathematician and philosopher of the 17th century, René Descartes, developed the logic of the spirit-body duality of nature, little did his contemporaries realize how much the subject would be alive today; that is, in terms of compatibility with ideas being expressed by many in science. In an essay entitled "Remarks on the Mind-Body Question,"[22] the currency of this subject was noted by Eugene Wigner when he said that "not many years ago, the existence of a mind or soul would have been passionately denied by most physical scientists . . . it was nearly universally accepted among physical scientists that there is nothing besides matter." But there seems to be a growing respect in the physical sciences for the view that matter does not account for emotions, thoughts, sensations, aesthetic appreciation, desires, morality, etc. In effect, this is the same as saying that mind and consciousness, as well as life itself, is something over and above matter. As noted by A. S. Eddington,[23] physics is no longer so tempted or disposed to condemn the spiritual aspect of our nature as illusory because of a lack of concreteness. The modern theory of biological evolution, as expressed in materialistic thinking, reflects disagreement with any such trend and, to some extent, this is indicated in the so-called reductionist controversy to be mentioned in Chapter 12.

Although less relevant perhaps to the foregoing, it is nevertheless pertinent here to draw attention to a seemingly directive aspect as related to the human brain. One of the unsolved

167

paradoxes in modern biology is the astonishing phenomenon that "in an extremely small fraction of time compared with the long history of animal evolution"[24] the size of the human brain precipitously increased and, then, just as precipitously, any further increase in size came to an abrupt halt. Harry J. Jerison, a Professor of Psychiatry, notes that brain evolution in living vertebrates before man was ever so conservative in terms of many hundreds of millions of years, that the earliest endocast for present-day man may be placed at about 250,000 years; and he noted that, on the basis of various studies, man's brain evolved to its present size within the past million years.[25] "As evolutionists," said Ernst Mayr, "we must ask ourselves why all the factors favoring an increase in brain size suddenly lost their power after the homo sapiens level had been reached."[26] He noted, in this connection, that there is no evidence which suggests that internal improvement of the brain can occur without an enlargement of cranial capacity. In terms of capacity, the brain appears to have exceeded, in a rapid jump, its evolving needs of an earlier time. In a word, it seems to have attained an end-goal that would meet the intellectual requirements for man for all time to come. All of this is to say nothing of the physiological changes that had to occur with respect to the human body as a whole to accommodate a shift in the center of gravity in consequence of the rapid increase in skull size to brain size. This, in a comparable short period of time. The workings of chance seem to have been overworked. There is more to conscious directionality, it would seem, than the modern theory of evolution recognizes. Now, it is quite true that the biological explanation for the precipitous increase in brain size to its present capacity is that the introduction of speech communication, greater imagery, improved behavioral responses, etc. carried forward this remarkable phenomenon in evolutionary terms. But this does not explain the astonishing absence of continued growth in brain size as mentioned by Mayr, nor does it reasonably explain the "rapid-fire" responsiveness of the presently recognized evolutionary processes on a broad front to meet the challenge of something new.

It seems that the materialists are constantly faced with giving explanations of a mechanistic nature even where this leads into questionable alleyways which are often supported, not by empirical fact, but by a great deal of conjecture. Excluding, as they do, anything other than mechanistic ideas and explanations necessarily omits from consideration even the more obvious implications of intelligent design. This is unfortunate. As we proceed, the more it will become evident, I believe, that some of the belabored explanations that flow from such an exclusion could be better explained in terms of design. In a wider aspect of the human brain enlargement question, for instance, the environment in its relationship to man could be taken into better account in a purposeful way. The environment on this planet has evolved by numerous processes in a unique manner to man as described in earlier chapters. It generally coincided in a sense of timely preparation with the phenomenon of the human brain which had to come to full scope and capacity in terms of potential in order to make use of it. Man could not simply make discoveries and inventions of the nature and scale as made without having a ready and fully capable capacity to do so. This capacity had to be in excess of immediate need even though this conjectural explanation defies the basic processes under which evolution is supposed to work. This is because evolution would require, in its usual manner of presentation, that the development of any organism be merely to the level of then existing need as imposed by the physical, environmental, cultural, etc. circumstances and not by virtue of any major jump ahead, coupled with a "completion" aspect. To say that the human brain came forward as a fully complete instrument from the time of its present endocast with the potential intellectual capacity from the beginning to make an amazing use of a compatible environment, while doing violence to these evolutionary concepts, does suggest a possible answer to what is beyond explanation in terms of such concepts, does it not?

Let us now return to make some additional observations about the goal-seeking tendencies in living things. Is it not significant that there is an obvious relationship between the

169

matter of goal-seeking of living organisms and the ultimate attainability (rather than unattainability) of such goals in the end? Let there be no doubt about the fact that living systems have today achieved ecologically well-balanced, useful, and purposeful end-goals in an overall context. Not simply ordinary goals. Rather goals that are remarkable for their obvious fitness to purposeful activities and pursuits which, in many cases, invoke highly complex mechanisms and parts of mechanisms (such as the eye and other mechanisms for sensory perception, ear drums for hearing, animal metabolism, wings of birds, brains, and so on). This is to say that there is an amazing relationship between the course on which life may move forward in an evolutionary sense and an ultimate logical realization that may be expected. We can look back intelligently at past or intermediate stages in the development of life as it now exists. In so doing, it is clear that each stage was preceded by an earlier stage and, in going from one stage to the next, the direction taken (in evolution progressively) follows a visibly marked course toward an apparent goal (the next stage) which *is there* in the end to be realized. It is not important as concerns this phenomenon to say that selection had time to bring this about or to say that, in the process of attaining goals, failures or "mistakes" occurred along the way. That is beside the point. There did not have to be the means at hand (traceable to the chemical elements) whereby eyes, ear-drums, brains, etc. could exist, much less the physical principles on which they operate. Equally important, living organisms sought out the attainable in the end. If we were to assume that the selective processes of evolution, together with their living subjects, were blind and uninformed of the attainable ends toward which they were working over countless generations, we have to recognize that, in terms of chance, all of this activity toward improvement would be for naught were it not for the coincidence of attainable goals; that is, meaningful, fit, and purposeful goals.

These observations can only help to strengthen the idea that, in time, a higher state of awareness of a "supernatural" reality in the human mind may be just around the corner—

caught-up now at an intervening stage reaching toward an attainable end—and this, it would seem, may be foreseen from what is presently observable as concerns other attained goals in living things during the course of evolutionary history. Man, it would seem, long ago achieved the mental capacity, but has yet to achieve a more direct break-through in his conscious awareness of a higher state. This may be, perhaps, one ultimate of goal-achievement of man in an earthbound capacity.

From the dawn of human history, it is recorded that man has looked to something higher than himself. This tendency in man suggests an incipient awareness of an ultimate goal to be achieved in the realization that something higher than himself does in fact exist. The trend of man's conscious awareness in that direction is analogous to the direction which all of life itself appears to have taken over the course of time in moving toward end results which are there to be achieved. All of this seems to be at the root of the research efforts to which Alister Hardy has directed his attention for a number of years; that is, in the study of man's "bent" in the direction of something higher than himself which he calls "the instinct for God" and regards it as fundamental to man as the sex instinct. As a part of his studies, as I understand them from his works, early and classical forms of supernatural thought have been reviewed to find clues in this direction. The human specie has, he maintains, looked beyond itself to a higher form of being. It has taken the form of the worship of the world of nature in its myriad forms, to inanimate objects, to deceased relatives, to other spiritual personages, to the biblical God, and so on. For instance, in both of his books as mentioned, he suggests a possible psychic side to human consciousness which may, in time, come to higher fruition. These concepts are founded upon some present empirical support. Having made this identification of the direction in which the life stream (including consciousness) is flowing, such a projection as to future conscious awareness is not unrealistic. It goes without saying that this concept is consistent, if not in support of, the idea of Teilhard de Chardin of a future convergence of consciousness into an "Omega Point," as well as of other writers that have

171

seen a course in direction of a teleological nature as related to evolutionary processes.

Even now man appears to be increasingly experiencing a mode of intellectual power that encompasses a spectrum of parapsychological phenomena that includes clairvoyance, telepathy, and other expressions of psychic phenomena. This is not to say that these experiences have been sufficiently demonstrated to gain universal acceptance, yet their occurrence is seemingly far too often to be disregarded. If true, it may well be said that this is the culmination of a process not unlike the processes which, over considerable time, developed characteristics in living systems on the basis of the same principle, i.e. that the directional movement or trend toward improvement is there to be realized in the end. The tendency in man from time immemorial toward a higher state, even with a blurred vision thereof, would seem consistent with these observations.

When one realizes that a basic principle appears to operate vis á vis the manner of construction of both inanimate and animate nature, the comments made earlier in this chapter take on even greater significance. I have in mind the so-called doctrine of emerging properties. It is indeed a revealing principle that pervades throughout the nature of things. In terms of design, it presents the picture of a designer who, like a carpenter, has carefully selected the materials with which to construct an edifice—but which materials do not of themselves, except in final form or configuration, serve a meaningful or useful purpose.

This may best be explained by calling attention to a few examples.

In living matter, cells are quite unlike the characteristic features of the structures that they build. They, too, appear to be simply atomic "building-blocks." When combined with billions of other cells, they form, for instance, a functioning human body. An observation of the activities of cells made by John P. D. John at the turn of the century is illustrative of this principle on the animate side of nature:

172

Here are a billion body-builders. Some were at work on a nerve who never heard of a muscle. Some were at work on a muscle who never heard of a nerve. Some are making eyes who never saw the light. Some are making ears who never heard a sound. Who taught these nerve-builders the nature of muscular fiber. . . . Who taught these muscle makers the nature of nervous energy. . . . Who taught the army of eye makers the nature of light, that they should construct an eye with lenses adapted to receive it. . . . Who taught the heart builders the principle of hydrodynamics; the lung builders the principle of osmose; the ear builders the principles of acoustics; the gland builders the principles of secretion;—in short, who taught the countless processions of infinitesimal workers the vast fund of knowledge that touches upon infinity? The workmanship of these minute artisans give unmistakable evidence of far-reaching design. Whose design? Not that of the busy workers, for every moment they are falling at their post by the million.[27]

On the non-living side, the same principle operates throughout in the chemical transformations in nature. As we considered in Chapter 5, the atoms do not (with the few exceptions as mentioned) appear to have a significance on their own, yet, when combined with other atoms, they produce specific and different kinds of properties. For example, two hydrogen atoms and one oxygen atom make the compound of water—an essence quite unlike the properties of the individual components of hydrogen and oxygen. As another example, twelve atoms of carbon, twenty-two of hydrogen, and eleven of oxygen make up the compound of sugar—a different substance. Then, too, at the macro-level of phenomena, as for example the phenomena considered in Chapter 6, we see countless examples of component parts of things which, while of little or of no importance on their own, make-up still other phenomena that are functional and purposeful in a relational sense of life and especially to man. Newly emerged properties, where seemingly appropriate, are seen to have inter-related at higher levels of aggregation with other matter and phenomena

173

that, combined, bear still new relationships in terms of function, fitness, and purposiveness in an overall ultimate sense. This is the manner in which, it would seem, a Designer would have undertaken the step-by-step process of the construction of a world of intended diversity and variety. If blind chance were to have been the causative factor of all of this phenomena, there would have been no need for such ultimate purposeful results as evidenced by the performance of the "neutral" constituent component parts of things.

Life itself is looked upon as of a different order than the atoms, molecules, cells, etc. of which it is composed. Erwin Schrödinger was convinced of this in his remarkable book "What is Life."[28] It is a new and independent essence, he said. For one thing it no longer acts like matter. This rationale, it would seem, is a sound basis on which to view the mind-matter relationship referred to earlier in this chapter rather than to view mind as solely the consequence of physico-chemical materialism.

I have previously called attention to Pantin's observation with respect to the emergence of new qualities that have arisen at different levels in the organization of things. He observed that at each level of structure, special properties appear and that these properties relate to the "configuration rather than to properties of the individual atoms and molecules of which they are composed."[29] "As in living organisms," he noted, "we find configurations which repeat themselves in the inorganic, although there is no inheritable variation upon which natural selection can operate as in living organisms."[30] Hein, as well, pointed out that the doctrine of emergent evolution confirms that "the historically later stages of the development of an organism arise out of, but are not strictly deducible from, knowledge of earlier states." It is, she said, "the emergence of something new, something which cannot be predicted from earlier stages and is to that extent richer than its cause."[31] Monod, in his book, described the multiplicity of machinery and function in the mini- sub-units which comprise the whole of the living cell. Each of the sub-units appear to be autonomous and yet, at the same time, cooperate with the whole in

174

its functioning. For instance, he described how the protein molecule channels "the activity of the chemical machine, assures its coherent functioning, and puts it together. . . ."[32] On several occasions, Monod compared the working of biological regulatory systems to the workings of computers. For instance in describing the highly mechanical and even "technological" aspect of the translation process operative within the DNA double helix, he referred to the successive interactions of the various components leading to the assembly of a polypeptide upon the surface of the ribosome as comparing to "a milling machine which notch by notch moves a piece of work through to completion—all this inevitably recalls an assembly line in a machine factory. . . ."[33]

Michael A. Simon, in his recent book "The Matter of Life," considered the "problem" of the emergence of whole living organisms which do not bear a resemblance to the parts of which they are made. He asked: ". . . How are we to account for the occurrence of properties on higher levels of organization when these properties have never appeared on a lower level?"[34] His answer, in terms of biology, is that DNA molecules appear to have been naturally selected from a number of physico-chemically equivalent possibilities, and is further explicable if the problem of the origin of these organisms is also explicable.[35] Additionally, according to Simon, emergence is not a particular problem for biology if there is not a fundamental difference between biological properties and physical and chemical properties and, in this regard, he said that: "We know that processes occur in nature whereby higher degrees of organization are produced out of elements at a lower degree of organization, such as the formation of atoms from elementary particles and the formation of molecules from atoms."[36] But, as we shall see in a later chapter, the modern synthetic theory of evolution minimizes the importance of elemental matter as an active or contributing agent in the results of life phenomena that both precede and succeed the activities of selective processes in organic evolution. There is an unwillingness to receive a strong hint of a basic plan and design inherently built-in to the inanimate matter as concerns the mech-

175

anisms and processes that find expression in living organisms. It is not enough to say that we have no positive proof of this for we have, as well, no positive proof of chance as is in fact relied upon to account for the role of elemental matter under the modern theory.

Do not the above observations lead us to lessen the importance attached in biology to the idea of random chance and cause us to divert our attention more specifically to the built-in latent potential capacities of the atomic elements themselves (as means), and the creative substances they are capable of engineering, as explanable in terms of an intelligent Designer of the universe and as the more immediate cause of the origin of self-replicating mechanisms in living things, the basic code of inheritance, the origin of mind and consciousness, the origin of species differentiation, and so on? If this be so, it makes the argument to chance even more deficient than it is, as we shall consider in Chapter 12.

# 11

## Design Solutions with Respect
## to the Origin of Life

Following an earlier era during which cosmic activity appears to have fully predominated, life arrived on the scene. It was something uniquely valuable to be carried forward by self-replication, endowed with an inheritable code of information, imbued with a "will to live," and goal-seeking toward attainable purposive ends. Interestingly, these qualities of life display the "prospective contrivance" aspect to which A. E. Taylor referred.[1] The mind and consciousness of man, as we have seen, is also forward-looking as though zealously endowed with a future destiny. The unique qualities of life assured the reversal of the entropic process of energy dissipation in the universe, suggesting than an aim of the preceding activity was the creation of life, but this alone was not, as we have considered earlier, an ultimate aim in and of itself.

The fact that life is reproductive and coupled with an hereditary code of genetic information in the DNA molecule, rather than being non-reproductive and not so coupled, furnishes a remarkable insight into the design-plan of life. At the same time it furnishes a basic clue to the purpose of evolutionary changes in living things over the course of time in a reconciliatory design context. As a part of this, we may see that the provision of these mechanisms in association with first life shows, in addition to their meaning in various other ways to be considered, a pre-conceived knowledge of important meaningful events thereafter to occur on Earth. This,

177

perhaps surprising to some, assumes the correctness of certain prevailing theories in science. Design, in this connection, is to be seen as explanatory of "why" these events occurred, with science explaining "how" they occurred. Here again, we shall focus our attention on the end results.

One may see numerous alternate engineering possibilities with respect to the existence, maintenance, and development of life on this planet, but it so happens that the provision of self-replication (coupled with the genetic code) appears, *in retrospect*, to have been the best, if not the only, solution with respect to certain major events that subsequently occurred and which have resulted in the formulation of well-accepted theories in science relating to:

1) The circumstances under which first life is thought to have arisen on Earth and thereafter continued;

2) The major physico-chemical and other environmental changes that have been historically associated with the history of the Earth;

3) The selective processes of organic evolution acting on the qualities of life.

Before setting forth the design concepts as mentioned above, it is first desirable to briefly describe each of the scientific theories as relevant here.

As concerns (1), it is theorized that life came to the Earth through a "narrow window" physico-chemically and historically speaking. In bacterial form, it is estimated that this occurred some 3.5 billion years ago. Life's origin, according to the theory, takes us back to a "primordial soup" where very special physico-chemical conditions are believed to have then, and only then, existed. It may be that the vision in science of a "soup" formula to be briefly considered here will, in time, give way to the idea of an origin of first life on Earth from elsewhere in space. This, by reason of the recent discovery, as previously mentioned, of the widespread existence of organic molecules in space and the possibility some of them may have been carried here in a comet or by some cosmic collision.

Indeed, a new book entitled "Lifecloud" written by astronomers Fred Hoyle and Chandra Wickramasinghe has advanced such a theory. But whichever of the two theories will ultimately prevail in science will not affect the design argument to be made in this chapter except to say it bears repeating that the further science pushes our understanding of the origin of the basic ingredients for life back toward the beginnings of the universe, the more we must come to realize the remarkableness of the latent potential sufficiently imparted initially to primeval material whether in an ocean "soup" or in a "celestial" environment.

Be that as it may, the present prevailing "soup" theory holds that the main chemical building-blocks of life, i.e. nucleotides and amino acids, were produced on Earth from molecules of water, methane, and ammonia interacting with electrical discharge (lightening).[2] There was no free oxygen because it is produced by plants which did not exist at the time. The absence of oxygen, noted Bronowski, permitted ultra-violet light from the Sun to penetrate through to the surface of the Earth.[3] Laboratory experimentation in recent times, under which certain life-originating organic compounds were artificially synthesized under simulated conditions, is thought to have captured certain of the requisite conditions for first life to have appeared, thereby lending support to the theory. For purposes here, it is unnecessary to set forth the stages which, in theory, are thought to have led to the first primitive living cell on Earth, following the production of the main chemical building-blocks of life as mentioned. Monod called attention to the "major difficulties" in the steps that would have had to follow, i.e. "the formation of macromolecules capable, under the conditions prevailing in the primordial soup, of promoting their own replication unaided by any teleomonic process."[4] Interestingly, he was quick to point out that the *a priori* probability was next to zero that these "major difficulties" could be resolved by chance circumstances, but he considered it to be unscientific and unobjective to speculate that there could have been any other cause.

There is nothing in science to indicate that life on Earth

has spontaneously originated other than during the earlier period of time as mentioned when the environmental conditions were quite different than they are today. Indeed, the French scientist Louis Pasteur firmly established that life does not arise spontaneously from inanimate matter as many had thought to be the case before he made his experimental observations. The only exception to this that is recognized in science is that of the early occurrence of life as mentioned. All present-day life on Earth is said, therefore, to be traceable (although the fossil record does not go back quite so far) directly, and without discontinuity, back to that first formulative period. In support of this, science points to several empirical factors. In the first place, it is known today that all of life is characterized by the same mostly invariable and rigid DNA molecular structure (except for its coding informational details). As noted by Bronowski, it is known that all forms of life "from a bacterium to an elephant, from a virus to a rose are controlled by the four bases in the DNA molecule. . . ."[5] To the same effect, essentially, is the comment of Shklovskii and Sagan: "The innerworkings of terrestrial organisms—from microbes to man—are so similar in their biochemical details as to make it highly likely that all organisms on the Earth had evolved from a single instance of the origin of life."[6]

As concerns (2) above, the general nature of the physicochemical change in the environment that is thought to have occurred after the early conditions when first life is thought to have arose was explained by Asimov as follows: ". . . As life advanced to the stage where photosynthesis became possible and oxygen and nitrogen replaced the ammonia and carbon dioxide of the atmosphere, some of the oxygen was converted by the impinging ultra-violet into the more energetic ozone. . . ."[7] It is thought that, at this stage, higher forms of life were able to develop. Asimov further explained the consequences of this as related to the possible development of life under present-day conditions and expressed the prevailing view that there is a good reason to doubt that the process (life creation out of non-life) can be repeated in the environment of today.[8] "As organisms evolved," according to Hein, "so did their environment and consequently we may speculate that the earliest forms of life which were spontaneously generated from inanimate matter were a composition of organic compounds which conceivably could not even survive in today's environment."[9] We have also considered, in Chapters 6 and 7, that changes in the environment of a geologic nature transformed the Earth over time in a most meaningful way that affected future life inhabitation and development.

In reference to (3), the cells of living organisms, once they appeared on Earth, were endowed (like the atoms themselves of which they are composed) with latent potential capacities to permit future change along constructive development lines. While structurally rigid and mostly invariant in their basic chemical organization, as to be considered later in this chapter, they nevertheless contain in their nuclei the self-copying material in DNA which controls their activity as well as the genetic code of inheritance. The coded information is open to variance by operation of certain of the basic selective processes mentioned in the last chapter which, in accordance with the modern theory of evolution, govern the activities, performances, and developments to occur in living organisms.[10] An exception relates to the recently reported discovery by the biochemist, George Pieczenik, that a yet unrecognized selective process seems to occur at the molecular level before the organism develops. This, on account of the significance he attaches to certain protective patterns in the genes of the DNA molecule.[11]

In summary of the foregoing, life first arose at an early stage in the geologic history of the Earth under a given set of unique physico-chemical conditions; the environmental conditions under which first life originated have changed to an environment of conditions that are believed non-productive of original life; all life today is re-traceable to the period as mentioned; the permissiveness to adaptive change found in the make-up of the DNA molecule in living systems, interacting with selective processes of evolution, has enabled the survival and development of life.

Now, if we trust to science with respect to the three general theories as earlier mentioned, it is most difficult to avoid the implication to intelligent design. This may be seen in both the occurrence of the events and circumstances on which the scientific theories are based, as well as in the self-replicative characteristic imparted beforehand to living cells. Both aspects are mutually inter-dependent on the other in a manner which strongly infers an advance contemplation and knowledge of forthcoming circumstances.

This would seem evident, first of all, from the provision for self-replication. From the standpoint of pure chance, it would have been just as well for life to have terminated as rapidly as it was brought into existence with no means of self-copying continuity in accordance with a structural standard. Further, there would have been no need for "chance" to have invented in the first place the highly intricate and complex mechanisms involved (the *a priori* probability occurrence of which was next to zero)—the basic pattern or arrangement for which was rooted inherently in the elemental matter of which they are constructed.

There are those who may say that the changing environmental events as theorized in science to have occurred in conjunction with the evolution of life might have been unnecessary in a well-designed world. It might even be said that life, as an occurrence, could have been planned as a permanent non-cyclical event without change or renewal of any kind—a complete final product of lasting duration. Perhaps it might also be said that the evolving preparatory events leading to the inhabitation of Earth by man, as described in Chapter 6, could have been circumvented in the design of things by an initial self-sufficiency in all these respects. But these speculations as to what might have been the case in a different world are nothing more than just that and are, of course, contradictory to what in fact occurred as envisioned in modern science. There is no reason to suggest, in this connection, that possible alternative creative possibilities of a speculative nature favor the idea of chance over that of intelligent design. As indicated before, we have no basis on which to question the means engaged to achieve remarkable ends which speak quite adequately on their own in the context of design. And, when measured in terms of the evident purposefulness of evolutionary change as described later in this chapter, any idea that the occurrence of the above alternative possible events would have presented a superior kind of creation would be most unconvincing.

As it happened (that is, in keeping with modern scientific thought), while one may see that various alternative engineering possibilities could have been engaged with respect to the occurrence of life, the best solution prevailed, e.g., the provision for self-replication without a provision for a continuous and spontaneous life generation. One alternative to this, as suggested above, would have been for life to be non-replicative and also lacking in the provision for continuous spontaneous generation, but any such alternative would have resulted in the discontinuity of life. A second alternative would have been for life to have occurred without provision for self-replication but with spontaneous generation of a continual nature, or, as a third alternative, life could have been open to both spontaneous generation and to self-replication. But if either of these alternatives had been engaged, the dependent and purposeful inter-relations as are now abundantly demonstrated between living things and their environment would have been incongruous to say the least. One may imagine the irrationality, disorder, incoherence, and lack of intelligibility of it all. Instead of a harmony there would have been a haphazard arrangement. Meaningful or ordered diversity would have been incongruous to say the least. One may imagine the appalling. The development of life into higher complex forms from simple organisms would have been precluded in an evolutionary sense of meaning.

The foreclosure of a continual life origination situation avoided what would have been a meaningless and chaotic state of affairs. The provision for self-replication, coupled with the genetic code of DNA, permitted an orderly and continually renewable creative life process. It provided the means for a meaningful multiplicity and diversity of life in a well organized and ingenious manner. In effect, it permitted the continuation of initial life, together with the great potential for differentiation and diversity in species. In a way, selection processes may be seen as having given a guidance aspect to a changing environment with DNA, in its tolerance aspect, acting much like a computerized sensor on a spaceship.

Further, from a design point of view, one may suppose that the reproductive process is the basic key to improvement in a changing environment in contrast to any alternate plan for a "one-time" static situation where no improvement or potential would have been possible as mentioned. The story of organic evolution evinces of itself a drive for an increase in quality and not so much in quantity. Teilhard de Chardin made a similar point when he said: "The rejuvenations made possible by each reproduction achieve something more than mere substitution and diversification."[12] The development of complexity in living systems, according to Shklovskii and Sagan, "is intimately connected with their self-replication."[13] Here is a possible aspect of "chance" that might be "directed chance" in the manner of expression of Teilhard. In a way, organic evolution appears to have followed a course of preparation over time to achieve certain end results in much the same manner as that which is evidenced in the progressive story of inanimate evolution.

The change in the initial life productive environment to that which was not initially productive of life is of itself suggestive of a designed control mechanism that gave meaning to biological evolution and accounts for the production of higher forms of life of a purposeful and functional nature. We have already seen, as in Chapter 6, that the epochal environmental changes were purposeful in the overall design aspects of the Earth in preparation for the development of higher life, especially man. Environmental change has resulted in improved forms of life to arise, as well, each at a higher level of organization than before, instead of an overall retrogresive decline in organization and improvement. This is, at least, the end product of it all. We can begin to see wherein and in what areas of biological evolution both design

184

and chance (with chance limited within a range of tolerance to be discussed later) have operated together to prepare the way for the greater suitability of living organisms. But the chance aspect, as limited, in no way diminished the fundamental framework of design. Processes of evolution, as mentioned, have only assisted in carrying forward the antecedent requirements for what may be seen as an intelligently designed creation.

The life cycle appears to be inextricably interwoven with the provision for reproduction in a sense of design. It would seem that the mechanism of self-replication was born of necessity with a clear telephatic view of life-spans of limited time duration rather than, as in most non-life aggregations, a duration of some degree of permanency. The recurrent life cycle, being logically complementary to reproduction, is an ideal solution to the building process toward purposeful and suitable end goals in living things. Assuming a manner of construction from the smallest units to the larger aggregations of living matter on which to build over a period of time, the limited life cycles have facilitated the potential for diversity and variety in living things. It has brought forth endless opportunities for forward progression at a rather rapid pace toward an improvement in quality and more highly organized and purposeful end results. It reflects a futuristic intent of getting on to more purposive ends without, at the same time, denying purpose in the short term. Each step (each life cycle) contributes in some almost imperceptible manner to the next step. It has brought about the harmony and the inter-relationships that exist among living things, and between living things and the environment. The success is exemplified in the fact that life has survived epochal change. Not only this, but it has brought about a perfectly intelligible situation whereby each living specie has achieved some particular function that shows purposefulness in an overall context.

In man, the course of a single life cycle permits a full unfolding of learning and productivity in conjunction with an interplay of free will—a full purposive life—that contributes to both the present and to successive human beings yet to

185

come into existence. The life cycle of man, therefore, may be seen as playing a dual role of participation in the present that shows an aspect of completion in all respects and, at the same time, bears a participatory relational aspect to the future. Other living things have a clearly lesser role to play and yet fulfill purposeful objectives on their own. In the animal kingdom, for instance, the purpose of many animals seems primarily to carry out some particular limited function and to reproduce in kind. Today, it is evident that man has obtained effective control and dominion over other life forms. This would seem to show a remarkable plan for the emergence of one dominant being that alone possessed the capability of giving directiveness to the whole of living things rather than, as chance would have it, being a diffused aspect of control and direction. The uniqueness of man and his breadth of mind and consciousness makes him an isolated exception from other forms of life. This is of itself strong evidence of intended design. If chance had dictated events, one could easily visualize other types of living forms that would have reached the level of human progress and achievement out of the more than one million animal species known to presently exist.

It is because evolutionary processes have been at work in a manner that has modified and diversified living things that, for one thing, the materialists of today rule out the concept of a designed and purposeful universe. Monod is a good example of this. It would seem, however, that one would expect a Designer, from any reasonable standpoint, to have made provision for living organisms to undergo physiological change as needed with respect to what may be seen as purposeful changing circumstances and, in addition, to permit the individuality that avoids the sterility of stereotyped carbon copies of beings.

Monod, in his book, clearly demonstrated the basic conservatism and rigidity of the chemical structure of the cell and the DNA molecule. He called attention to the fact that the present-day cell has been in existence for several billion years and is characterized by an invariant basic chemical organization with molecular control networks to assure a functional coherence which, in evolution, he said, has provided an "extraordinary stability" of certain specie.[14] The basic structural integrity of the genes was described by E. L. Tatum, of the Rockefeller Institute and a Nobel Prize winner, speaking to the National Academy of Sciences (1963), as follows: "The genes specify all the specie and the individual characteristics of every living organism. They determine the potentialities or limits of variability of these characters. Interaction of environment and organism can modify the expression of a character, but only within these gene-determined limits, and only as a consequence of mutation can new limits of variability be said to serve as raw ingredients for selection and evolution."[15]

One of the points made by the materialists, notwithstanding the rigid structural standard of the genetic code and the translation mechanism in the DNA molecule, is that the sequence of the base pairs of the DNA double helix is non-repetitive. Monod, for example, said: ". . . it should be underscored that the sequence is entirely 'free,' inasmuch as no restriction is imposed upon it by the overall structure, which can accommodate all possible sequences."[16] This so-called freedom of chance variation, as by mutations, on the hereditary code of life brought the further comment from Monod: ". . . since they constitute the *only* possible source of modifications in the genetic text, itself the sole repository of the organism's hereditary structures, it necessarily follows that chance *alone* is at the source of every innovation, of all creation in the biosphere."[17]

Yet, the discovery of Pieczenik, as mentioned, is evidence of a sort of built-in self-determination at the level of the genes in DNA that serves to negate the carefree assertions of Monod that a wide-open game of roulette is taking place in the occurrence of creative innovation in living things. And, as mentioned in the introductory chapter, and as evidenced elsewhere throughout this book, the meaningful end-results of the activity of the atoms as reflected well up the ladder of both inanimate and animate evolution are much too perfectly linked, fit, and suitable, to allow for the kind of free-ranging concept at the level of DNA as expressed by Monod.

In still other ways, the view of Monod has been strongly criticized. In reference to Monod's book and comment as above noted, for instance, Hardy was critical of his thought that the chance variations of the DNA code really govern evolution. It is a fallacy, he said, "to suppose that they controlled the course of its direction. It is *selection* that *guides* the process, and selection is far from random."[18] His point is significant here in that it shows that the course of direction in evolution is basically not random but selectively guided by external environmental factors, including behavioral selection in his view and in that of a growing number of biologists, which act on the "endless range of variation" provided by the "remarkable shuffling processes" brought about by "apparently" random DNA mutations, and the chance interplay and re-combinations of the genes.[19] It should also be noted, as by Pantin, that the rigid limitation of the properties of matter demand that only a limited number of classes of chemical machinery may exist, and it must be said that the concept of randomness does not involve by any means the freedom to make anything possible. Then too, as indicated previously, the genes determine the potentialities or limits of variability of these characters even though from time to time subject to mutation or recombination. The basic job of the genes of DNA—in carrying out their function, according to C. H. Waddington, "is to remain as stable as possible, with as little change as may be, while they are passed on from cell to cell, or from individual to individual, through many generations."[20]

In terms of design, one of the amazing things to consider is that despite all evolutionary changes in the form, shape, etc. of living organisms, the structural integrity of DNA has remained essentially unchanged. For all the continuous chemical activity in the evolutionary stream of life it is remarkable, said Hardy, "that there is little or no essential difference in the general form of the DNA molecules at different stages in their long evolutionary history from the lowest organisms to man; it is only in the details of their coding arrangements that are different. Even in bacteria the system is essentially the same."[21] In further reference to the recent discovery of George Pieczenik, it was found that there are certain constraints in the way in which the genetic message in DNA is arranged. According to Pieczenik, the DNA sequences seem to exist to protect themselves and their coded information from recoding.[22]

Pollard sees the expression of great design in the creativity of evolution that is highly manifest "in the way in which DNA codes thread their way through such a manifold maze of chance and accident."[23] He said that the means by which living systems store and transmit the information required for writing the "language of life" is "a very ingenious coding system using four coding symbols which is remarkably like the punched tapes used to give instructions to a modern electronic computer."[24] The important point that is missed by the materialists is the fact of the remarkable end-results that have come about in consequence of the preservation of a structural standard and the permissiveness to change which is a significant feature thereof. "This," said Pollard, "would in no way *explain* except by way of saying that an incredible number of chances capitalizing on a continuously varying environment not casually related to them, has in fact accomplished so remarkable a result."[25]

It is perplexing that the materialists have failed to find a purposeful aspect—an overall picture of design—in consequence of the activity of evolutionary processes. This, in relation to the needs of diversification and variability in the natural world of living things in the manner considered herein. The significance of this lies in the fact that the mechanisms and processes of evolution permit change, survival, and the development of living things while, at the same time, retaining the basic structural organization. This is a remarkable complement to the design aspects of self-replication, life-span, etc. that, of themselves, appear to represent the best solution to an overall general plan of a designed world. As Pollard pointed out, there is no reason to suppose that a Designer of the universe would not work "within the chances and accidents which provide nature with her indeterminism and her freedom."[26] "Nor can it be expected," he said, "that a Designer would have desired to create puppets which would have stifled any concept of meaning and purpose in consequence of the creation."[27]

The processes and mechanisms we have been considering would appear to have been constructed in general with a view toward permitting a certain freedom and ability to undergo change (throughout the span of time that the Earth itself has undergone great change) and thereby permitted living things to mold themselves, so to speak, to differing environmental circumstances and conditions and, at the same time, to evolve into highly purposeful and functioning entities that are in evidence today.

That there had to be an initial source of the hereditary information in the DNA molecule is considered a major unsolved problem in biology today. An important thing to remember, in this connection, is that selection did not take hold and commence to operate until after this phenomenon first occurred. As to the origin of life itself, there are few who do not recognize the emergence of life as a "by-product of the chemical elements of which it is composed."[28] But is it reasonable to ascribe the ultimate source of life or the informational code in DNA to the primordial soup? The answer is extremely important. We must turn again in amazement to the atoms and the latent potential capacity they have shown to create fit and suitable properties throughout nature that strongly suggests pre-conceived knowledge and design.

From our discussion in the preceding chapter, is it possible that the atoms fall into structural patterns in response to conscious activation? If this is a phenomenon that may give an aspect of guidance in the evolution of living things, does it not also suggest a conscious direction has been involved with respect to atomic activity in still broader aspects to include atomic inanimate activity as well? The two aspects of nature, as we have seen, are much too inter-related to find direction in one but not in the other; that is conscious direction. That they both depend on the same ingredients and the source of direction in non-life, as well as in life, may best be attributed to "outside" help if conscious activation has anything to do with it. In a way, the discussion of inanimate and animate nature in the next chapter will give some cohesion to these views.

# 12

## The Chemistry of Design

The current controversy on the part of many in science that biology should be reduced to physics and chemistry, according to Michael A. Simon in his book "The Matter of Life," centers around the question of whether the living organism is "an arrangement of chemical substances organized and interacting according to the same principles as applied to inanimate matter, or whether it is in some sense an entity 'over and above' the aggregation of matter of which it is composed."[1] Quite possibly, the controversy as stated may be beyond an easy solution if it should turn out that both parts of the question are answerable in the affirmative. At any rate, Simon went on to raise the question as to the uncertainty of the origin of organisms and whether such origin is significant throughout, e.g. is there "a necessary connection to anything in the microcosmic level."[2] As part of this, he raised the related question whether operations in entities of a higher level may be accounted for by laws governing a microlevel.[3] These questions point up the close intimacy between inanimate and animate matter and the uncertainty that exists with respect to the issue of a dividing line between the two aspects of nature.

There are, to be sure, a number of similarities, as well as dissimilarities, that are presently recognizable between inanimate and animate nature. Perhaps, in briefly considering some of them here, we will gain a better insight into the empirical problem raised above and its relevance to the question of chance or design. As mentioned in Chapter 5, living substance is the product of only a small portion of the whole of the available atomic elements that are also found in inanimate substances, yet both living and non-living things hold certain kinds of atomic elements in common in their make-up.

As noted by Pantin, some complex inanimate systems show many of the features we associate with living things.[4] For one thing, the interrelationship between living things and purely chemical things is underscored by developments in biochemistry showing the nature of viruses and colloids that tend to narrow the gap between the two worlds of nature.[5] Hein noted that recent successes in synthesizing DNA, and even viruses from artificially synthesized change of DNA, give additional support to the thesis of the continuity of the inanimate and the animate, saying: "Indeed we have seen how difficult it is to designate a fixed point which divides the living from the non-living. The unit of life itself is a matter of dispute."[6] Then too, there are phenomena in inanimate matter which nearly duplicate certain qualities of animate matter. One of the examples cited by Hein is that one of the chief characteristics of living things, dissymmetry of the carbon compounds, may be explained as having a non-biological origin. Our two hands have identical five fingers which are mirror images of one another and are not superimposable. Hein noted that this dissymmetry occurs in carbon compounds "when a molecule may take two forms which are identical in terms of the atoms and groupings of atoms which it contains, but when the atoms are differently disposed in space. . . ."[7] On the same subject, Bronowski said that we still do not know why life has this strange chemical property and it follows "that we must be able to link evolution with chemistry," noting that this was one of the obsessions of Louis Pasteur in whose time it was known that some crystals are so arranged that there are right-hand versions and left-hand versions.[8] As another example, the power of self-replication and growth is to be found in living things as well as in crystals, even though these powers are expressed differently and are far more limited in crystals than on the animate side of things.

A recent and interesting discovery was reported several

years ago by Dr. Cyril Ponnamperuma, the Director of the Laboratory of Chemical Evolution of the University of Maryland. In the process of trying to re-create some molecules that may have led to life, researchers at the Laboratory made the unexpected discovery of what appeared to be a chemical metabolic pathway in existence before the beginning of life. They produced what appeared to be a chemical sequence of acids used by practically all organisms in the process of respiration. Dr. Ponnamperuma, according to one account, postulated that when life began it possibly did not invent the compounds which were involved in a sequencive reaction used by living things in the respiration process, but that the sequences were already existing chemically or, in other words, "life today may be a recapitulation of pre-life chemically speaking."[9] If this be so as concerns certain life processes, will other yet unexplained life phenomena be traceable someday back to a chemical pathway at the atomic level of things? Mention has already been made of the thoughts expressed by some highly respected scientists that mind and consciousness, in rudimentary form at least, may be re-traceable to the atomic level. This, of course, is a speculative matter and not likely representative of a prevailing view. What about the first coded information for the DNA molecule? One cannot help but be mindful that present explanations in the biological sciences for the origin of such phenomenon are also speculative and uncertain.

On the side of dissimilarity of animate to inanimate substance, Pantin called attention to the fact that living things run contrary to the entropy principle of the second law of thermodynamics.[10] Further, he noted the breadth of the reproductive processes in living things with respect to which the element carbon plays a predominant role; that what animated living organisms do is quite different from what happens to inanimate material; that parts of organisms are functional and exhibit organization at many levels simultaneously (such as in cells, organisms, colonies, etc.); and that the material substances of the two are different, as, for example, the complex chemical substance of the DNA molecule.[11] To this, of course, could be added a large number of other highly unique qualities found in life, as previously mentioned. In man, this would surely include, among other things, mind and consciousness, original thought, expression of values, etc.

The foregoing discussion reflects the distinct nature of "life" as something separate and apart from its atomic composition and, at the same time, shows the importance of that composition (at least) to the organization and structure of life. The similarities may well suggest that the design blueprint for life pre-existed in the make-up of the atoms, either in terms of their potential for meaningful patterned architecture, or in their substance, or both. The dissimilarities, on the other hand, would appear to support the views so well expressed by Edwin Schrödinger, in his previously mentioned and remarkable book "What is Life," that life is of a different and independent essence from its atomic constituency.[12]

The view in modern biology of the role played by elemental inanimate matter in the origin of life was expressed by Ledyard G. Stebbins in his book "Processes of Organic Evolution" as follows: ". . . the properties of life depend only to a small degree on the substances of which living matter is composed. To a much greater degree living things owe their nature to the way in which the components are organized into orderly patterns, which are far more permanent than the substances themselves."[13] This no doubt expresses a conservative view based on a lack of any specific knowledge to the contrary. It is a view which suggests that the life-originating process was not of such a nature that life would have emerged necessarily from special properties inherent in elemental inanimate matter, but rather stresses the architectural arrangement or ordered patterns in which they are organized. In his description of the mechanisms of the DNA molecule, Monod said that the "architectural plan" for pre-formed and complete structure of the living cell "was present in its very constituents."[14] However, he expressed the materialistic viewpoint that the structure did not pre-exist anywhere and must have come into being spontaneously and autonomously, without outside help and without the injection of additional information."[15] This is another way of saying that the atomic architectural arrangement or pattern that resulted in the structure of the living cell, while put together from certain elements of the atoms, was purely haphazard and random—although recognizing that, when so put together, did produce the structure of the living cell because the contributing atoms arranged themselves in a proper architecture.

In an intelligently designed universe, in the context herein, a Designer would have been the responsible agency for the whole of living and non-living matter, both being instrumentalities of a creation which implies the make-up of different things for different purposes and with life, mind and consciousness, as a subsequent occurrence, to give meaning and purpose to it all. The occasion of the origin of physicochemical substances and of their fully complementary laws, containing the inherent capacity for the origin of life at a later stage, may be seen as of no less importance from a construction standpoint than the events to transpire at a later stage. In accordance with such a view, no conflict is to be seen with respect to increasing evidence that tends to narrow the distinction between the living and non-living worlds of nature. The continuity and linkage between the two are of the same creative process. Any thought of the necessity of maintaining a clear distinction at the interface between the two aspects of nature in support of a special creation is superficial in this context. Even though it may well have been the case, there is no need for the infusion of a special life-giving principle for the first time at the interface between the two worlds, as in the thinking of the so-called vitalists. As in the view of Teilhard de Chardin in his book "The Phenomenon of Man,"[16] life was "incipient" in the very ingredients. It simply raises a question of the means and manner of the creation and nothing else. It does not detract from the event of the actual fruition of first life on Earth as a new essence at a later point of time as something very special—a culmination of earlier creative processes. A division of labor, so to speak, in terms of design and creation. Although there are definite distinctions between the living and non-living, it would seem that these are of kind

196

and, while living organisms are in fact far more complex and intricate in their structural configuration and substance, it is clear that they are designed to carry out different unique purposes and functions, strongly implying an overall scheme of things.

This view is not, as some might think, the simple reduction in importance of the characteristic features of living things to the lifeless characteristics of inanimate chemical substance. That is the materialistic view. The dispute with the materialists is a simple one. Take the DNA molecule for instance. It has no equivalent to anything we know of at present in the universe. Certainly, the atoms had the latent potential capacity from the beginning to give this result, but were the atoms so designed as to intentionally achieve the result, or did the result occur in consequence of purely random occurrences? The materialists give little thought to the source of the "architectural plan" referred to by Monod. That part of it is simply physics and chemistry. In such a view, the elements of the atoms that are involved in life processes are seen in an entirely different context than is appropriate to the view of a designed creation.

One of the problems with the materialistic view is that the chemical elements are looked upon as representative of "ends" in whatever state they may be found at the time with no attribute of necessary consequence yet to come; that is, they are not to be seen as the necessary "means" to bring about something quite different in essence. Looking backward in time before first life, the materialists would say that nothing required the relevant atoms involved in life processes to be productive of life even though looking at things, after the fact, the materialists would surely say that the relevant atoms were necessary means to the end results of life. There is a very narrow distinction here and one that is crucial. It marks the difference between chance and design. Such a view defies the fact that different kinds of properties do in fact emerge throughout nature from constituent elemental components that bear no resemblence to such properties. As in the case of phenomena we have considered in earlier chapters, elemental matter is simply the "means" to produce end results that interrelate with life in general and to man in particular. While further investigations of science may, or may not, provide more fundamental clues to the mysteries of the method of the atomic means, the ends, as products of the means, are in no event to be ignored as related to the question of chance or design. The few kinds of basic atomic elements had to have more than what Monod attributed simply to autonomy. They had to have, as well, the necessary selectivity and the goal-seeking potential for the properties of both living and non-living matter which are not only compatible with one another but also with respect to end results. This, in order to achieve the remarkable ends that are everywhere evident, and with the interconnecting harmonies as we have seen. Clearly, atomic composition has carried out specific assignments as to which meaning and purpose is to be found in the manner previously mentioned. The more we have seen how both inanimate and animate matter have come together on a broad scale in terms of perfect fitness, suitability, unity, and the like, the more we must attribute this to an external agency that planned, designed, and executed the entire project through the medium of special qualities intentionally imparted to elemental matter and its associated natural forces and laws. The end results may be seen as furnishing to us the best evidence as against materialistic dogma. It simply does not make sense to say that all of the elements that guided inanimate nature into a harmonious relationship with animate nature would not have played a necessary and active role in the development of life processes as well. Exactly how this may have come about is conjectural at present. Whether by reason of a compatibility or power built into the atoms and their compositions that either are activated and coordinated externally, or internally, or both, we do not know. Whether or not a greater understanding of the mysterious particles in the nuclei of the atoms will shed some new light on this in the future is, of course, an unknown quantity. As indicated in Chapter 5, it does give one reason to pause and to question whether the bewildering new "zoo" of elementary particles may somehow have a more important role to play in the construction of matter in the universe than is presently attributed to them.

It would seem that the more we move back into the atomic level of things in order to account for the occurrence of certain basic features that are characteristic of both inanimate and animate phenomena, the stronger becomes the appeal to a designed universe, and the more remote and extreme the appeal to random chance. The materialistic view feeds upon the element of time to make "anything" possible. The view requires eons of time on which to lean upon and, even then, the advance predictive possibility alone of achieving a DNA molecule was "next to nothing." As we have seen, that is only one of countless remarkable achievements in the overall picture, even though perhaps the more impressive from our point of view. It does not seem right to say that the basic atomic elements as are involved in both non-living and living systems and substances could have possessed at random from the early time of the origin of these atoms in our universe (16 to 20 billions of years ago) the latent potential capacity for the end results in evidence. That is, without at the same time giving recognition to greatly reduced, if not essentially the elimination of, opportunities for random chance and the further enhancement of the view of an intelligence which created elemental matter in a purposeful manner and with a clear view of an intended objective. Indeed science today, to the extent it narrows the gap between the inanimate and animate worlds of nature and attributes more and more to the atomic level of things as a responsible agency in life processes, only strengthens this view and furthers the recognition that both worlds of nature have been guided or directed to compatible and interlocked ends. Then again, when we add to the picture the principle of emerging properties that is shown to operate in both living and non-living matter, as considered in an earlier chapter, the harmonious manner of the construction medium is exposed in a way that defies the idea of chance and, at the

199

same time, displays a remarkable advance knowledge and intent in the creation. For one to know that the plan for self-replication, coded heredity information with respect to the first DNA molecule, specie differentiation, the will to live (rather than the will not to live), goal-seeking and achievement, and even possibly mind and consciousness, was present in the very constituents of elemental matter is a strong indictment of the materialistic view.

# 13

## Conclusion

From the time of the discovery by Copernicus that the Earth is not central to its solar system, but rather that the Earth in fact revolves around the Sun as other planetary objects, there have been many who have described man as forever destined to relative insignificance and said that his belief in a supernatural is myth and superstition. Quite often in current literature one sees man described as an unimportant creature inhabiting a rather small planet revolving around a minor Sun on the outer fringe of an ordinary galaxy.

In matter of fact, however, from a vantage point on a planet that seems to be just as good as any other, man's mind and consciousness, like the mysterious essence of light and the force of gravity, now penetrates to great depths in the vastness of space even to the edge of the universe. The significance formerly attached to the Earth before Copernicus should be deemed superseded by a realization that man is the central and significant feature of his solar system (and perhaps well beyond). He appears to hold the present or potential ability to exercise effective dominion and control over the whole of it. A fair exchange of real meaning and significance for an ancient view of relative unimportance. Such an accomplishment did not come about by virtue of any concatenation of illusions or by distorted views of reality, but rather in consequence of a concrete conjunctiveness of countless fit and suitable antecedent conditions in an interplay with the mind of man.

To say that the mind and consciousness of man is simply

the by-product of a purely accidentally evolved physico-chemical central nervous system, rather than as an intended event in a cosmic scheme of things, is to disregard much of that which we have considered throughout many of the chapters in this book which bears no mechanistic relationship to such a system.

From the original primeval fireball as a point of "beginning," it would seem that matter and energy, together with universal laws, were set in motion as a deliberate act to produce the goal-seeking phenomena as necessary to attain life-related significance and, in particular, a very special significance to mind and consciousness as exemplified in man. This, I submit, is the empirical record before us that may not be ignored.

The fact that the end-results of the phenomena of the natural world, both inanimate and animate, have realistically combined in a most meaningful way with man alone shows a regularity and invariance aspect which reminds one of the criteria engaged in successful scientific inquiry that leads to the establishment of well-accepted theories. The scientist, noted Eric C. Rust, "is concerned with what things of the same kind and events of the same type have in common. He looks for universal characters and relations."[1] In this manner, we have covered in this work (quite comprehensively) the relationship of cosmic (including inanimate) phenomena to living systems which, in all their remarkable multiplicity, diversity, and variety, go the "extra distance" to be quite perfectly relevant, appropriate, and suitable for the particular usages and purposes of mankind, presently and prospectively. The essentials for the whole of these relevant and suitable phenomena are not limited to the Earth and man as we have seen, but are available in one form or another throughout the universe wherever they may conveniently coincide with mind and consciousness. The one thing that the components of nature have in common with one another (quite invariably and regularly), as well as in respect to end-results, is the means to further an on-going and endless stream of mental and creative activities. This, to say nothing of their actual or potential role for the existence and general support of life processes.

This was not so much in evidence in the past as it is today in consequence of our far greater understanding of the natural world.

If we view the invariant aspect of man's relationship to the phenomena of nature to be only one empirical approach to the proof of intelligent design, how then are we to relate this to still other differing kinds of empirical approaches that, as have been seen, carry the same consistent conviction to design? Certainly the analogy and general "fitness" approaches are themselves to be seen today in a much broader context. It is when we appreciate that the triad of these somewhat distinctive approaches each converge in support of design, rather than of chance, that the reliability quotient in terms of proof is to be found oriented in the experience of the methods of science itself. This, in the manner described in Chapter 3. To those whom I have convinced that the whole of the presently known phenomena of nature may be seen to infer design, rather than chance, the need of course for such a triangulation of proofs may seem quite superfluous. But those who are not so convinced may find it difficult to deny the compelling logic that finds support in the "effect to cause" methods found to be highly reliable in scientific investigations.

The evidence to show design is no longer subject to fair criticism on the idea that we do not know what other worlds are like as a point of comparison. We appear to have passed beyond prior limitations in knowledge that dimmed our perspective (as we have considered) on the nature and make-up of our universe and its countless, yet restricted, opportunities for similarity in formulation and design. It has been a broad increase in knowledge of cosmic and inanimate nature that has led the way to our better understanding of design from non-design, both in the Earth environment and beyond. At the same time, this has contributed immensely to our understanding of design on the animate side of nature. It is again submitted that discovery, as manifested in end-results, has increasingly pointed in one direction alone to show not only countless new inferences to intelligent design but also a continual erosion of what formerly was claimed to show the contrary. There is no satisfactory explanation for this distinctively unilateral and progressive trend. As we move on from one new discovery to the next, we may expect the same pattern if for no other reason than the fact that this is what the past has always shown to be the case (as demonstrated herein).

But is the foregoing simply one view among many possible diverse views on the nature of things? For example, an essay by Fred Hoyle entitled "Ten Faces of the Universe" explains that the way we look at the universe depends on our individual perception of our place in it. Included among Hoyle's list of views are those of the Physicist's Universe, the Mathematicians's Universe, the Biologist's Universe, Everyman's Universe, God's Universe, etc.[2]

As indicated in the beginning of this work, none other than two possible views of the universe are involved here in an ultimate sense, i.e. the conflicting views of unintended chance or intended design as the cause of the origin of things. There is no other alternative. It is in relation to these that we must take our final measure of the question. In the process, however, we have examined the relevant phenomena of nature from many different-sided aspects in a cross-section of scientific fields of endeavor. Even though individual perceptions may well differ with respect to the individual phenomenon we have considered, what could be more reliable to us than the views included herein that have been reasonably based on observations derived in no small degree from different fields of science?

In this, I return to make the point that, while absolute certainty lies beyond our "empirical" reach on this subject, on the basis of strict principles of logic, we have come close indeed to such near-certainty that it should not really matter. This may be said, I feel, even without availing one's self of scriptural texts, religious experience, or ontological and cosmological arguments that appeal to logic and pure reason. For the more presumptions to design inherent in this approach which are based on reliable and high quality observation of an undeviating nature, the less likely and more highly improbable the chances of error. The idea of a chance creation, rather than being viewed as a "possibility" or (by those of the materialistic view) as a "probability," is caught up in a complicated web of design that leaves no room for any real credibility. The record shown here favoring an intelligently designed creation, notwithstanding weaknesses that may be implicit in one's subjective thinking, is much too deeply-rooted in broad-based empirical knowledge having objective foundations than to be simply passed on as the more reasonable view.

The view of the philosopher Immanuel Kant was that the order we behold in nature is all mind-dependent and based on our varying experiences. Thomas McPherson, the contemporary British philosopher, analyzed Kant's argument on this to say that it does not constitute a serious objection to the view of an ordered and designed world.[3] This, even though some people, he noted, see things differently than others with different cultures, observations, illusions, variations, etc. While it does not help the view of design, one of the stronger responses to Kant is to say (according to McPherson): "It is true that we bring concepts to our experience of the world, but we also acquire them from our experience of the world; there is a kind of two-way traffic here."[4] It is a matter of how the "notion of order" is to be understood—not that order is not really present or absent to be understood.[5]

The notion of order and design we have considered in the many facets as presented in this work fully bears out a "two-way traffic" between the mind of man and his physical surroundings. Nature, as noted in Chapters 1 and 7, had to be reciprocally and intrinsically in harmony with man's mental activities in the first place for man to be creative with respect to his surrounding in the manner mentioned in Chapter 7. This is to say nothing of all the remarkable cosmic (and inanimate) phenomena described in Chapters 4 through 6, as well as in Chapter 8, that made it all possible in the absence of man.

The general approach taken in this work has been to present a step-by-step overview of the major and most critical events that, so far as we know, have occurred from the origin of our universe down to the present. This has included, insofar as practical, a consideration of the end-results of the whole of the major known phenomena of nature, and if perchance there are omissions to be noted they are the consequence of inadvertence rather than of intention. In the end, irrespective of unknowns as to certain aspects, a broadly based and coherent picture overwhelmingly supports the premise that the view of design is the only one of the two views that human reason, common sense, and intuition may adopt. This is not to suggest that our reasoning processes and senses are infallible but, as correctly pointed out by Richard Taylor, we do in fact rely on them. "We assume," he said, "rightly or wrongly, that they are trustworthy guides with respect to what is true, and what exists independently of our senses and their origin; and we still assume this, even when they are our only guides."[6] In addition, if we allow ourselves to be governed by strong trends, we may well presume that the view of design will continue increasingly to be revealed in the context and manner as presented.

This work's basic objective has been to follow the pathway of empirically-based observation in support of a designed universe rather than to emphasize the writer's personal views on meaning and purpose. The view of the biblical God enters the picture, however, by force of the inventory of natural phenomena that has been described. Quite obviously, certain preconditions and requirements had to be met in order for this universe and the things within it to have come about in the first place. From observation, it would seem clear that a single thread runs throughout (in relation to the common objective as mentioned) in the parts at least with which we are knowledgeable, and without signs of conflicting or disunited purposes. The phenomena we have considered thus exhibit a remarkable uniformity in constituency of substance and law, and an inter-connectedness which does not suggest that multiple causative entities are behind ultimate events in the universe. The phenomenal means-to-ends relationships that are everywhere evident are related to both the parts and the whole and suggestive of a creative power of great foresight that had to know, in the previously quoted words of J. N. Shearman, "how to make a present arrangement of things with a view toward the future . . . the end result had to be foreseen in order to bring . . . (it) . . . about and an intelligence . . . (that) . . . directed them so as to produce the orderly arrangement of parts which . . . (is) . . . observed to exist."[7] It would seem quite clear that one is required to step outside of the material existence of "natural" things in our known universe to seek out an antecedent and pre-existing intelligence. Otherwise, one has to unreasonably account for the origin and remarkable creative power of material substance on its own. As Tennant indicated, the dice had to be loaded from the start if one were to reasonably attribute these results to chance—a sort of "un-random" chance.

Even the atoms, with their acknowledged latent potential capacity from the beginning to produce the marvels of the universe, are not at all the entire story of the creation, as we have seen. The properties of elemental things do not alone account for a great deal of other phenomena, some of which are not even casually related to one another. The manner in which the construction process has evolved strongly infers the existence of an external coordinating essence that harmonized the multiplicity of various activities and channeled them into meaningful, fit and purposive end results. It has no appeal to say that some internal natural life force, within the substance of things, could bring about such inter-related meaning and coordination. It does appeal, however, that the Designer of our universe is vested with such an awesomess of power, knowledge, and intellect that it would seem remiss to deny the attributes ascribed to the biblical God. This is especially so when we take into mind that the biblical account of Genesis fits quite comfortably into the sequential occurrence of events that have been reviewed herein. In this regard, too, it would seem reasonable that a Designer would have made known through revelations to man a code of conduct to accompany the freedom of choice in relation to a moral order. Indeed, such a code was presented to man through Moses and refined in meaning and interpreted in the life of Christ.

There are many today who express difficulty with the view

of a designed universe because of the absence of a physical or more demonstrative presence of the essence of God. I believe both F. R. Tennant and Martin J. Heinecken set forth reasonable explanations that could account for this, that is, in a way that makes sense in relation to the views put forward earlier in Chapters 8 and 9. First of all, in the view of Tennant, we have to accept that the best designed world for the human being is one that involves a moral order rather than an unburdened one of pure happiness. The fact that man is endowed with a plastic personal freedom of choice is itself indicative that the former is the one chosen for our earthly purposes. According to Tennant: "The best world, then, must include free agents, creatures that are in turn 'creators' in the sense that their 'utterances' are not God's positings but their own."[8]

In such a world of devolved freedom, it would seem self-defeating if man's quest for the highest were not to be his own. Said Tennant: "God must not be too certainly knowable to us, as well as not too active on us. Otherwise, . . . over-abundance of light would preclude that 'groping after God,' which is the obverse of revelation to a developing and free agent such as man."[9]

In Heinecken's view, only absolute power can give freedom and not thereby limit itself or lose sovereignty.[10] Heinecken made the following quotation from Kierkegaard to make his own point which carries somewhat of an implication that man's independence should remain inviolate:

> Creation out of nothing is once again the expression of omnipotence for being able to make things independent. It is to him who made me independent, while he nevertheless retained everything, that I owe all things. If in order to create man God had lost any of his power, then he could not have made man independent.[11]

Is the choice of good over evil, therefore, an intended ideal to which man must aspire? Certainly, it is to him an attribute of personal free will. As indicated in Chapter 8, we have every reason to expect that, wherever intelligent life may be found throughout the universe, there would exist the freedom of thought and expression in some form or another that would likely relate to the same moral values of good and evil. If this be so, is it not suggestive of a goal and purpose, or at least an end-result to be achieved wherever intelligent beings are found to exist? As we have seen, good and evil are associated with mind and consciousness—an apparent "imperfection" of evil in a world that otherwise shows the highest degree of perfection. The matter of evil and its consequences stand out uniquely in man, his mind and consciousness, and the fact that it does so within the framework of a remarkably designed world in other respects implies a special meaning and significance. As previously noted, we may see here a basis for trial, error, and accountability in a choice between good and evil. We should not presume, therefore, that these characteristics are not of themselves the hallmarks of design and ultimate purpose. In a way, evil may not be a "problem" but rather a consequence of personal freedom, itself purposeful.

It has been a chief aim of this book to show that we dwell within a universal labyrinth of design far too bewildering to attribute to chance. The means of achieving the presently discernable end-results were much too well-ordered from the "beginning" to ascribe events to anything other than a pre-conceived and singularly executed plan. A plan under which the power to control and coordinate the elements and forces pre-existed to later extend into the perfectly precise and intricately harmonized arrangements as are found in nature. A truly professional undertaking that gives no hint of either amateurism or that of an indistinct natural guiding force caught up in the middle of it all. It is most reasonable to assume that the value qualities of life were also made to order. As we have seen, the discoveries of man have unerringly unfolded an ever-enlarging panorama of the design of things. While this, on its own, may not reveal the final purpose of creation, it is perfectly reasonable to expect the trend of discovery will continue until, sooner or later, even the most unthinking of men throughout the world will come to realize the importance of choosing those noble qualities which spring from a challenge of the higher and beyond.

# Bibliography

## CHAPTER ONE

1. McPherson, Thomas. *The Argument from Design.* N. Y. and London: The MacMillan Press Ltd., 1972, Chap. 6, p. 64.
2. Taylor, A. E. *Does God Exist?* London and N. Y.: MacMillan, 1945, p. 101.
3. Hurlbutt, Robert H., III. *Hume, Newton, and the Design Argument.* Lincoln, Nebraska: University of Nebraska Press, 1965, pp. 151-153.
4. Tennant, F. R. *Philosophical Theology,* Vol. II, Chap. 4. Cambridge University Press, 1928 and 1930 (reprinted in 1968), p. 79. Used with publisher's permission.
5. Hein, Hilde S. *On the Nature and Origin of Life.* © 1971 by Hilde S. Hein. N. Y.: McGraw-Hill Book Company, 1971, p. 59 (The History of Science Series; ed. Daniel A. Greenberg). Excerpts herein used with permission of the publisher.
6. Kapp, Reginald O. *Facts and Faith—The Dual Nature of Reality.* London: Oxford University Press, 1955.
7. Pollard, William G. *Chance and Providence*: *God's Action in a World Governed by Scientific Law.* N. Y.: Charles Scribner Sons, 1958, pp. 55, 60. See also by the same author: *Man on a Spaceship.* Claremont, California: Publication by Claremont Graduate School and University Center for the Claremont Colleges, 1967, pp. 50-51. Excerpts herein are used with permission of the author.
8. Eddington, A. S. "Decline of Determinism," *The Mathematical Gazette,* Vol. 16, No. 218, as reprinted in the 1932 Annual Report of the Board of Regents of the Smithsonian Institution, Wash., D. C., pp. 143-144.
9. Jeans, Sir James. *The Mysterious Universe.* New York: The MacMillan Co., New Rev. Ed., 1931, p. 33.

10. Rust, Eric C. *Science and Faith*. New York: Oxford University Press, 1967, pp. 171-172.
11. Reprinted with permission from *Collier's Encyclopedia*. N. Y.: P. F. Collier & Son Corp. © 1957, Vol. 18, pp. 143-144. "Spinoza, Baruch" by David Bidney.


## CHAPTER TWO

1. Monod, Jacques. *Chance and Necessity*. N. Y.: Alfred A. Knopf, Inc., 1971, p. 180 (London: Collins, 1971), trans. by Austryn Wainhouse. (Originally published in France as *Le Hasard et La Necessite* by editions du Seuil, Paris: 1970.)
2. Ibid., pp. 145-146.
3. Bronowski, J. *The Identity of Man*. Garden City, N. J.: The Natural History Press. American Museum of Science Books edition, 1966, p. 4.
4. Simpson, George G. *The Meaning of Evolution*. Yale University Press, 1949, p. 344.
5. Reid, Leslie. *Earth's Company*. London: John Murray, 1958, pp. 1-2.
6. Tennant, F. R. *Philosophical Theology*, Vol. II, Chap. 4 (reprinted in 1968). Cambridge University Press, 1928 and 1930, pp. 87-88.
7. Reprinted with permission from *Collier's Encyclopedia*, N.Y.: P. F. Collier & Son Corp., © 1957, Vol. 2, p. 475. "Atomism" by John W. Dowling.
8. Hick, John. *Arguments for the Existence of God*. London: McMillan and Co., Ltd., 1970, pp. 9-10. In N. Y.: Herder and Herder, 1971, p. 10. © John Hick, 1971.
9. Hein, Hilde S. *On the Nature and Origin of Life*, p. 92.
10. Asimov, Isaac. *Only a Trillion*. London and N. Y.: Abelard-Schuman, 1957, pp. 103-110. © 1957 Isaac Asimov. Used with permission of Harper & Row, Inc.
11. Du Noüy, Lecomte. *Human Destiny*. New York: Longman's Green, 1947.
12. Asimov, Isaac. *Only a Trillion,* p. 105.
13. Wigner, Eugene P. *The Unreasonable Effectiveness of Mathematics in the Natural Sciences*. Richard Courant Lecture in Mathematical Sciences delivered at New York University, May 11, 1959; reprinted therein by permission from "Communications in Pure and Applied Mathematics," Vol. 13,

No. 1, February, 1960, p. 227. Copyright by John Wiley and Sons, Inc. Used with permission of John Wiley and Sons, Inc.

14. Palade, George E. In an address to the National Academy of Science meeting in 1963.

15. Kapp, Reginald O. *Facts and Faith—The Dual Nature of Reality.* London: Oxford University Press, 1955.

16. Kant, Immanuel. *Critique of Pure Reason,* trans. N. Kemp Smith, Chapter III, Sec. 6. Quoted in Thomas McPherson's *The Argument from Design.* London: MacMillan, 1968; N. Y.: St. Martin's Press.

17. Calder, Nigel. *The Key to the Universe,* N. Y.: The Viking Press, 1977, p. 185.

18. Monod, Jacques. *Chance and Necessity,* p. 146.

19. Kierkegaard, Soren. *The Journals of Soren Kierkegaard,* Entry No. 616, p. 181, trans. by A. Dru; *Soren Kierkegaard's Philosophical Fragments.* Princeton: Princeton University Press, 1936; D. F. Swendon trans. N. Y.: Oxford University Press, 1951.

20. Kessel, Edward L., a contributed essay to *The Evidence of God in an Expanding Universe,* ed. John Clover Monsma. © 1958 John Clover Monsma. N. Y.: G. P. Putnam Sons, 1958, pp. 50-51 (Toronto: Longman's, Green, 1958). This and other excerpts from the book are used herein with permission of the publisher.

21. Mascall, Eric. *The Christian Universe.* U. S. A.: Morehouse-Barlow, 1966.

22. Davis, George Earl, a contributed essay to *The Evidence of God in an Expanding Universe,* ed. John Clover Monsma. N. Y.: G. P. Putnam Sons, 1958, p. 71.

23. Taylor, Richard. *Metaphysics.* Englewood Cliffs, N. J.: Prentice Hall, Inc., © 1963, pp. 102-119.

24. Baisneé, Jules A. *Readings in Natural Theology.* Westminster, Maryland: The Newman Press.

25. Hick, John. *Arguments for the Existence of God,* p. 11. See also: Hick, John. *Philosophy of Religion.* "The Design Argument," Appendix III, 2nd Ed. Englewood Cliffs, N. J.: Prentice Hall, Inc., 1970.

26. Reid, Leslie, *Earth's Company,* p. 2.

27. Tennant, F. R. *Philosophical Theology,* Vol. II, Chap. 4, p. 79.

28. Romer, Alfred S. *The Procession of Life*. London: Weidenfeld and Nicholson, 1968.

29. Rust, Eric C., an essay contributed to *Science and Religion,* ed. by John Clover Monsma. N. Y.: G. P. Putnam Sons, 1962, p. 106.

30. Nambu, Yoichiro. "The Confinement of Quarks." *Scientific American,* November, 1976, pp. 48-60.

31. Berry, Adrian. *The Next Ten Thousand Years: A Vision of Man's Future in the Universe*. London: Jonathan Cape Ltd., 1974. Coronet Books, Hodder and Stroughton, Coronet edition, 1976, p. 182. Also, published N. Y.: E. P. Dutton, 1974; in paperback: New American Library, 1975. © Adrian Berry 1975. Excerpts herein reprinted by permission of the author.

32. Calder, Nigel, *The Key to the Universe,* p. 11.

33. Davis, George Earl. An essay contributed to *The Evidence of God in an Expanding Universe,* ed. John Clover Monsma. N. Y.: G. P. Putnam Sons, 1958, p. 71 (Toronto: Longman's, Green, 1958).

## CHAPTER THREE

1. Ray, John. *The Wisdom of God Manifested in the Work of the Creation*. London: Printed for Samuel Smith, 1691.

2. Derham, William. *Physico-Theology* or, *A Demonstration of the Being and Attributes of God from His Works of Creation*. London and Dublin: Samuel Fairbrother, 1730.

3. Paley, William. *Natural Theology* (1802), abridged ed. by F. Ferre (Indianapolis: Bobbs-Merrill, 1963); reprinted by St. Thomas Press, Houston, 1972.

4. *Bridgewater Treatises*. "The Power and Goodness of God as Manifested in the Creation." London: William Pickering, 1836.

5. Paley, William. *Natural Theology,* pp. 1-6.

6. Clark, Robert E. D. *The Universe: Plan or Accident?* Philadelhphia: Muhlenberg Press, and London: Paternoster Press, 1961.

7. Ray, John. *The Wisdom of God Manifested in the Work of the Creation,* p. 65.

8. Paley, William. *Natural Theology,* pp. 280-286; 207-212; 285.

9. Shearman, J. N. *The Natural Theology of Evolution*. London: George Allen and Unwin, Ltd., 1915.
10. Aquinas, St. Thomas. "The Existence of God." *The Summa Theologica*. Quoted in Introduction to St. Thomas Aquinas, ed. by Anton C. Pegis. N. Y.: Random House, Inc., 1948, Modern Library College Editions, p. 27.
11. Heinecken, Martin J. *God in the Space Age*, 1st ed. Philadelphia and Toronto: The John C. Winston Company, 1958, p. 329. Copyright © 1959 by Martin J. Heinecken. Permission to use by Holt, Rinehart, and Winston, publishers.
12. Broms, Allan. *Thus Life Began*. Garden City, N. Y.: Doubleday & Co., Inc., 1968, p. 20.
13. Bertocci, Peter Anthony. *Introduction to the Philosophy of Religion*. Englewood Cliffs, N. J.: Prentice Hall, 1951, p. 330.
14. Ibid., p. 330.
15. Hume, David. *Dialogues Concerning Natural Religion,* ed. Kemp Smith. Oxford, 1935.
16. McPherson, Thomas. *The Argument from Design*. N. Y. and London: The MacMillan Press Ltd., 1972, pp. 1; 45.
17. Hurlbutt, Robert H., III. *Hume, Newton, and the Design Argument,* p. 151.
18. Kant, Immanuel. *Critique of Pure Reason*.
19. Taylor, A. E. *Does God Exist?* p. 57.

## CHAPTER FOUR

1. Henderson, L. J. *The Fitness of the Environment*. N. Y.: The MacMillan Co., 1913. (Boston: Beacon Press, 1958, passim.)
2. Ibid., p. 5.
3. Ibid., pp. 267-271.
4. Ibid., pp. 267-272.
5. Ibid., p. 53.
6. Pantin, C. F. A. "Organic Design," 8 Adv. Sci. pp. 138-150, 1951, *Brit. Assoc. for Adv. of Science Report*.
7. Bertocci, Peter Anthony. *Introduction to the Philosophy of Religion*. Englewood Cliffs, N. J.: Prentice Hall, 1951.
8. Ibid., p. 308.
9. Tennant, F. R. *Philosophical Theology,* Vol. II, Chap. 4, p. 86.

10. Ibid., p. 86.
11. Bertocci, Peter Anthony. *Introduction to the Philosophy of Religion,* p. 331.
12. Ibid., p. 333.
13. Reprinted from Wallace I. Matson, *The Existence of God.* Copyright © 1965 by Cornell University, p. 110. Used by permission of the publisher, Cornell University Press.
14. Lack, David. *Evolutionary Theory and Christian Belief.* London: Methuen and Co. Ltd., 1957 (parenthetical portion supplied).
15. Shklovskii, I. S. and Sagan, Carl. *Intelligent Life in the Universe,* (being an extension and revision of I. S. Shklovskii's *Universe, Life, Mind,* authorized translation by Paula Fern). Delta Book published by Dell Publishing Co., Inc., and reprinted therein by arrangement with Holden-Day, Inc., New York, 1966, pp. 228-229.
16. Ibid., p. 228.
18. Henderson, L. J. *The Fitness of the Environment,* Chap. I.
19. Pantin, C. F. A. *The Relations Between the Sciences.* Cambridge University Press, 1968, p. 62.
20. Ibid., p. 145.
21. Ibid., p. 145.
22. Sullivan, Walter. *We Are Not Alone.* N. Y.: McGraw-Hill Book Company, 1964. Signet Books, Rev. ed. The New American Library, 1966, p. 146.
23. Pantin, C. F. A. *The Relations Between the Sciences,* pp. 149-150.
24. Ibid., p. 172.

## CHAPTER FIVE

1. Merrison, A. W. "Elementary Particles," in *Growing Points in Science.* The Department of Education and Science of the British Government, 1972, p. 1.
2. Garrett, Alfred Benjamin; Haskins, Joseph Frederic; and Sisler, Harry Hall. *The Essentials of Chemistry,* 2nd ed. Ginn & Company, 1959, pp. 38-39.
3. Weisskopf, Victor F. *Knowledge and Wonder: The Natural World as Man Knows It.* Garden City, New York: Double-

day & Company, Inc.; Anchor Books, 1963, p. 95. Copyright © 1962, 1966 by Doubleday & Co., Inc.

4. Ibid., p. 100.

5. Ibid., p. 100 See also Hecht, Selig. *Explaining the Atom.* New York: Viking Press, 1947, pp. 12-13.

6. Gamow, George. *Matter, Earth, and Sky,* 2nd ed., © 1965. Englewood Cliffs, N. J.: Prentice Hall, Inc., 1968, pp. 592-593. Reprinted by permission of the publisher.

7. From *Exploration of the Universe,* updated Brief Ed. by George Abell. Copyright © 1964, 1969, 1973 by Holt, Rinehart and Winston, Inc., pp. 377-378. Reprinted by permission of Holt, Rinehart and Winston.

8. Greenwood, W. Osborne. *Biology and Christian Belief.* London: Student Christian Movement Press, 1938.

9. Buehler, John A. "Chemical Laws and God," in *The Evidence of God in an Expanding Universe,* ed. John Clover Monsma. N. Y.: G. P. Putnam Sons, 1958, pp. 161-162. (Toronto: Longman's, Green & Co., 1958.)

10. Clark, Robert E. D. *The Christian Stake in Science.* Chicago: Moody Press Edition, 1967, p. 35; published by special arrangement with Paternoster Press, London.

11. Teilhard de Chardin, Abbé Pierre. *Man's Place in Nature,* trans. by René Hague from Editions Albin Michel. 1956: London: William Collins & Co. Ltd. Fontana Books (Collins) 1966, p. 23 (N. Y.: Harper & Row, 1966).

12. Gamow, George. *Matter, Earth, and Sky,* p. 3. Reprinted by permission of the publisher, Prentice-Hall, Inc.

13. See, for instance, "The Confinement of Quarks" by Yoichiro Nambu in *Scientific American,* Nov., 1976.

14. Garrett, Haskins and Sisler. *The Essentials of Chemistry,* pp. 258-262.

15. Reyner, J. H. *The Universe of Relationships.* London: Vincent Stuart, Ltd., 1960, p. 11.

16. Ibid., p. 42.

17. Ibid., p. 11.

18. Ibid., p. 11.

19. Ibid., p. 15.

20. Ibid., p. 15.

21. Weisskopf, Victor F. *Knowledge and Wonder,* p. 105.

22. Ibid., p. 126.

23. Pollard, William G. *Man on a Spaceship.* Claremont, Cali-

fornia: Claremont Graduate School and University Center for the Claremont Colleges, 1967, pp. 49-51.

24. Weisskopf, Victor F. *Knowledge and Wonder,* pp. 105-106; 128.

25. Garrett, Haskins and Sisler. *The Essentials of Chemistry,* pp. 257-262.

26. Maurer, Elmer W. "Laboratory Lessons," in *The Evidence of God in an Expanding Universe,* ed. John Clover Monsma. N. Y.: G. P. Putnam Sons, 1958, pp. 201-206. (Toronto: Longman's Green & Co., 1958.)

27. Jean, Frank Covert; Harrah, Ezra Clarence; Herman, Fred Louis; Powers, Samuel Ralph. *Man and His Physical Universe.* Ginn and Company, Rev. ed., 1949, p. 214.

28. Buehler, John A. "Chemical Laws and God," in *The Evidence of God in an Expanding Universe,* ed. John Clover Monsma, pp. 161-162.

29. Battersby, A. R. "Chemistry of Natural Products," in *Growing Points in Science.* The Department of Education and Science of the British Government, 1972, p. 94.

30. Jones, Ewart. "Chemistry," in *Growing Points in Science.* The Department of Education and Science of the British Government, 1972, p. 93.

31. Reyner, J. H. *The Universe of Relationships,* p. 26.

32. Ibid., p. 11.

33. Greenwood, W. Osborne. *Biology and Christian Belief.*

34. Eddington, Sir A. S. *Science and the Unseen World: "Space, Time, and Gravitation."* The MacMillan Company, 1929, p. 14. (Swarthmore Lecture, 1929.)

35. Ibid.

36. Ibid.

37. Merrison, A. W. *Elementary Particles,* p. 4.

38. Cline, David B.; Mann, Alfred K.; Rubbia, Carlo. "The Search for New Families of Particles," *Scientific American,* Vol. 234, No. 1, January, 1976, p. 45.

39. Nambu, Yoichiro. "The Confinement of Quarks." *Scientific American,* November, 1976, p. 48.

40. Casper, Barry M. and Noer, Richard J. *Revolutions in Physics.* N. Y.: W. W. Norton & Company, Inc., © 1972, p. 435.

41. Merrison, A. W. *Elementary Particles,* p. 3. (Abbreviation supplied.)

42. Glashow, Sheldon Lee. *Scientific American,* Vol. 233, No. 4, October, 1975, p. 50.
43. Ibid., p. 50.


## CHAPTER SIX

1. Eicher, Don L. *Geologic Time.* Englewood Cliffs, N. J.: Prentice Hall, Inc., 1968, p. 19.
2. Hartwig, G. *The Harmonics of Nature.* London: Longman's Green & Co., 1866.
3. Buckland, William. Treatise VI, "Geology and Minerology Considered with Reference to Natural Theology," in the Bridgewater Treatises on *The Power, Wisdom and Goodness of God as Manifested in the Creation.* London: William Pickering, 1836, p. 98.
4. Deitz, Robert S.; Holden, John C. "The Breakup of Pangaea," in *Scientific American,* Vol. 223, No. 4, pp. 30-41, October, 1970; republished by W. H. Freeman and Company (San Francisco), 1970, p. 2.
5. Moorbath, Stephen. "The Oldest Rocks and the Growth of Continents," in *Scientific American,* March, 1977, pp. 92-104.
6. Ibid., pp. 94-96.
7. Dietz, Robert S.; Holden, John C. "The Breakup of Pangaea," p. 2.
8. See Moorbath, Stephen. "The Oldest Rocks and The Growth of Continents," pp. 92-104.
9. Hoyle, Fred. *Highlights in Astronomy.* San Francisco: W. H. Freeman and Company, 1975, pp. 14-18.
10. Gamow, George. *Matter, Earth, and Sky,* p. 400.
11. Moorbath, Stephen. "The Oldest Rocks and The Growth of Continents," p. 92.
12. Ibid., p. 21.
13. Ibid., p. 21.
14. Ibid., p. 21.
15. Kurtén, Bjorn. "Continental Drift and Evolution," in *Scientific American,* March, 1969, as published in the offprint (No. 877). San Francisco: W. H. Freeman and Company, p. 2.
16. Swartzendruber, Dale. An essay contributed to *The Evidence of God in an Expanding Universe,* ed. John Clover

Monsma. N. Y.: G. P. Putnam Sons, 1958, pp. 187-191.
(Toronto: Longman's Green, 1958.)

17. Jean, Harrah, Herman, and Powers. *Man and His Physical Universe,* Rev. ed., 1949, p. 619.
18. Ibid., p. 619.
19. Ibid., pp. 619-620.
20. Ibid., p. 620.
21. Ibid., p. 621.
22. Zimmerman, Lester John. "Soil, Plants, and 4000 Year-Old Explanation," in *The Evidence of God in an Expanding Universe,* ed. John Clover Monsma. N. Y.: Putnam Sons, 1958, p. 194. (Toronto: Longman's Green, 1958.)
23. Pollard, William G. *Man on a Spaceship,* pp. 10-11.
24. Hubbert, M. King. "The Energy Resources of the Earth," in *Scientific American,* September, 1971. San Francisco: republished in *Energy and Power,* W. H. Freeman and Company, 1971, pp. 31-40.
25. Knopf, Adolf. "Time in Earth History," in *Genetics, Paleontology and Evolution,* ed. Glen L. Jepsen, George Gaylord Simpson, and Ernst Mayr; Atheneum on reprint arrangements with Princeton University Press, 1949, first Atheneum Edition, p. 6.
26. Berry, Adrian. *The Next Ten Thousand Years.* London: Jonathan Cape Ltd., 1974. Coronet Books, Hodder and Stroughton. Coronet edition, 1976, p. 185. Also, N. Y.: E. P. Dutton, 1974. In paperback: New American Library, 1975.
27. Dyson, Freeman J. "Energy in the Universe," in *Scientific American,* Sept., 1971; republished in *Energy and Power,* San Francisco: W. H. Freeman and Company, p. 25.
28. Garrett, Alfred Benjamin; Haskins, Joseph Fredric; and Sisler, Harry Hall. *The Essentials of Chemistry,* 2nd ed. Ginn & Company, 1959, pp. 76-81.
29. Parke, Thomas David. "Plain Water Will Tell You The Story," in *The Evidence of God in an Expanding Universe,* ed. John Clover Monsma. N. Y.: G. P. Putnam Sons, 1958, p. 75.
30. Ibid., pp. 75-76.
31. Watson, Lyall. *Supernature.* London: Hodder and Stroughton, Ltd., 1973. Coronet Books. Coronet edition, 1974, p. 34.
32. Ibid., p. 35.
33. Ibid., p. 35.

34. Hartwig, G. *The Harmonics of Nature.*
35. Oort, Abraham H. "The Energy Cycle of the Earth," in *Scientific American,* Sept., 1970; republished in *The Biosphere.* San Francisco: W. H. Freeman and Company, 1970, pp. 14-24.
36. Ibid., p. 14.
37. Ibid., p.18.
38. *The Weather Machine* (WNET-TV-Channel 13, New York), on a grant from Champion International Corporation, December, 1974; Published © 1974 in brochure by Champion International Corporation. Used with permission.
39. Garrett, Alfred Benjamin; Haskins, Joseph Fredric; Sisler, Harry Hall. *The Essentials of Chemistry,* pp. 55-95.
40. Gates, David M. "The Flow of Energy in the Biosphere," in *Scientific American,* September, 1971; in *Energy and Power.* San Francisco: W. H. Freeman and Company, 1971, pp. 43-55.
41. Paley, William. *Natural Theology,* p. 291.
42. Allen, Frank. An essay contributed to *The Evidence of God in an Expanding Universe,* ed. John Clover Monsma. N. Y.: G. P. Putnam's Sons, 1958, pp. 19-21. (Toronto: Longman's Green, & Co., 1958.)
43. Hartwig, G. *The Harmonics of Nature.*
44. Huang, Fu Shu. "A Nuclear Accretion Theory of Star Formation," in *Astronomical Society of the Pacific,* Vol. 69 (October, 1957), pp. 427-430. Quoted in Sullivan, Walter. *We Are Not Alone.* N. Y.: McGraw-Hill Book Company, 1964. Signet Books, rev. ed. The New American Library, p. 96.
45. Sullivan, Walter. *We Are Not Alone,* p. 73.
46. Pollard, William G. *Man on a Spaceship,* p. 10.
47. Heard, Gerald. *Is God Evident?* New York and London: Harper & Brothers Publishers, 1948, pp. 59-61.
48. Ibid., p. 59.
49. Temperley, H. N. V. *A Scientist Who Believes in God.* London: Hodder and Stroughton, 1961.
50. Display sign, NASA Center, Houston, Texas.
51. "THE MOON—What Was Discovered." *Awake!* N. Y.: Watchtower Bible and Tract Society of New York, Inc., Vol. LIV, No. 10, May 22, 1973, pp. 5-8.
52. Ibid, p. 8.
53. Berry, Adrian. *The Next Ten Thousand Years,* p. 182.

54. Hoyle, Fred. *Highlights in Astronomy,* p. 47.
55. Berry, Adrian. *The Next Ten Thousand Years,* pp. 60-63.
56. Parker, Bruce C. *International Herald Tribune* (W. P. by Victor Cohn), September 10, 1973.
57. Asimov, Isaac. *Only a Trillion,* p. 108.
58. Taylor, Richard. *Metaphysics,* 2nd ed., Chapter 5. Englewood Cliffs, N. J.: Prentice Hall, © 1974, p. 38.
59. Ibid., p. 41.
60. Rust, Eric C. *Science and Faith,* pp. 171-172.
61. Fuller, R. Buckminster, paraphrased in "Inside Buckminster Fuller's Universe" by Harold Taylor. *Saturday Review,* May 2, 1970, pp. 56-69. (Fuller is the author of *Operating Manual for Spaceship Earth,* © 1969 by Southern Illinois University Press.)
62. Dyson, Freeman J. "Energy in the Universe," *Scientific American,* Sept. 1971. Republished in *Energy and Power,* San Francisco: W. H. Freeman and Co., p. 27.

## CHAPTER SEVEN

1. Heim, Karl. *The World: Its Creation and Consumption,* trans. by Robert Smith. London: Oliver and Boyd, 1962.
2. Berry, Adrian. *The Next Ten Thousand Years,* p. 187.
3. Ibid., p. 189.
4. Pollard, William G. *Man on a Spaceship,* p. 13.
5. Hart-Davis, Duff. "Design for No-Waste Living," in *Sunday Telegraph* (London), October 27, 1974, pp. 8-9.
6. Ibid., p. 8.
7. Pollard, William G. *Man on a Spaceship,* pp. 14-15.
8. Ibid., p. 11.
9. Ibid., p. 14.
10. Pell, Claiborne. "The Oceans—Man's Last Great Resource," in *Saturday Review,* October 11, 1969, pp. 19-22; 62-63.
11. Ibid., pp. 19-20.
12. Pollard, William G. *Man on a Spaceship,* pp. 44-49.
13. Wigner, Eugene P. *The Unreasonable Effectiveness of Mathematics in the Natural Sciences.* Richard Courant Lecture in Mathematical Sciences delivered at New York University, May 11, 1959. Reprinted therein by permission from "Communications in Pure and Applied Mathematics," Vol. XIII, No. 1 (February, 1960), pp. 1-14. Copyright by John Wiley and Sons, Inc. Excerpts used with permission.

14. Ibid., pp. 233; 237.
15. Pollard, William G. *Man on a Spaceship,* pp. 44-45.
16. Wigner, Eugene P. *The Unreasonable Effectiveness of Mathematics in the Natural Sciences,* p. 237.
17. Pollard, William G. *Man on a Spaceship,* p. 49.
18. Habgood, John S. *Religion and Science.* Birmingham, England: Hodder and Stroughton, 1964, p. 66.
19. Rust, Eric C. *Science and Faith,* p. 159.
20. Hoffer, Eric. "The Golden Mean," in *Smithsonian Magazine,* December, 1975, Vol. 6, No. 1, pp. 111-125.
21. Berry, Adrian. "Putting the Universe in Sequence," (London) *The Daily Telegraph,* December 1, 1969, p. 12.
22. Hoggart, Verner E., Jr. *Fibboniaci and Lucas Numbers.* Boston: Houghton Mifflin Co., 1969.
23. Berry, Adrian. "Putting the Universe in Sequence," p. 12.
24. Hoffer, Eric. "The Golden Mean," p. 111-125.
25. Berry, Adrian. "Putting the Universe in Sequence," p. 12.
26. Ibid., p. 12.

## CHAPTER EIGHT

1. King, Ivan R. *The Universe Unfolding.* San Francisco: W. H. Freeman and Company, 1976, p. vii.
2. Ibid., p. viii.
3. Adapted from *Exploration of the Universe,* updated Brief Ed. by George Abell. Copyright © 1964, 1969, 1973 by Holt, Rinehart and Winston, Inc., pp. 420; 426. Reprinted by permission of Holt, Rinehart and Winston.
4. Gamow, George. *Matter, Earth and Sky.* 2nd ed., p. 586. © 1965. Reprinted by permission of Prentice-Hall, Inc., Englewood Cliffs, New Jersey.
5. Abell, George. *Exploration of the Universe,* p. 391.
6. Kessel, Edward L. *The Evidence of God in an Expanding Universe,* ed. by John Clover Monsma, pp. 50-57.
7. Bonansea, Bernardine. *Science and Religion,* ed. by John Clover Monsma. N. Y.: G. P. Putnam Sons, 1962, p. 100.
8. Reprinted from Wallace I. Matson, *The Existence of God.* Copyright © 1965 Cornell University. Used by permission of the publisher, Cornell University Press.
9. Seagrave, Sterling. *Smithsonian Magazine,* Vol. 8, No. 1, April, 1977, pp. 43-44.

10. Davidsen, Arthur F. (London) *The Daily Telegraph,* April 21, 1977, p. 1, as reported by their Science Correspondent, Adrian Berry.

11. Berry, Adrian. *The Daily Telegraph* (London), July 18, 1977, p. 6.

12. Snow, C. P. In British Television Interview (BBC-2) on May 11, 1976.

13. STARS—Where Life Begins. "Time Magazine," December 27, 1976, p. 30.

14. Wheeler, J. A. *Our Universe: The Known and the Unknown.* "American Scientist," Spring 1968; quoted in Berry, Adrian. *The Next Ten Thousand Years,* p. 117.

15. Seagrave, Sterling. *Smithsonian Magazine,* Vol. 8, No. 1, April 1977, p. 47.

16. Paley, William. *Natural Theology (1802),* abridged ed. by F. Ferre. Indianapolis: Bobbs-Merril, 1963.

17. Ibid., p. 294.

18. Ibid., pp. 293-294.

19. Ibid., p. 290.

20. Tennant, F. R. *Philosophical Theology,* Vol. II, Chap. 4.

21. Jeans, Sir James. *The Mysterious Universe.* New York: The MacMillan Co., 1931.

22. Reprinted with permission from *Collier's Encyclopedia.* N. Y.: © P. F. Collier's & Son Corp. "Gravitation" by Paul R. Heyl, Vol. 9, p. 227.

23. Berry, Adrian. *The Next Ten Thousand Years,* pp. 183-184.

24. Dyson, Freeman J. "Energy in the Universe," *Scientific American,* Sept. 1971. Republished in *Energy and Power,* San Francisco: W. H. Freeman and Co., p. 20.

25. Ibid., p. 20.

26. Ibid., p. 20.

27. Ibid., p. 23.

28. Ibid., p. 25.

29. Berry, Adrian. *The Next Ten Thousand Years,* p. 184.

30. Dyson, Freeman J. "Energy in the Universe," *Scientific American,* Sept. 1971. Republished in *Energy and Power,* p. 26.

31. Watson, Lyall, *Supernature.* London: Hodder & Stroughton, Ltd., 1973. Coronet Book edition, 1974, pp. 87-88.

32. Heard, Gerald, *Is God Evident?* N. Y. and London: Harper Bros. Publisher, p. 48. See also, Reyner, J. H. *Universe of Relationships.*

33. *The Dusty Universe.* Field, George B. and Cameron, A. G. W., editors. Published for the Smithsonian Astrophysical Observatory by Neale Watson Academic Publications, Inc., New York, 1973.
34. *Darwin, Evolution, and Creation,* by Zimmerman, Paul Albert, editor, and others. St. Louis: Concordia Publishing House, 1959, pp. 99-100.
35. Monod, Jacques. *Chance and Necessity,* p. 180.
36. Heinecken, Martin J. *God in the Space Age.* Philadelphia and Toronto: John C. Winston Company, First ed. 1959, p. 122.
37. Wald, George. Quoted in "Origin of Life" by William L. Lawrence, in *New York Times,* October 27, 1963, Sec. E-7.
38. Romer, Alfred. *The Procession of Life.* London: Weidenfeld and Nicholson, 1968.
39. Clark, Cecil H. Douglas. London: Epworth Press, 1966.
40. Miller, James. "New Quest for Life in Space," in *Readers Digest,* June 1973, p. 43.
41. Hick, John. *Arguments for the Existence of God,* p. 35.
42. Dyson, Freeman J. "Energy in the Universe," in *Energy and Power,* p. 19.
43. Ibid., p. 19.
44. Gribbin, Dr. John. *Astronomy* journal, issue of May, 1977.
45. Berry, Adrian. *The Daily Telegraph* (London), July 18, 1977.
46. Ibid.
47. Hoyle, Fred. *Highlights in Astronomy,* pp. 136-138.
48. Sagan, Carl. *Across a Cosmic Sea, Mars Beckons, The Denver Post* (Denver), August 1976.
49. Asimov, Isaac. "The Next Frontier?" in *National Geographic Magazine,* July, 1976.
50. Clarke, Arthur C. An article in *The Sunday Telegraph* (London), 1976; see also the same author in "Man's Destiny in Space," in *The Sunday Telegraph,* August 9, 1970, p. 6.
51. Sagan, Carl. *Across a Cosmic Sea, Mars Beckons.*
52. Berry, Adrian. *The Iron Sun: Crossing the Universe Through Black Holes.* N. Y.: E. P. Dutton, 1977. In paperback: Warner Brothers, 1979.
53. Dyson, Freeman J. *Perspective in Modern Physics,* ed. by Robert E. Marshak. London: Interscience Publishers, 1966.
54. Dyson, Freeman J. Quoted in ". . . And Man Remade the Firmament," by Adrian Berry in *The Daily Telegraph* (London) (Mag. Sec.), November, 1973, pp. 44-50.

55. Dyson, Freeman J. "Energy in The Universe," in *Energy and Power,* p. 26.
56. *Ibid.,* p. 27.


# CHAPTER NINE

1. Willey, Basil. *The Religion of Nature.* London: The Lindley Press, 1957 (The Essex Hall Lecture), p. 14.
2. Aquinas, St. Thomas. Referred to in Bertocci, Peter Anthony, *Introduction to the Philosophy of Religion,* p. 338.
3. Tennant, F. R. *Philosophical Theology,* p. 81.
4. Teilhard de Chardin, Abbé Pierre. *The Phenomenon Of Man.* London: William Collins & Sons, Ltd.; N. Y.: Harper & Row, 1959.
5. Bertocci, Peter Anthony. *Introduction to the Philosophy of Religion,* p. 338.
6. Hoyle, Fred. *Highlights in Astronomy,* pp. 18 and 21.
7. Wyllie, Peter J., in an address, February 24, 1977, to the American Association for the Advancement of Science's annual meeting at Denver as reported in the *Denver Post,* February 25, 1977, in an interview with Jim Kirksey.
8. Ambroggi, Robert P. "Underground Reservoirs to Control the Water Cycle," in *Scientific American,* Vol. 236, No. 5, May, 1977, pp. 21-27.
9. Ibid., pp. 25-26.
10. Ibid., p. 27.
11. *Darwin, Evolution and Creation,* by Zimmerman, Paul Albert, ed., and others. St. Louis: Concordia House, 1959, p. 93-94.
12. Bakker, Robert T. "Dinosaur Renaissance," in *Scientific American,* April, 1975, p. 58.
13. Bakker, Robert T. and Galton, Peter M. "Dinosaur Morphyly and a New Class of Vertebrates in Nature." Vol. 248, No. 5444, in *Scientific American,* March, 1974, pp. 168-172.
14. Romer, Alfred S. In "Time Series and Trends in Animal Evolution," in *Genetics, Paleontology and Evolution.* Atheneum through arrangement with Princeton University Press (copyright 1949), 1963, pp. 103-120.
15. Ibid., p. 107.
16. Mayr, Ernst. *Populations, Species, and Evolution.* Cambridge,

Mass.: The Belknap Press of Harvard University Press, 1970, p. 19.
17. Ibid., p. 250.

## CHAPTER TEN

1. Aquinas, St. Thomas. "The Existence of God," in *The Summa Theologica*. Quoted in *Introduction to St. Thomas Aquinas,* ed. by Anton C. Pegis. N. Y.: Random House, Inc., 1948. Modern Library College Editions, p. 27.
2. Hein, Hilde S. *On The Nature and Origin of Life.* © 1971 by Hilde S. Hein. N. Y.: McGraw-Hill Book Company (ed. by Daniel A. Greenberg), p. 58.
3. Du Noüy, Lecomte. *Human Destiny.* New York: Longman's Green, 1947.
4. Coulter, John M. and Merle. *Where Evolution and Religion Meet.* The MacMillan Company, 1924.
5. Stebbins, G. Ledyard. *Processes of Organic Evolution.* Englewood Cliffs, N. J.: Prentice Hall, Inc., 1966, pp. 2-3.
6. Mayr, Ernst. *Population, Species, and Evolution,* p. 5.
7. Hardy, Sir Alister. *The Living Stream.* N. Y. and Evanston: Harper & Row, 1965.
8. Hardy, Sir Alister. *The Biology of God.* Copyright © by Alister Hardy. London: Jonathan Cape Ltd., 1975. Extracts herein used with permission of the author.
9. Ibid., p. 35.
10. Ibid., p. 43.
11. Ewer, R. F. *New Biology,* Vol. 13. London: Penguin, 1952, pp. 117-119, and Acta Biotheoretica, Vol. 13 (Leiden, 1960, pp. 161-184). Quoted in Hardy, *Biology of God,* p. 44.
12. Taylor, Richard. *Metaphysics,* p. 95.
13. Ibid., p. 100.
14. Hardy, Sir Alister. *Biology of God,* p. 55.
15. Ibid., p. 206.
16. Wright, Sewall. *Process and Divinity.* (Open Court, La Salle, Ill., 1964), ed. by W. L. Reese and E. Freeman, pp. 113-114; quoted in Hardy, Sir Alister, *Biology of God,* p. 206.
17. Haldane, J. B. S. *The Inequality of Man.* London: Chatto & Windus, 1932, p. 114; quoted in Hardy, Sir Alister, *Biology of God,* p. 206.

18. Hardy, Sir Alister. *The Biology of God,* p. 209.
19. Ibid., pp. 45; 18.
20. Ray, John. *The Wisdom of God Manifested in the Work of the Creation.*
21. Habgood, John. *Religion and Science.* Birmingham, England: Hodder & Stroughton, 1964, p. 67.
22. Wigner, Eugene. "Remarks on the Mind-Body Question," in *The Scientist Speculates,* I. J. Good, ed. London: William Heinemann Ltd., 1961; N. Y.: Basic Books, Inc. 1962.
23. Eddington, A. S. *Science and the Unseen World,* Swarthmore Lectures, 1929. N. Y.: The Macmillan Company, 1929, pp. 32; 50.
24. Hardy, Sir Alister. *The Biology of God,* p. 52.
25. Jerison, Harry J. "Paleoneurology and the Evolution of Mind," in *Scientific American,* Vol. 234, No. 1, January, 1976, pp. 90-102.
26. Mayr, Ernst. *Populations, Species, and Evolution,* p. 386.
27. John, John P. D. *Science of God and the World.* Lectures and Addresses, Vol. I, copyrighted by Jennings and Graham and published by The Methodist Book Concern, N. Y. and Cincinnati, 1907, p. 23.
28. Schrödinger, Erwin. *What is Life? The Physical Aspect of the Living Cell.* Cambridge, England: Cambridge University Press, 1946, p. 2.
29. Pantin, C. F. A. *The Relations Between the Sciences,* p. 131.
30. Ibid., p. 131.
31. Hein, Hilde S. *On The Nature and Origin of Life,* p. 43.
32. Monod, Jacques. *Chance and Necessity,* p. 46.
33. Ibid., p. 108.
34. Simon, Michael A. *The Matter of Life.* New Haven and London: © Yale University Press, 1971, pp. 154-155.
35. Ibid., p. 158.
36. Ibid., p. 150.

## CHAPTER ELEVEN

1. Taylor, A. E. *Does God Exist?* London and N. Y.: MacMillan, 1945.
2. Simon, Michael A. *The Matter of Life.* New Haven and London: © Yale University Press, 1971, p. 163.
3. Bronowski, J. *The Ascent of Man,* London: British Broad-

casting Corporation, 1973, p. 314. Also published in U.S.A. by Little, Brown and Company.

4. Monod, Jacques. *Chance and Necessity,* pp. 140-143.
5. Bronowski, J. *The Ascent of Man,* p. 317.
6. Shklovskii, I. S. and Sagan, Carl. *Intelligent Life in the Universe,* p. 183.
7. Asimov, Isaac, *Only a Trillion.* London and N. Y.: Abelard-Schuman, 1957, pp. 110-111. © 1957 Isaac Asimov. Used with permission of Harper & Row, Inc.
8. Ibid., p. 111.
9. Hein, Hilde S. *On The Nature and Origin of Life,* p. 126.
10. Monod, Jacques. *Chance and Necessity.*
11. Pieczenik, George, reported in "A New View of Evolution," in *Time Magazine,* April 4, 1977, p. 47.
12. Teilhard de Chardin, Abbé Pierre. *The Phenomenon of Man.* London: Wm. Collins & Sons Ltd.; N. Y.: Harper & Row, 1959; revised edition, 1965; Fontana Edition, 1965.
13. Shklovskii, I. S. and Sagan, Carl. *Intelligent Life in the Universe,* p. 186.
14. Monod, Jacques. *Chance and Necessity.* p. 122.
15. Tatum, E. L. An address given to the annual meeting of the National Academy of Sciences in 1963.
16. Monod, Jacques. *Chance and Necessity,* p. 106.
17. Ibid., p. 110.
18. Hardy, Sir Alister. *The Biology of God,* p. 33.
19. Ibid., p. 33.
20. Waddington, C. H. "Biology," in *Growing Points in Science,* p. 119.
21. Hardy, Sir Alister. *The Biology of God,* p. 32.
22. Pieczenik, George. *Time Magazine,* August 4, 1977, p. 47.
23. Pollard, William G. *Man on a Spaceship,* p. 33.
24. Ibid., p. 33.
25. Ibid., p. 34.
26. Ibid., pp. 50-51.
27. Ibid., pp. 50-51.
28. Hein, Hilde S. *On The Nature and Origin of Life,* pp. 129-148.

## CHAPTER TWELVE

1. Simon, Michael A. *The Matter of Life,* p. 28.
2. Ibid., p. 29.

3. Ibid., p. 31.
4. Pantin, C. F. A. *The Relations Between the Sciences,* p. 124.
5. Bertocci, Peter Anthony. *Introduction to the Philosophy of Religion,* p. 167.
6. Hein, Hilde S. *On The Nature and Origin of Life,* p. 164.
7. Ibid., p. 141.
8. Bronowski, J. *The Ascent of Man,* p. 313.
9. Ponnamperuma, Dr. Cyril. Reported in *The Houston Post* (UPI), April 22, 1974.
10. Pantin, C. F. A. *The Relations Between the Sciences,* p. 51.
11. Ibid., pp. 74-76.
12. Schrödinger, Erwin. *What is Life? The Physical Aspect of the Living Cell,* p. 2.
13. Stebbins, G. Ledyard. *Processes of Organic Evolution,* p. 1.
14. Monod, Jacques. *Chance and Necessity,* p. 87.
15. Ibid., p. 87.
16. Teilhard de Chardin, Abbé Pierre. *The Phenomenon of Man.*

## CHAPTER THIRTEEN

1. Rust, Eric C. in *Science and Religion,* pp. 107-109.
2. Hoyle, Fred. *Ten Faces of the Universe.* San Francisco: W. H. Freeman and Company.
3. McPherson, Thomas. *The Argument from Design,* p. 15.
4. Ibid., p. 20.
5. Ibid., pp. 16-19.
6. Taylor, Richard. *Metaphysics,* 2nd ed. © 1974. Prentice-Hall, Inc., p. 118.
7. Shearman, J. N. *The Natural Theology of Evolution.*
8. Tennant, F. R. *Philosophical Theology,* Vol. II, Chap. VII.
9. Ibid., Vol. II, Chap. VII.
10. Heinecken, Martin J. *God in the Space Age,* p. 58.
11. Kierkegaard, Soren. Quoted in Heinecken's *God in the Space Age,* p. 59.

# Index

231

233